THE
DESERVING

THE
DESERVING

What the Lives of the Condemned Reveal About American Justice

ELIZABETH VARTKESSIAN

BLOOMSBURY PUBLISHING
NEW YORK · LONDON · OXFORD · NEW DELHI · SYDNEY

BLOOMSBURY PUBLISHING
Bloomsbury Publishing Inc.
1359 Broadway, New York, NY 10018, USA
50 Bedford Square, London, WC1B 3DP, UK
Bloomsbury Publishing Ireland Limited,
29 Earlsfort Terrace, Dublin 2, D02 AY28, Ireland

BLOOMSBURY, BLOOMSBURY PUBLISHING, and the Diana logo
are trademarks of Bloomsbury Publishing Plc

First published in the United States 2026

ISBN: HB: 978-1-63973-139-8; eBook: 978-1-63973-140-4

Library of Congress Control Number: 2025934763

2 4 6 8 10 9 7 5 3 1

Typeset by Six Red Marbles India
Printed in the United States by Lakeside Book Company

To find out more about our authors and books, visit www.bloomsbury.com
and sign up for our newsletters.

Bloomsbury books may be purchased for business or promotional use. For information
on bulk purchases please contact Macmillan Corporate and Premium Sales Department
at specialmarkets@macmillan.com.
For product safety–related questions contact productsafety@bloomsbury.com.

To Jonny, Avery, and Ara, for the gift of this life.
To my clients. All were children deserving to exist in a society that
fostered their potential, not supported their ruin.
To the future. With hope we will do better for each other.

Author's Note

The condemned, as used in the subtitle, includes those facing execution as well as those carrying out sentences in prisons and other carceral facilities.

There are many complicated legal issues involved in the court cases included in this book. As I'm not a lawyer, I have focused on highlighting the complexity of the law where it is meaningful to help the reader understand the moral conundrum posed, and distilling, by the same principle, for the sake of clarity and brevity. Please see the endnotes for references, resources, and further reading.

Finally, as a member of a legal defense team, I have also had to address attorney-client privilege. This is a protection that exists between me and my client and is what permits the kind of trusting relationship that is necessary to the work of a mitigation specialist to develop. Living clients were asked permission to be included in the work, were given the opportunity to review and give feedback, and consented to having parts of their lives shared. In addition, with the exception of two men who I could not successfully anonymize, all clients and witnesses in this book have been given fictional names, and, where necessary, details regarding places and dates have been changed. Those clients living and deceased each shared with me how they hoped their lives would lead to a greater awareness and change for the better. That is the aim of this work. I hope to have achieved it.

Contents

Foreword

In 1998, the photographer Deborah Luster and the poet C. D. Wright began a project that would last several years: creating portraits of the incarcerated in Louisiana's prisons. Wright wrote of *One Big Self*: "What I wanted was to unequivocally lay out the real feel of hard time."[1] Louisiana then had one of the highest incarceration rates in the nation. It still does, which means it also has one of the highest incarceration rates in the world.[2]

The story of how Luster began the project tells us something about her. She'd turned to photography after losing her mother to murder, reeling from loss and anger. The camera gave her a source of strength: the power to document. The day her mother's killer was sentenced, the image of the courtroom gallery struck her—this gathering of her own family and the family of the convicted: "So many lives destroyed or damaged by this greedy, stupid act. I wondered if there remained a single soul untouched by violence."[3]

As I read her account, I thought of my own journey. I began fighting against the death penalty in 1982 when I became a spiritual adviser for Elmo Patrick Sonnier, a condemned man in Louisiana who had been convicted of murder and about whom I wrote *Dead Man Walking* (1993). As I learned about his life, his experiences, the pain he caused, I came to understand the profound loss of dignity that comes with taking a life. Portraiture can be a restoration of dignity. I think Luster recognized this. One photograph in particular struck me: the cover of Elizabeth Vartkessian's remarkable book *The Deserving: What the Lives of the Condemned Reveal About American Justice.*[4]

The image shows an inmate at the East Carroll Parish Prison Farm in Transylvania, the first institution Luster visited. This man decided that his portrait would show a version of himself from another time. He stretched out his hand, holding a photo of himself as a boy. This gesture, the man's outstretched arm with the boy's photograph, becomes the portrait. It is so hard to look away. It reminds us of the possibilities that violent crime forecloses, both for victims and for perpetrators.

The Deserving is the first book I'm aware of, at least for a general audience, to pull back the curtain on a lifesaving field most have never heard of: mitigation. It is a relatively young field, filled with the scrappy, resourceful, impassioned energy of people like Elizabeth. Mitigation work is a kind of portraiture. It is the essential craft of presenting the whole person to a jury. And through the jury, the world. Sadly, our prisons and death rows are overflowing with people whose defense teams failed them when it came time to present all the factors that led that person to that crime. Our prisons are full of people who themselves were cruelly abused, veterans suffering from post-traumatic stress, the mentally ill. Lisa Montgomery, a federal capital defendant whose defense team I consulted, was one of the most abused persons I have ever heard of in my life. Although Lisa's crime was unspeakably horrendous, who could judge that her violent act was not related to the torture and trauma she had endured? The horrors of her capital crime simply cannot be extracted from the fuller context of her life circumstances.

We are all better than our own worst act, but so many of the imprisoned have been treated as if their crime is all they are. "Human dignity is inviolable." So states the European Union's Charter of Fundamental

Rights, echoing the Universal Declaration of Human Rights to which the United States is a signatory. *Inviolable*. It means that our dignity is inherent; it is neither given to us nor can it be taken away. Until such time as that dignity is recognized and the death penalty is abolished, along with all forms of dehumanization, we need the work that is mitigation. It is mercy work. When someone charged with a crime appears in court, often the crucial factor in determining that person's fate is mitigation. It stands between the condemned and the ultimate punishment, with which no human should be empowered.

It's a frightening time. I didn't think I would see the day when we would allow the killing of people by lethal gas. But I sat down to write this foreword shortly after the state of Louisiana executed Jessie Hoffman with nitrogen gas at Angola, where Luster and Wright bore witness a quarter of a century ago. This after more than fifteen years without a state killing. Last year, Alabama executed four men using nitrogen hypoxia, starting with Kenneth Eugene Smith. Elizabeth Bruenig, who reported on the execution, wrote that after the gas began to flow, Smith writhed and gasped for twenty-two minutes, struggling for air before he finally died. (The state of Alabama has banned Bruenig from its prisons because of her reporting.)[5] Like Luster, Bruenig came to her work reporting in prisons after someone close to her was murdered. Such victims have had to make the fundamental choice between mercy and vengeance. Mercy is not the same as forgiveness, Bruenig notes; indeed, it does not require forgiveness, but rather a relinquishment, a laying down of weapons, a refusal to let harm continue. I see this as holy. "Families of murder victims routinely perform exceptional feats of mercy," she writes.[6]

I believe mercy is stronger than vengeance. Mitigation specialists are mercy incarnate; they show love by their actions. They are the historians for the least of us, and they do their work in spaces that are designed to strip dignity. They do not judge. And they ask that we do the same. Standing in spaces of trauma and suffering, they return to learn more, dig deeper, connect more closely. Their proximity to suffering and pursuit of truth are the embodiment of faith. Their work gives me a renewed hope for justice.

—Sister Helen Prejean, July 2025

Introduction

B efore I'd ever set foot inside a prison, my colleagues gave me some advice: dress plainly. I settled on dark pants, a button-down shirt, a sweater, and gray or beige sneakers. A forgettable outfit that caused the least concern going through security. Underwire bras often set off the handheld metal detectors that the officers waved over the front and back of my body, so I learned to wear a sports bra. I left most jewelry at home save a necklace and a couple of silver rings. Blending in culturally was important, too. In my few months in Texas I had learned to address every man as "sir" and every woman as "ma'am," regardless of age. I clumsily embraced "y'all."

It was February 2005, I was twenty-three years old, and I was meeting Edward, also in his twenties, for the first time. I left my apartment in Houston at dawn for Livingston, about seventy miles northeast of the city. I had made the journey enough times by then to know I would need to stop along the way to change a ten-dollar bill into a roll of quarters so I could buy food and drinks from the vending machines, should Edward want anything. My visit was scheduled for eight A.M., and the prison could refuse to allow it if I was late.

The sun was up by the time I exited the highway onto a farm road, passing a barbecue joint, a number of trailer homes, and finally a Baptist church whose billboard encouraged passersby to turn their lives to Jesus. One minute later I could see the large white water tower of the Polunsky Unit, where Texas's death row had been located since 1999. That's where Edward lived.

I walked through a metal detector while the items I'd brought with me crept through an X-ray machine. After the initial inspection, an officer half-heartedly thumbed my white glue-top notepad (spiral-bound notepads were not allowed), eyeballed my two pens, unfurled the roll of quarters, and handed back my driver's license. At a window in the same cramped entrance, I traded my identification for a visitor badge, which hung like a placard around my neck.

I walked through a series of small enclosures, each one required to be shut fully behind me before the next one opened for me to enter. After that, I proceeded alone outside, down a narrow cement pathway that connected the entrance to the visiting area. I was flanked by two sets of prison cells. In front of me and off to my right was a block of dark-gray units, each with two horizontal windows. Those cells were for men serving long-term sentences, including life without the possibility of parole. Some of these men were outside on the lawn around me, trimming grass and tending flower beds of bright pink and yellow that lined the cement path. A nearly identical block was on the left. It was easy to miss the difference from the outside: one window instead of two toward the top of each unit. That was death row.

Four months earlier I had made the drive from Washington, D.C., to my new, as-yet-unseen home in Houston. I was moving to Texas to start working for a small, recently formed nonprofit called the Gulf Region Advocacy Center (GRACE) that represented poor defendants in criminal cases, mainly ones that involved the death penalty.[1] At that time Houston, the largest city within Harris County, was ground zero for capital punishment. The late 1990s and early 2000s were the peak of capital punishment in the United States generally, but especially in

Texas specifically.[2] Texas executions hit a record high in 2000, when forty individuals were put to death in the state, representing just over 47 percent of all executions in the United States. To put that number in perspective, in 2024 twenty-five people were executed in the entire country. Even so, Texas remained prolific, representing 20 percent of executions, with five death sentences carried out.[3]

The GRACE office operated out of the overcrowded attic of a house owned by the founding director of the organization, the attorney Danalynn Recer, who also lived catty-corner to the building. I was among the first paid employees in this space, which was a constant hive of activity. My specific role in the attic office was not as an attorney but as a mitigation specialist. I was not entirely sure what that entailed, though I knew the job existed on the criminal defense side. I wasn't alone in knowing nothing about the role. Few people had heard of mitigation specialists in 2004,[4] and though the profession has grown since then, most people, even those engaged in the legal field, remain unaware of it. I've often wondered if the word *mitigation* itself doesn't play a part; it tends to complicate and obscure a relatively straightforward concept, which is that a person convicted of a crime needs to be seen in the fullness of their experience. Only then can justice be dispensed.

A mitigation specialist's job is to investigate the life of an accused or convicted person.[5] This person—now client—has most often been either accused or convicted of murder. The task of the mitigation specialist is to provide relevant context about the client's life for those deciding the most appropriate punishment. Relevance is potentially everywhere; the trajectory of a person's life is shaped by so many factors. Thus, the mitigation specialist casts a wide net to gather information. Records matter. Institutions and institutional language about clients matter. The history of their community matters, as do people who know directly about them or their families and the circumstances in which they were raised.

At the time I went to work with Danalynn, I knew virtually nothing about criminal law and wasn't versed in the mechanics of the death penalty. My primary experience with capital punishment had come through a brief stint volunteering for an attorney during my senior year of college, during which I summarized the trial transcript of a woman in Alabama who had been sentenced to death for her role in a murder for hire. The story presented to the jury was this: The defendant, Annie, was said to have given a nephew fifty dollars in exchange for him carrying out the murder of her lover. The victim had a history of terrorizing Annie, including standing over her while she was in bed, holding a running chain saw and threatening to kill her. She was convicted and sentenced to death. Never mind the evidence, which struck me as weak at best; what stuck with me was the extreme abuse Annie had experienced. I wondered how a death sentence could possibly be appropriate in such a circumstance. I thought about Annie a lot after reading about what she had endured. I couldn't shake the feeling that her conviction represented a deep injustice. I struggled to understand how the abuse, which was in full view of the court and to the jury, wasn't seen as a reason to spare her.

DEATH LOOMED LARGE in my mind when I was a child—genocides, specifically—and I am certain it fueled my interest in understanding why people harm one another. I am the daughter of an ethnic Armenian, and many within my father's family were victims of the genocide perpetrated by the Ottomans in 1915. My mother, who was born and raised in Poland in the 1950s, grew up in a culture shaped by the knowledge and memory of internment camps and the sudden disappearance and loss of loved ones. Each of my parents carried distrust, a basic skepticism of other people and their motives. Secrecy was central, perhaps to their sense of safety, and certainly to the way I experienced early life. In 1991, when I was ten years old, heading to Poland for the first time, my mother mentioned that she had siblings and other relatives she had never told me about. When I was in my twenties, my father told me that his father had been a long-haul truck driver with several families, wives and children, throughout Iraq. Some ten years later, while I was visiting my family home in California, my father mentioned that he himself had been briefly imprisoned by the Ba'ath Party in the 1970s. Even before I was aware of them, I sensed that such hidden experiences shaped my home, my life, and therefore myself. The past trickled into the present in ways I yearned to better understand.

In college I majored in political philosophy; I was preoccupied with understanding how values such as justice, liberty, and equality structured the formation of nation states. Later I completed a degree in comparative social policy, which was the extension of the theories I had studied into real-world application. I studied how values—culturally created and ranked—shaped different national approaches to social systems such as housing, health care, and employment. It was eye-opening to trace how the moral compass of a nation directed the creation of its welfare state. Nations with a clear vision of fostering equity within their population, I observed, have universal health care, free higher education, and paid parental leave of many months. Such policies incentivize preventive care, a well-educated citizenry, strong family units, and community support. These nations' criminal legal systems tend to adopt this same ethos of investment in people. Countries with strong social support policies—many Nordic countries, for example—do not have capital punishment, nor even true life without parole.[6] They also have fewer homicides per capita.[7]

A chance meeting with one of Danalynn's colleagues made me aware of her work with GRACE. I reached out to Danalynn directly about potential openings at the office. Nearly as soon as I sent the email, she responded. About a month later we met in person at a coffee shop. I arrived early and picked a corner table, where I waited anxiously for her to arrive. Ten minutes later she rushed in with a Big Gulp–size beverage, dressed simply in a shirt and jeans. I noticed several cans of Diet Coke in her purse. She placed her bag on the floor and sat across from me. She got right to it:

"What would you say to someone on death row who tells you they want to give up their appeals?"

"I'd ask them why," I said uncertainly. "I'd ask what was happening at that moment. Maybe something that was making it harder to survive? Maybe they needed more support?"

The rest of her questions were similarly open-ended yet probing.

If I asked Danalynn now what she saw in me that day, I have a feeling she would say something about curiosity, the fact that I expressed an interest in the thoughts, feelings, and experiences of the condemned. And perhaps that I wasn't sold on being an attorney, that other roles in defense interested me, even if I didn't know what they were. Danalynn herself hadn't planned on becoming an attorney. She worked as a mitigation specialist for years before the office that employed her was stripped of federal funding and closed, forcing her to switch gears. She was a workaholic motivated by her views: it started with an initial fury at the injustice involved in the death penalty that deepened as she got to know clients and their families. She was inquisitive, dogged, skilled at adding clarifying context. At her core she understood how precarious life could be and how essential humanizing the accused was to the fulfillment of justice. She believed in mercy.

At the end of our thirty minutes together, Danalynn asked when I could get to Texas.

I answered without even asking what she was offering. "I just need a car."

"Good," she said. She would see me in Houston as soon as I could get there. She left the coffee shop as quickly as she'd come. I stayed a bit longer, staring at an empty Diet Coke can sitting on the table—a bit of proof.

THE JOB OF the mitigation specialist developed in the late 1970s after the U.S. Supreme Court declared that judges or juries could hand down a death sentence only after the background of the convicted person was considered. (The case is fascinating and will be explained in chapter 2.) Most lawyers didn't know how to develop this kind of evidence, so the earliest people to fulfill the mitigation function in capital cases were anthropologists, social workers, journalists, and others similarly trained in extensive information gathering and synthesis. In 1976, before mitigation evidence—defined as "anything in the life of a defendant which might militate against the appropriateness of the death penalty"[8]—became a requirement, lawyers were not generally taught how to investigate, much less present, the context of a convicted person's history and experience.

In 1989 the American Bar Association adopted professional guidelines for the appointment and performance of counsel in death penalty cases, which included direction on the need for and use of mitigation in capital cases.[9] These guidelines included one of the earliest official mentions of the mitigation specialist.[10] Over the years, as the guidelines were expanded and updated, the roles of mitigation and mitigation evidence became more involved and more codified.[11] By 2003 the mitigation specialist had been clearly defined as the person tasked with harvesting information about the client's background and functioning, a process critical to the litigation of death penalty cases.[12]

The 2003 guidelines are the professional North Star for mitigation specialists detailing their central role on the defense team and directing how the work of collecting life history information must be carried out. I still find those guidelines beautiful for the way they acknowledge the connections between development, behavior, and harm.

> A mitigation specialist is also an indispensable member of the defense team throughout all capital proceedings. Mitigation specialists possess clinical and information-gathering skills and training that most lawyers simply do not have. They have the time and the ability to elicit sensitive, embarrassing and often humiliating evidence (e.g., family sexual abuse) that the defendant may have never disclosed. They have the clinical skills to recognize such things as congenital, mental or neurological conditions, to understand how these conditions may have affected the defendant's development and behavior, and to identify the most appropriate experts to examine the defendant or testify on his behalf. Moreover, they may be critical to assuring that the client obtains therapeutic services that render him cognitively and emotionally competent to make sound decisions concerning his case. Perhaps most critically, having a qualified mitigation specialist assigned to every capital case as an integral part of the defense team ensures that the presentation to be made at the penalty phase is integrated into the overall preparation of the case rather than being hurriedly thrown together by defense counsel still in shock at the guilty verdict. The mitigation specialist compiles a comprehensive and well-documented psychosocial history of the client based on an

exhaustive investigation; analyzes the significance of the information in terms of impact on development, including effect on personality and behavior; finds mitigating themes in the client's life history; identifies the need for expert assistance; assists in locating appropriate experts; provides social history information to experts to enable them to conduct competent and reliable evaluations; and works with the defense team and experts to develop a comprehensive and cohesive case in mitigation.[13]

My colleagues trained me, as Danalynn had trained them, as she had been trained by her mentors in the 1990s, those now largely credited with developing the profession. Pioneers in the field—Cecilia "Cessie" Alfonso and Katharine Baur, social workers in New York and New Jersey; Russell Stetler, a former journalist out of California; Craig Haney, a social psychologist in California; and Marie Deans[14] in South Carolina and later in Virginia, who founded Victims' Families for Alternatives to the Death Penalty (later Murder Victims' Families for Reconciliation) after the murder of her mother-in-law—were operating throughout the country. Danalynn was influenced by the anthropologist Scharlette Holdman, who began working as a mitigation specialist in Florida in the late 1970s.[15] Her training in anthropology allowed her to develop a deep understanding of those who had killed. She understood intuitively that someone who has killed was not born that way but shaped by a myriad of forces that ultimately led to tragedy.[16] Scharlette is widely credited with developing the multigenerational approach to mitigation development that is emblematic of the profession today. She also coined the term *mitigation specialist*, though she told me once that she wished she had called the profession something different. The title doesn't adequately describe the role mitigation specialists play in excavating the forces that shape a life.

As for working with those of Danalynn's cohort who were trained and influenced by mentors like Scharlette, the attic office in Houston was my apprenticeship. I learned from my fellow staff members and from the volunteer attorneys who spent six to twelve months working with us before returning to their criminal defense practices. Learning how to carry out mitigation investigation was and continues to be an evolving, active discipline, the rules both official and unofficial, based on experience and what has worked. Each lesson I absorbed came from listening, observing, and doing.

Since taking those first steps in 2004, I have gathered and presented mitigation evidence in about a hundred death penalty cases and consulted with capital and other types of criminal defense teams on hundreds more. Sometimes the trial has not yet taken place; sometimes it's over; many of my clients have already been convicted and find themselves engaged in the lengthy appeals process in either the state or federal courts. I've worked in clemency stage proceedings, including one case in Georgia in 2020 where my client was granted executive clemency about six hours before he was scheduled to die, and another where my client was wrongfully convicted and sentenced to over eighty years in prison in Connecticut in his early twenties. He was released in December 2022. I've worked with clients who have been sentenced to many decades of incarceration, life without any opportunity for parole, and death, and those who have been killed by the state.

In 2012 the Supreme Court extended the mitigation requirement to cases involving youth under the age of eighteen and facing a potential sentence of life without the possibility of parole. Though not required in all other criminal cases, the power of mitigation evidence to change outcomes for individuals facing the loss of liberty has filtered into wider criminal defense practice. This is especially true as thirteen states, the District of Columbia, and the federal government have enacted "second look" policies that allow for judicial review after an incarcerated person has served a portion of a lengthy sentence.[17] It is only a matter of time before mitigation specialists and the work they do are synonymous with access to justice.[18]

OVER THE LAST two decades I have traced, researched, and documented virtually every system that society has erected for the collective good as it relates to a client: departments of education, Head Start programs, special education services, disability assistance, environmental protection agencies and efforts to remediate Superfund or other extremely toxic geographic sites, social security support services, military recruitment processes, all four branches of the armed forces, post-service veterans' support, hospitals, clinics, access to medical insurance, public housing developments, departments of sanitation, emergency services, sheriffs' departments, state law enforcement agencies, coroners, crime labs, departments of corrections, probation and parole services, rehabilitation centers, youth homes, foster care systems, and every other type of agency or entity that has touched the client's life.

I have tracked contact with fire departments, investigated when emergency services became available to a given area, mapped population patterns across generations, identified the cargo ships in which my clients' ancestors were brought over to the United States, reviewed immigration records and policies, followed the paths from enslavement to sharecropping onward, traced interactions between law enforcement and local residents, and consulted historic studies and research related to the passage of laws. I have visited historical societies, state archives, vital statistic offices, and criminal, civil, traffic, misdemeanor, and probate courts in forty-two states and reviewed decades of local newspapers and correspondence between lawmakers.

I have spent time with thousands of people over the years—parents, siblings, aunts, uncles, cousins, nieces, nephews, grandparents, and grandchildren, in biological and adopted families; fellow classmates (and sometimes their family members) from elementary, middle, and high school, college, trade school, and Job Corps programs, along with teachers, custodians, bus drivers, cafeteria workers, coaches, principals, administrators, librarians, groundskeepers; co-workers, and supervisors; doctors, nurses, clinicians, dentists, secretaries, and admissions staff at medical facilities; military colleagues, recruiters, and test administrators; church members, ministers, priests, nuns, imams, youth group members and leaders, Sunday school teachers, choir directors and members, and Bible study groups; summer camp participants, youth leaders, and adult chaperones; boyfriends, girlfriends, spouses, one-night stands, longer-term relationships; roommates, neighbors (immediate and throughout the community), family friends, and family enemies; psychologists, psychiatrists, counselors, social workers, previous attorneys, previous investigators, and paralegals; prison guards, wardens, prison mental health staff, former fellow inmates, current fellow inmates, substance abuse counselors, prison educators, and spiritual advisers; victims of other crimes, surviving victims, family members of murder victims, and other impacted community members; jurors, bailiffs, judges, prosecutors, court reporters, and other court staff. It is typical for me to talk to hundreds of people in a single death penalty case, and many of those individuals must be visited multiple times. In other types of cases it is common to visit several dozen, and many more than once.

I have never worked in an organization focused on freeing innocent people from prison, though on occasion I have found myself involved in cases where clients didn't carry out the crime for which they were convicted. But I want to be clear that most of my clients, all but one of whom have been men, are responsible for the violent death of another person. That death wasn't an accident. It wasn't self-defense. My clients didn't kill for compassionate reasons, like euthanasia for the sick and dying. Such moral justifications do not apply. The murders my clients committed were often brutal, extreme, and irrational. These are the types of crimes that leave many wondering: What kind of person is capable of doing such a horrible thing?

Working with people who have killed means working with some of the most traumatized individuals in society. Because of the harm they have caused, the lessons that can be learned from their experiences are often ignored. The work of mitigation investigation itself involves learning all that is possible about those traumas. Certain factors repeat: underresourced, isolated, and forgotten communities; poor educational systems; lack of safe and healthy housing; sexual, physical, and emotional violence; neglect; and missed or misdiagnosed mental illness. Though this is not an exhaustive list, these factors represent the macro and micro assaults that have compounded on individual clients. I have come to believe that if everyone knew what I know about how murder happens, we wouldn't try to stop it through sentencing and surveillance; we'd try to stop it by making sure that no one ever is harmed or neglected in the way that my clients have been.

"But your client had a choice." Over the last two decades I've heard that thousands of times, even from the most sympathetic. At a certain point this notion of individual choice began to strike me as incorrect or, rather, woefully incomplete. I believe the onus is on the justice system to enlarge it. The law looks to address extreme behavior, and individual choice is an especially insufficient point of departure if you want to address extreme behavior. There is a need to account for the reality of individual choice while also accounting for community responsibility—the role of collective choice in the ways people come to harm one another.

Through my work with clients I've observed that the most important choices in a life—the ones that shape who a person ultimately becomes—are often those that are made for the person even before accessible memories of the experience have been formed. Who your parents are; how you are cared for and treated as an infant; whether you are provided with healthy food, clean water, and a living environment free from violence, instability, and environmental toxins like lead paint; whether you have access to caretakers with the capacity to emotionally engage with a developing person, or opportunities for meaningful education; your neighborhood—all these factors that inform every person's development result from choices that my clients did not make or even play a role in making. They were determined by social and familial circumstances that my clients did not choose for themselves but would nonetheless be the most formative to the people they became.

I truly believe that if my clients could have chosen something different, they would have. The truth is that by the time someone is on the verge of committing a murder, their trauma responses have been formed and well-honed. That includes the capacity to assess options and reason through stress, which has most often been severely limited. Their neural pathways are paved. The choice my client faces, in that nanosecond, is no choice at all.

Most of us know that promoting wellness is far more effective than emergency care. And sometimes working with my clients feels like working in an emergency room. I can see the chances to prevent the crisis that have been missed. But the fact that there are patterns—types of traumas and experiences endemic to the lives of those who have killed—means that there are also preventive measures. There are ways of stopping murder—of stopping harm in many instances—before it happens.

•

A KEY FUNCTION of the mitigation specialist, in addition to tracing the threads of a client's life through research and extensive interviewing, is ensuring that, in the theater of the legal process, a client's humanity is not lost. What does it mean about the America system of justice that such a task—to humanize the human—is necessary? For all the work being done around reducing mass incarceration, I have seen little reckoning with how dehumanization—a feature at the core of perpetrating harm—is built into the fabric of the legal process itself. And needlessly so; we could just as easily choose to restore and protect a person's dignity. Rather, our collective choice has been to prop up a superbly destructive system that produces huge amounts of generational harm and wastes human potential. There are many ways a legal system can function. We have chosen to create one that functions this way.

A core lesson of working with people who have killed is that the less you know about someone, the easier it is to cause them harm—to kill, torture, abuse, enslave. A criminal legal system, just like any other created social system, is culturally shaped, historically informed. Hold that concept in balance with how the history of America is a history of othering. See the equivalence. This is not a judgment, but a fact. And while the criminal legal system has refined itself in some ways to give the appearance of improvement, little fundamental progress has been made because the core issue—our collective empathy problem, including and especially across race, class, and ability—has never been addressed. Mitigation investigation, with its values of equity, dignity, and human connection, and the evidence it produces provide one antidote.

I LOVE WORKING as a mitigation specialist. It is a gift and a privilege to spend time with people I might not otherwise have the opportunity to know. And in that process, I have learned that what most people want, regardless of race, gender, income, ethnicity, or politics, is fundamentally the same: to be seen, valued, and cared about. I believe, despite all I have seen and experienced, that people are more parts good than bad, but need reminding of the ways in which we are more the same than different. The most effective way to perpetrate harm is to lose sight of another's humanity—and this brings me to the present.

I struggled with the decision to write this book. My work is connective and intimate, and I did not come to any of these relationships intending to share them with the world. Throughout the drafting of this book, I wondered if doing so was right. A friend, the poet and attorney Dwayne Betts,[19] reminded me once that books can go places I can't. The written word can reach deeper, farther, and it can be carried inside one's mind and heart in ways that the spoken word alone cannot. Holding on to that truth helped me navigate the complicated feelings I have held throughout this project.

The fact that many of these are not my stories means I tried as best as I could to do right by others. Each living client whose story is featured in the work was asked if they wanted to be included in the book and given the chance to read what was written and give feedback and, if they were comfortable, permission. In some instances, clients at the inception of their representation also signed retainers allowing for the use of their stories in service of the public good; others signed consents. Names of clients and witnesses, as well as details that would make a person easily identifiable, have been changed. In addition, I have stuck as closely as possible to sharing information that already appears in public records, like trial transcripts or briefs in which witnesses have given sworn statements about their experiences, where many of the hardest pieces of information have been shared in court proceedings.

There are two cases, though, where I do not use pseudonyms. In these two cases, I had previously written publicly about the men, rendering it far less likely that I could successfully anonymize them. Their stories felt essential to one of the main points of the book—that knowing a person in their fullness influences our assessment of what someone deserves in the aftermath of a tragedy. It also allowed me to highlight the many other victims involved in our legal system—loved ones of those whom society has cast aside, members of legal teams who develop bonds and friendship with the outcast, and the trauma that seeps into the spaces of lives that continue long after a sentence has been carried out. Their experiences are shared from a place of compassion and love.

EDWARD AND I are now both in our midforties. His once-lustrous hair has thinned with age, revealing a bald spot at the crown of his head. His goatee, which was also once perfectly black, is now salt-and-pepper. The last time I saw Edward, he noted my graying hair, and we joked about how we were growing old together. We have known each other for over twenty years. Other than members of his immediate family, I have known Edward for longer than almost anyone else in his life. And the same can be said for him. Other than my immediate family and a few friends, Edward has known me longer than anyone else in my life.

This book occupies the space between our first meeting and the present. It was written on weekends, in early mornings before the sun was up, in the middle of the night when my mind struggled to find peace, in my head as I drove between witness visits or out to various prisons to sit with clients. It was written in and on my heart. There will no doubt be people who think that I should have done more to protect others I have written about, or perhaps not written this at all. As author Samuel Beckett wrote, "Try again. Fail again. Fail better." I hope I have failed better.

Holding the humanity of my clients in balance with the fact that they have done harm may feel impossible at first, but I hope that coming to know these individuals as I have will show readers a path to understanding not only these men but many more whose stories have tended to be presented one-dimensionally. Think of mitigation as adding dimensions, an essential skill for us all—if there will ever really be a justice system, or indeed equality, in America or elsewhere.

It might seem as if the spaces I occupy house nothing but suffering or the heaviness that comes from hopelessness. It may even feel as if the problems contained here are insurmountable. There is a great amount of tragedy and much hard work to do, no doubt, but there is also enormous hope for the future. The answers I went looking for in 2004 are clear: we cannot incarcerate our way out of violent crime. The stories of people I have worked with and learned from during my career matter if we want to prevent future harm. They show a path toward helping people to heal parts of themselves and grow in ways that will tip life—all our lives—in another direction.

Chapter One

The Long Way Around

The walk from security at the entrance of the prison to the Polunsky Unit's visitation room took two minutes. A prison official was waiting for me in the vestibule of the visiting area, where I had walked alone after I cleared the metal detector and my items were x-rayed. She worked in the inmate records department and was my escort. Before heading to the visiting area, we stopped by her office, where I signed the logbook. Then, side by side, we proceeded down a sterile hallway that felt much like a hospital corridor. She asked about the drive from Houston and chatted about the weather. I responded in kind, to be polite, but I would have rather walked in silence. This place was designed for men to leave only in a coffin, and I didn't feel comfortable making small talk there. We passed a group of inmates, all men of color. I nodded my head toward them and said a barely audible hello. My escort did not. Her silence made me feel uneasy: Had I done something wrong? I drew my notepad to my chest and kept my eyes to the ground until we reached the visiting area.

I arrived early enough to secure one of the unit's two private legal booths, allocated first come, first served. This was the most private setting I could have with a client and provided the least distraction. In the main visiting area there would be a lot of activity, with officers bringing inmates in and out for social and other legal visits. Since death row inmates live in solitary confinement, being out of the cell with any visitor was also an opportunity to see other guys from the unit, shout out to someone, have a quick conversation.

As I waited for Edward to arrive, I wrote notes to myself about the things I wanted to ask. I kept the door behind me open and walked out occasionally to check a large wall-mounted clock by the vending machines. I didn't wear a watch; I didn't want to risk looking distractedly at the time while visiting a client.

It was nearly an hour before Edward appeared, handcuffed with his arms behind him, wearing a billowing white state-issued jumpsuit with the letters DR stenciled on the back. The prison required that death row inmates be escorted to the visiting area by four or more officers, rather than the usual two for those with lesser sentences. Edward entered his side of the legal booth. The large steel door behind him slammed shut. He then squatted low so the officers could open a slot in the door and release his restraints without being in the same space with him.

Something compelled me to stand up on my side of the booth and wait until Edward was unshackled. When the cuffs were off, he rubbed his wrists, where red marks remained. On our separate sides of the glass panel, we picked up our phones and wiped them down with our clothing, an attempt at sanitization. We then perched uncomfortably on small metal stools that were bolted to the ground.

Edward was about average height and chubby, though it was hard to get a good sense of his size under the large jumpsuit he wore. His face, light brown in color, was round, and his cheeks full and pink. His slicked-back hair was straight and jet-black. I noted his goatee and his big brown eyes. Even though it was February and hovering around fifty degrees outside, the sleeves of his jumpsuit were cut off to the tops of his biceps, revealing his arms fully. I spotted tattoos of what I knew to be his mother's and sister's names on his biceps. The tattoos were black and crooked, which made me wonder if he had received them in prison.

Before making the ninety-minute drive to meet Edward, I'd reviewed the information from his case file, which included trial transcripts, his trial attorney's file, and the files from his state appeals attorney. A lot of the information was redundant and bureaucratic and provided only the barest of bones about Edward as a person. I learned that he was the oldest of six children born to his mother, Maria, from four separate relationships. Maria was originally from Mexico and had come to the United States undocumented around age eighteen. Edward was born within a year of her arrival; his father was a married older co-worker. For this reason Edward was raised not knowing who his father was until shortly before he was arrested for capital murder and his mother facilitated a meeting between the two. Maria's second son died in an apparent drowning in the bathtub when Edward was three years old. Child protective services did a cursory investigation and determined his death to be accidental. The agency popped into Edward's life a few times thereafter, initially removing him but eventually sending him back to Maria.

Maria's expanding family moved on average every two years before Edward turned sixteen. His grades were poor, even in basic classes like art and physical education. He smoked PCP-soaked marijuana, which was widely available in the 1990s,[1] and was involved in a couple of armed robberies with several of his cousins before being arrested for murder. The murder took place about a month after his eighteenth birthday. Edward and another teen attempted to rob a convenience store in the middle of the day. Upon entering the store, which was full of people who had stopped for gas, a snack, or to use the restroom, Edward and his companion lost control of the robbery and began shooting. A young man with a wife and two daughters under the age of three at home was shot and died before making it to the hospital. Another man was shot in the leg and survived. Everyone in the store was horrified and scarred by the experience.

In the bedlam, it was never clear which young man, Edward or his acquaintance, had fired the fatal shot, despite numerous witnesses being present. Remarkably, the law in Texas does not always distinguish between the shooter responsible for firing the deadly shot and another shooter.[2] The fact that Edward participated in a robbery during which a man lost his life was enough for the state to pursue the death penalty. Understanding this, Edward's codefendant, who was slightly older, quickly confessed and accepted a sentence of forty years to life. Edward also confessed shortly after his arrest, but for reasons unknown he wasn't offered a deal.[3] His case went to trial fast; by the time he turned nineteen, he had been convicted of capital murder and sentenced to death. He was twenty-six years old the day we met. I was nearly twenty-four.

I introduced myself and explained that I was working with his attorneys to help on his case and that I had some questions for him. Edward was immediately agreeable, which was a relief. I had already met one man who was not interested in talking to me about his life before death row. Edward was different. "If you are here to help me, that's cool," he said.

With that, I launched into the series of personal questions I had thought about for the hour before our visit started. I figured that if he was willing to tell me anything I wanted to know, there was no reason not to dive right in.

I knew from reviewing the file that when Edward was about ten, he and his younger half brother had been sent to Mexico to live with an aunt for about two years. I am not sure why, but I decided to start there.

"Tell me about moving to Mexico," I said.

"When we got there, I thought we were just going to stay for a little bit, but we stayed out there for a couple years."

"How often did you speak to your mother?"

They didn't have much contact, he said. "It was hard. I didn't understand what was going on."

Just prior to Edward's arrival in Mexico, his aunt had experienced a late-term miscarriage and lost twin boys. Absent any other information from his mom or his aunt, he considered the possibility that he had been sent there with his brother to replace those twins. "I think about how much my aunt missed her kids," he said. "It was probably better for her to have us around."

When I asked how he felt about it all, he repeated flatly that it was hard. "I got used to it." He seemed to have accepted that he was there to make things "better" for his aunt in the wake of her loss.

I might have recognized such statements for what they were—openings, clues, leads to pursue—but I was still so green then. I moved on to my next question. I had a long list.

THE PREPARATION I received before my first visit to death row happened in a series of short, separate conversations with different colleagues. Bring quarters. Blend in. Be on time. No spiral notebooks. Write everything down. I was told to stay at each visit until visiting hours ended or the client asked me to leave. At first this struck me as odd and a bit rude, especially if it was clear that the conversation had come to an end. True, perhaps, if a mitigation visit was a social call, but it wasn't. The point was to collect information that could help make sense of the client's behavior, which meant observing details that might be slow to reveal themselves. Sticking around for extended periods of time, for many hours, gave me a chance to observe whether the client's style of interaction changed over time. Did he fatigue at a certain point, and, if so, when and how did that manifest? Did he return to the same questions or stories repeatedly? Did he laugh at odd moments, like when we were talking about something serious? Did his body language change over time from one of openness, fully facing me, to more closed as the conversation wore on or topics shifted to areas where potential trauma or shame lived? Could he follow a logical course of conversation beyond an hour or two? Was the end of the visit abrupt or communicated indirectly, such as placing the phone down without saying goodbye and having that represent the end of our time together? Such details were just as important as anything stated directly.

Every death row inmate at the Polunsky Unit lived in solitary confinement. Televisions were forbidden. The most a death row inmate could have was a radio, and if the inmate caught a disciplinary case, that could be taken away. Opportunities to be outside the cell were precious, and virtually no client ever wished to return to the maddening solitude, which meant visits could go on for hours. Tape recording was never permitted; it could trigger evidence rules and also limit personal disclosures. It was important to write down everything or nothing—the client might read handwritten notes, so a summary could misrepresent what the client had said. If I stopped taking notes, that could indicate that whatever was being shared wasn't meaningful. If I started to take notes again, that might indicate that something said at that moment was more important than other information that had been shared. I was being watched by the client the entire visit. Consistency was key.

I'd been told to make sure to type up my handwritten notes from client visits within forty-eight hours, or I would forget much of what I observed. This "forty-eight-hour rule" was and remains the benchmark across the profession. The drafted memo detailing the visit also had to include my impressions of the client: his demeanor and ability to maintain eye contact, his tone and cadence, whether I noticed any muscle twitches, spasms, or other automatic movements. It was important to track this information because each occurrence could provide a clue to how a client's brain worked. Such observations could even indicate where potential damage might be found, thus giving clues to lines of investigation—maternal drinking, a brain injury, substance use. The body offered involuntary clues that needed to be seen and memorialized or could easily be missed or forgotten.

One colleague gave me a crash course in the stages of litigation in a capital case. She sketched this out in nine labeled boxes on a piece of paper, each box representing a stage of the case from trial through state and federal appeals. After conviction and sentencing, which occurs at the trial court, there is an automatic direct appeal to the state supreme court. Once the state supreme court has affirmed the conviction and sentence, the case then moves through levels of state appeals, followed by levels of federal appeals. Only after a case has gone through all nine boxes can a death warrant can be signed, which sets the date for execution. Each of these stages can last anywhere from a few months to a decade; it is hard to predict. Edward's case was at the start of his federal appeals, which meant that it was necessary to look back at what both his trial and state appeals defense teams might have failed to do. The federal appeals were the last that his case needed to go through before an execution date could be set. In other words, if there were errors to correct, this was the last chance to raise the issue before Texas killed him.

BY THE END of that first visit, Edward had answered all my questions. I let him know I would be back to see him in two weeks. We said goodbye, putting our hands up to the glass as though we were touching, and I exited the unit in silence, without an escort.

Driving back to Houston, I thought about how much Edward had spoken, prompted by my questions, and yet how little he'd conveyed about his thoughts or feelings. His language had been repetitive. Not defensively so, I thought. There were just certain things he said: "I got used to it." His answers had been short—not so much curt as truncated. Not withholding, either. He was chatty. Engaged. But as I thought about the visit, I realized how little information had been relayed and how ready Edward was to agree whenever I tried to summarize what I'd heard. "That's what's up," he often said. I knew Edward had moved a lot as a child, and it seemed that each move was sudden and unexplained. There were lots of "I don't know" responses when I asked why the moves had taken place. I guessed that as a child he must have felt a lot of insecurity and confusion, almost as a matter of routine. A routine of nonroutine.

When I arrived back at the office, close to six P.M., one of the attorneys who had been representing death row prisoners—though not Edward—for several years was there. She asked about the visit.

"It was great," I said. "Edward answered all my questions."

She asked me to explain. I described how Edward had seemed open to talking about anything, so I'd started with his move to Mexico at the age of ten, which struck me as a major event in his childhood, and we'd proceeded from there.

Her brow furrowed. And she said something I think about often: "How someone actually handles trauma is not given in a response to a question. It's provided in the description of daily life before and after an event."

She went on to describe a different way of collecting data: by tracing how behaviors shift in the aftermath of a traumatic experience. To an observer lacking context, the behavioral changes themselves might appear completely unrelated to the event, perhaps years in the past—a reaction to a sound, say, or a sudden aversion to a place. Understanding a response to trauma requires knowing, as much as one can, about a person's baseline behavior before the traumatic experience. A direct question like "How was your life afterwards?" wouldn't necessarily yield the important information that the person was suddenly hypervigilant or avoidant. That type of direct questioning assumed a level of personal insight that most of us do not possess.

I would have many debriefing conversations like this with colleagues in my early days, regular reminders of how much I had to learn and of the value of being around more experienced practitioners who could facilitate my development.

I'd been so ill-equipped initially, but I quickly learned to ask myself: What can we learn if we think about not only what the client says but also what he doesn't say? This became an important way to think about other areas of investigation: witnesses, official records, even defense lawyers whose final word on a client ("stubborn" or "defiant," say) foreclosed meaningful investigation. I learned to focus on behaviors. And I learned to ask about daily life. Instead of "Tell me about Mexico," I might have said to Edward, "Describe how you would wake up in the morning," or "Walk me through a typical morning with your aunt. What would happen first?" Edward's early experiences had included sudden separation from a parent with no warning and little understanding of why it was happening ("When we got there, I thought we were just going to stay for a little bit, but we stayed out there for a couple years"). He'd been left in a foreign country where he did not speak the language or understand the culture and customs, with no sense of how long the situation would last. He'd been given a new, unknown caretaker who was experiencing a devastating loss. These were all experiences that any child would need time and support to understand and unpack. During that first visit, my questions hadn't allowed me to explore any of these areas with Edward.

How do we hear the ways in which a child struggles? I had a better chance of learning about Edward's challenges by having him walk me through his days before and after Mexico: how he got to school, what items he carried with him. What was the usual routine before bed? What happened if he needed the bathroom in the middle of the night? How did he obtain food when he was hungry?

Later on, as my skills developed, I'd learn that the direct questions I had initially asked Edward about his life were not just pointless; they were potentially damaging to the trust that I needed to build. By going straight to an unmooring life event, my questions might have come across as hunting for particular answers, implying a lack of interest in the rest of his life, including the utterly tedious moments. What I needed to do was create a structure for us that allowed a relationship to develop, a place where Edward could share all of his experiences, not only the most difficult ones.

Danalynn and the rest of the team also taught me to take a broader view of where experience actually begins. What do we miss if we only look at a client's life from the time they were born? Isn't a person shaped by their parents' and grandparents' experiences too? This made intuitive sense to me. I am the daughter of an ethnic Armenian, and many within my father's family were victims of a genocide that took place before the Holocaust, in 1915. My mother, who was born and raised in Poland in the 1950s, grew up in a culture shaped by the experience of internment camps. I wasn't involved in the events my parents and their parents had lived through, namely ethnic cleansing, but those events influenced their behavior, which influenced my behavior. Even my desire to understand hidden experiences and invisible dynamics was partly rooted in my parents' secrecy, shaped by their parents' experiences.

But there is also a biological component, the subject of the developing scientific field of epigenetics. Research has shown that traumatic experiences can influence genetic expression and how that expression is passed on to one's offspring.[4] Studies conducted in the 1990s with the adult children of Holocaust survivors showed that they were more likely than others to have mood and anxiety disorders, as well as post-traumatic stress disorder (PTSD). Evidence also showed that many children of Holocaust survivors had low cortisol levels. Cortisol interacts with certain parts of the brain to influence a person's motivation, mood, and fear level, and low cortisol levels have been linked to PTSD.[5] Later research with pregnant women who survived the attacks on the World Trade Center showed that the saliva of their babies also had low cortisol. The effect was most prominent in babies whose mothers had been in their third trimester on the day of the attacks.

What could I learn about Edward if I began the investigation into his life before his birth? To understand why Edward's life had proceeded as it had, and how he had internalized various traumas, I needed to understand his family, and in particular the experiences of his caretakers. I needed to start with getting to know his mother.

MARIA LIVED ALONE in a one-bedroom apartment located in a sprawling three-story complex. About a week after I met Edward, I made my third attempt to visit with her. I passed through a broken gate that was hanging off its hinges and entered the parking lot, which was full of crater-size potholes. The first two times I tried to visit Maria, there had been no answer when I knocked, so here I was again, hoping that this would be the moment we would meet. I stood at the door, waiting with the intense nervousness—I still feel it to this day—that comes with another core rule of mitigation investigation: no appointments or contact to arrange a time to meet. Just show up.

There's a reason we call a mitigation interview a "visit." My colleagues taught me to go to the home of a potential witness unannounced. It is the professional standard, even if there is reason to believe an individual would willingly make time to help. This rule, too, appeared counterintuitive to me at first—and potentially risky for the relationship I would need to build with the interviewee. However, here was the logic: a mitigation interview is an interaction designed to obtain reliable evidence. Reliable evidence means not giving the witness a chance to talk to others before the visit. It means guarding against them calling other people to come over and participate in the visit, thereby limiting disclosures. Any person adjusts their behavior based on who is in the room, and the presence of others can make it harder to share difficult memories or experiences.

Showing up and simply starting the conversation is also the best way to guard against someone changing their mind at the last moment and skipping out entirely. When your loved one faces murder charges, your immediate feelings of fear, grief, anger, and shock are not the only sources of pain. The news (local, national, sometimes international) media will have likely picked up stories about the murder. People in the immediate area know who is accused and have heard about the crime, including (and especially) its most sensational details. Shame descends on the family and others close to the client.[6] Most people, no matter the love they feel for the client, find it extremely challenging to talk about something so hard to comprehend—that this family member or good friend might be responsible for the death of someone else. It's understandable that even those who want to help and are initially open to meeting could become anxious and avoidant.

In addition to the emotional reasons that a well-meaning person might dodge contact, there are other problems with arranging interviews ahead of time. People are unlikely to answer the phone to an unknown number, but if the mitigation specialist leaves a voicemail explaining the purpose of the visit, there is no way to know who else might intercept that message and what repercussions the witness could face. Any attempted contact through social media or email bears the same risks.

Mitigation investigation was and remains in-person work. It's also community-based work. When I show up at the home of a potential witness, they are able to see my face and read my body language: nonverbal cues such as my facial expressions, eye contact, or gestures. And I can read theirs. Evidence is expressed by one's body and environment. More can be gleaned about a person—their habits, beliefs, and values—in a single visit to their home than in any number of conversations over the phone or by video.[7] The items on a person's wall, the presence or absence of furniture, how a home is cared for and maintained, whether there is central air or heating, if there is a particular scent or odor, whether there is a place to eat with others, if the paint on the walls is chipped, if there are pets and how they are treated, and who stops by the home or calls—these are important clues that cannot be obtained through other means. Many of these everyday facts could be altered or obscured if someone knew to expect a visit. It is rare to have a conversation with a witness just once, and all follow-up visits are unannounced as well, though there might be multiple, dozens even, during the course of an investigation.

So, with my heart pounding in my ears, I found myself again knocking at Maria's door one evening. This time I heard a dead bolt turn, and a woman answered. Her hair was black and wavy and pulled back in a ponytail. Her eyes were the same as Edward's, large and brown. I had been taught how to introduce myself; I delivered the standard greeting, "Hi. My name is Liz. I am here to visit with Maria." I waited for her to respond. She confirmed she was Maria. "It's good to meet you," I said. "I am here to visit with you about your son Edward." A sudden flash of what looked like exhaustion crossed her face. She seemed to force a smile as she welcomed me inside. There had been turnover on Edward's defense team, and I was the fifth person working for him to appear at her door in the space of two years.

The front room of Maria's apartment, the main living area, was clean but cluttered with various papers and unopened mail stacked on surfaces and plastic bags strewn around, some empty and some filled with belongings. The walls were bare, minus a few pictures of Edward and his siblings. Other personal touches such as throw pillows and plants were absent. No knickknacks. Maria lived there, but the space didn't seem fully inhabited.

This was my first time meeting a client's mother. Once again, my inexperience showed. I started with a series of census-style questions about her family: the names of her parents, their ages when she was born, the names of her siblings and their ages. I hoped to get a handle on Edward's family tree. I thought that was a neutral place to start. Maria didn't seem to know the answers to most of the questions, and the exchange quickly became tense. I would ask something seemingly straightforward, and she would meekly shake her head from side to side and say she did not know. Feeling like I wasn't getting anywhere, I switched topics. I asked for the names of Edward's friends when he was growing up. Maria didn't remember much about them—just vague impressions and not their names. In fact, she couldn't name a single person with whom he'd spent time. She did not like having other kids at her place, she explained, nor letting her own kids spend time at their friends' houses.

Multiple times it looked like Maria was on the verge of tears, yet I stayed until she said she needed to get ready for work the next day. After we'd spent several hours together, I left. I walked to my car, feeling uneasy about the interaction. Maria had struck me as timid, ashamed, and fragile. I hadn't learned much about her or Edward. I sensed that I had approached the interaction all wrong.

MY BREAKTHROUGH WITH Maria happened two months later. As usual, I appeared unannounced at her door, but this time she smiled and looked genuinely happy to see me. I had been stopping in to spend time with Maria every two weeks. On the advice of my colleagues, I aimed on each visit for general conversation rather than asking direct questions. I found that in some ways the long way around an intended subject turned out to be the more direct route. Maria began to make eye contact, her posture opened, and even her voice became smoother and more relaxed. She asked about my life, including my family, and showed interest when I told her that my parents were immigrants, my mother from Poland and my father from Iraq. On hearing that my mother had waited tables at a diner and my father had often worked two to three jobs to make sure our family had enough money, she nodded in recognition. Maria knew what it was like to work twelve, fourteen, or even sixteen hours a day.

I could identify with some of her experiences, too. We talked about what it was like for her to move to the United States without being able to speak English. One of her first employers would sometimes refuse to give Maria her paycheck until she asked for it in English. She told me how bad she'd felt during those exchanges. I recalled how small and worthless I'd felt when my father's brother, who lived near us and spoke

English, addressed me in Armenian even though he knew I could not speak the language.

As I spent time with Maria and others who had known Edward throughout his life, I was also collecting documents from courthouses, hospitals, schools, and other institutions and agencies that Edward's family had interacted with, not just over his lifetime but well before it. The standard for gathering information in a mitigation investigation is to go three generations back from the client's birthday and, if applicable and possible, three generations forward as well. It is essential to be able to construct and trace a family tree, which can show emerging patterns of mental health concerns. I think about author Ernest Hemingway, who took his own life, and how his family tree was marked with half a dozen other suicides across generations.[8] Family trees also show eras within a family—births, marriages, divorces, deaths—the cast of characters rotating and changing in ways that can highlight some person or event with a particular impact on the client. Rather than rely solely on any one witness's account of an experience, by Edward or anyone else, I needed to corroborate information through multiple sources.

It was in the process of gathering criminal, civil, and traffic records for everyone Edward had shared a home with that I came across his stepfather, Steve. What I discovered there left me with many questions, especially about the nature of Steve's relationship with Maria, who was listed as the victim in one of the court records. Even though I knew about the case, rather than ask about it directly, I waited for Maria and Edward to bring up this period in their lives.

From Edward I eventually learned that in late 1990, when he was eleven years old, Steve began living with their family full-time. They moved into a two-bedroom mobile home. Maria and Steve ended up having three children together, bringing the total to seven people sharing less than a thousand square feet of space. Edward told me that he didn't spend much time at the trailer. At first, he made it sound like he just hadn't cared for the tight quarters. But over time, Edward divulged more about his constant efforts not to be at home. He wouldn't go back to the trailer for several days at a time, opting instead to sleep outside, without shelter or bedding, in the woods that surrounded the mobile home park. By the age of twelve, he had learned that Steve drank beer upon waking until he blacked out in the afternoon. When he recovered from blacking out, Steve was often abusive and violent.

As I sat with Maria one day, the conversation meandered toward her relationship with him. I asked how they met. Steve had been Maria's neighbor. Maria was living in a one-bedroom apartment at the time; Edward and her other son were with her sister in Mexico. Maria sent them away because she couldn't watch them and work as much as she needed to in order to pay the rent. Child protective services had already been to her apartment a few times during Edward's early life, and she didn't want to get into trouble for neglecting her kids.

Before having much direct contact with Steve, Maria noticed that he drank a lot. The signs were familiar because some of her family members had problems with alcohol. Steve looked sweaty, his eyes bloodshot, his gait off. Maria felt uneasy around him. To avoid trouble, Maria was nice to him when they spoke, though she was afraid. She felt as though he watched her. Steve was often hanging around her apartment when she came home at night, which made her increasingly uncomfortable.

One night while Maria was making dinner, Steve came by, asking to borrow a pot to cook pasta. When she opened the door, he pushed his way into her apartment.

"He picked me up like a sack of potatoes, put me over his shoulder, and carried me to his apartment. I screamed and tried to make a lot of noise and even broke one of his windows during the attack, but no one came to help, and he did not stop. He did whatever he wanted to me."

While Steve raped Maria, she thought about the fact that she still had food on the stove and that her apartment door was wide-open. Her mind went elsewhere until Steve had finished. Maria then calmly returned to her apartment and called the police. This option had only recently become a possibility for Maria. She was one of the 2.7 million people who had received amnesty from the 1986 Immigration Reform and Control Act, which allowed Maria and anyone else who had entered the United States without documentation prior to 1982 to apply for a green card.[9] Before that point, she had no legal rights and could not have made such a call without risking deportation—a risk she would not have taken, for reasons I came to understand as I got to know her. Even with that status change, it took courage for Maria to call the police. Steve was subsequently arrested and sent to jail.

Maria didn't have anyone to talk to about the rape. She didn't have health insurance to see a therapist, and local authorities provided no support through victim services or any other agency.[10] She moved again, picking a two-bedroom apartment in the same complex, on the ground floor facing the parking lot, so she wouldn't have as far to go from her car to the front door. Maria wanted to leave the complex entirely, but she wasn't able to find anything affordable. Then, after close to two years living apart from her sons, Maria went to Mexico to collect them. By that point they had acclimated, and now they felt like Mexico was their home. "I got used to it," Edward told me, "and then boom boom boom, she took me back." But Maria didn't want to live alone anymore.

Within just a few months, Steve's case was resolved with a plea agreement to time served in jail. From records, I knew that about ten years before he raped Maria, Steve had been accused of indecent exposure in Virginia and then later charged with burglary in Texas. His family could afford to hire counsel for each of these cases, as well as their own mental health experts, in service of his defense. It was the kind of legal support unheard-of for my clients.

After Steve was released, he returned to the same apartment complex. It wasn't long before he found Maria again. She had reported the attack and submitted to the resulting law enforcement process—she had described what happened in detail, she had pressed charges, she had engaged with the law—and Steve was right back.[11] Maria believed, based on what she'd experienced, that the police wouldn't be able to keep Steve away from her. She was tired of not knowing when Steve might come by or what he would do to her; her anxiety was becoming unbearable. Then Steve said he wanted to marry her. To Maria, in that moment, saying yes seemed like the best of a set of bad options: if she didn't have the resources to move and couldn't prevent him from harassing her, she might as well keep him where she could see him. This might be a way to manage the randomness of his behavior, she thought, and bring some stability to her life. Maria told me she'd hoped that, as her husband, he would treat her better. Admittedly, her reasoning seemed unusual to me, and I wondered if what was happening was familiar to her in some way. Her explanation conveyed a degree of being worn down by the time Steve had raped her and then returned to the apartment complex.

They married, and Maria's life did not improve. Steve continued to drink and became increasingly violent. Maria tried to keep the kids in a separate room so he wouldn't hurt them. She locked the door, but he would use a knife to pick the lock. The abuse didn't stop when she became pregnant with Steve's child. He once dragged Maria across the floor by her hair and slammed her head through the wall, leaving a hole, all in front of Edward, who was around twelve years old at the time. Later, when Steve had passed out, leaving her to clean up the debris from the damage, Maria noticed that a beam was right next to the spot where her head had crashed through. "I wouldn't be talking to you today if Steve had put my head through the wall a few inches over," she said, laughing nervously.[12]

Maria's story shed so much light on Edward's life. Even though he hadn't been present when Maria was raped, his life was directly impacted by the repercussions of the assault. Maria brought her children back from Mexico shortly after the rape because she was afraid to live alone. She made this decision even though Edward and his brother had become accustomed to their new lives with her sister and were thriving. To this day, Edward speaks about how that period in Mexico was the best time of his life: he had parents, structure, and safety. "In Mexico I felt loved. I felt wanted. It was different from what I felt with my mom. With my mom there were times no matter what I did I'd get beat. It was just expected. My mom didn't show love the same way my aunt did. With my aunt there would be something to eat when you got home. She was giving all of us love."

When Edward returned from Mexico, Maria was shut down and emotionally unavailable. Her temper, which had been significant before, was worse. She had no patience for Edward, who needed a lot of reminding to do what he was told. As the oldest son, he was expected to clean the apartment, make food for himself and his brother, and watch his brother after school. "But I wasn't an adult," he told me. At school, Edward repeated third grade because of challenges with problem-solving and completing tasks; at home, he failed to meet Maria's demands. Maria, who had a hard time understanding English and struggled to communicate clearly in any language when she was frustrated, did not understand that Edward wasn't being lazy or defiant. Maybe if Edward had been able to speak better Spanish, he could have articulated what he needed help with, but despite having spent more than a year in Mexico, he hadn't become conversant.

As our visits continued, Maria told me that during this time in her life, she was often frustrated, overtaken by anger. It wasn't unusual for her, when Edward failed to do what he was told, to grab something near to hand—a phone, a hanger, a shoe, a belt, a bicycle chain—and pummel him anywhere on his body until he cried out for her to stop and promised to do better next time. I was aware of some of this—I had collected records from the Texas Department of Family and Protective Services, which indicated that teachers had noticed bicycle chain marks on Edward's body. Although reports were made, I saw no evidence that anyone at the agency followed up.[13]

That evening in Maria's living room, as she spoke of Steve and all she had survived, I realized that tears were streaming down my face. The only light in the room was the faint glow of a standing lamp in the corner. The sun had set long before. I hoped she couldn't see me well enough to notice. Later, driving home, I felt guilty. The next day at work, when I told my colleagues what had happened, the consensus was that I would need to tighten my grip on my responses to make sure I wasn't impacting whether a person felt able to share information with me. My tears could suggest to Maria that I thought she was a terrible person for how she treated Edward, or that I was fragile and couldn't handle the details, or something else that could, inadvertently, make it harder for her to share more about her life.

Though I felt frustration at how my emotions had showed up in that visit, I also felt like I had achieved something positive. I had helped to create a space where Maria felt she could share the details of her rape, which she hadn't told to anyone except law enforcement. Maria deserved such a space. She deserved to be able to share her experience of motherhood too, free of judgment. Even so, I could never shake the sense that our encounters held so many seemingly incompatible truths: that it was somehow cruel and unfair of the criminal legal system, and of me as its agent, to draw out and ultimately expose Maria's traumas in order to help contextualize her son's life. It was unfair to dredge up protective services reports of Maria's abuse when she herself was a victim and a survivor who had never been treated like one. And yet there was also something empowering about the way, through the mitigation process, she could use her own pain to help someone she loved.

I wasn't trained to take on all I learned from Maria. I wondered how I could continue to feel the intensity of such exchanges without eventually breaking down in front of a witness. While learning about the harms visited upon Edward, Maria, and others in his family, I began to find ways of separating myself in the moment. During one of our visits, Edward described how Steve would grab anything from around the trailer park to beat him with, just like Maria did. For a while, Steve used a discarded two-by-four. Family pictures showed the piece of lumber leaning against a wall. I listened to Edward, watching his face closely and trying to observe rather than reflect. After I left the prison, I stopped by a home improvement store. I stood in the lumber aisle and stared at the two-by-fours, imagined one of them striking Edward's fourteen-year-old body, the impact, the vibrations. Hopelessness swelled in my chest. I had managed not to cry in front of Edward, but that day I cried the rest of the way home.

THE INVESTIGATION CONTINUED to expand organically, and the potential breadth of the work kept growing. Every visit with Edward, he provided new information about friends, neighbors, teachers, co-workers, and others. I knew I would find and visit them. But Danalynn had also taught me that some of the most important witnesses were often people that a client would never mention.

"Think about someone you went to high school with," she said. "Someone who, if I showed up at your doorstep and told you they were facing murder charges, you wouldn't be surprised."

Someone came to mind immediately.

I doubt he'd recall my name. We didn't hang out with the same people. Actually, he didn't really hang out with anyone. He tended to keep to himself, was often harassed by other kids at school, looked messy and disheveled most of the time, sat in the back of class with his head down on the desk, and was often absent. Such observations likely wouldn't come from a close friend or family member.

Danalynn continued, "Do you think this person would mention you as a witness to interview?" I had no reason to think he would remember me at all, and yet, from a mitigation perspective, I had valuable information about him. If getting a full picture of a person was required, I needed to cast a wider net.

Still, it was impossible to know in advance which of these more incidental acquaintances might have information that would meaningfully add to the picture I was developing of Edward's life. In one document I discovered the name of a former neighbor who was listed as Edward's babysitter. Edward had been a toddler at the time, too young to remember her, and so he never mentioned her. The chances that, decades later, she could provide anything useful were slim, but I had been taught to try.

Having located an address for Edward's former short-term babysitter, I pulled up to a single-story brick home near one of the airports in Houston. The house was surrounded by a chain-link fence and had a reinforced security door with a dead bolt. I didn't see a doorbell. I knocked loudly, hoping that someone inside could hear me. A woman who looked to be in her late sixties answered the door wearing a long floral house robe. I introduced myself with the script that had started to feel more natural. She invited me inside. She remembered Maria only after I showed her a picture.

We sat across from each other on large recliners while a Mexican telenovela played in the background. She had lived in the same apartment complex as Maria, she explained. She hadn't really been Edward's babysitter; she had only let Maria list her that way so child protective services wouldn't bother the family. Several neighbors had called the police to report Maria as negligent. Though this woman remembered Edward as a cute and pudgy baby she would have gladly looked after, she too had to work and was unable to care for him. She was sorry she couldn't help me more.

Rather than getting up immediately, I sat for a few more minutes. I asked her what the apartment complex had been like when she lived there. She described it as three stories with a courtyard and swimming pool. I asked where her apartment was located in relation to Maria's, and she mentioned that she passed Maria's on the way to her own. When Maria left the window blinds open, the woman said she would see Edward chained to the bed with little bowls and a bottle nearby. She suspected that Maria had no other way to make sure that Edward stayed safe while she was working long hours. As far as this woman knew, no one came to change Edward's diapers, feed him, or hold him. She shook her head. "What else could she do?"

The question stuck with me. What else? Wasn't there a better way to keep Edward safe? At that time Maria wasn't in the country legally. This was before she was given amnesty. Head Start, which is available regardless of immigration status, didn't become available in Houston until the late 1980s, at least five years after this time in Edward's life. There were childcare subsidies coordinated by states, but those were enacted even later, in 1990. There were local childcare programs targeted to low-income families, but the mere existence of such programs

didn't mean Maria could have accessed them.[14] Couldn't she have
relied on neighbors or friends to watch Edward? Most of the people
she knew were just like the neighbor I had met, individuals who were
also undocumented, and worked long hours like her. Couldn't she have
paid someone? Maria made just enough money to pay rent and afford
necessities. There wasn't extra. And bringing Edward to work with her
meant risking her job. Maria told me she'd never wanted to give him up
for adoption. Even if she had, it would not have been safe for her to drop
him at an agency, or a hospital, or a church.[15] How could it be the case
that the best option a working mother had was to leave her son chained
to a bed? I tried to think of a safe, free place she might have taken him.
I couldn't think of one.

I FOUND OUT more about the forces that had shaped Maria by gathering documents, spending time with Edward's family members, and
researching the small town in Mexico where Maria was from. Maria's
mother died during the birth of her youngest son, whose father was
unknown. Maria's father had left their marriage years before, after one
of her younger brothers was run over by a delivery van and died from
his injuries. After Maria's parents' relationship fell apart, Maria and
her mother relocated from Mexico City to the small village where her
mother was raised. By the time of Maria's mother's death, her father had
remarried and started a new family, which she wasn't welcome to join.

For the next six years, Maria, twelve years old, was left to raise the
baby, David, and another brother, Mateo. Her older sister had been
sent off to live with an aunt in another part of the country, leaving
Maria as the eldest and therefore in charge. Although an uncle lived
nearby, he was focused on his own children, one of whom lived with
serious physical and mental disabilities. Their family grew food to sell

at local markets, but harvests were poor, and hardship, combined with the demands of his family, meant he had neither the time nor the will to provide care or protection for Maria, David, and Mateo. The three stayed in the clay dwelling where their mother had bled to death after delivering David. They had no running water, electricity, or regularly available food. Maria fed David water with a little milk, while on good days she and Mateo subsisted on tortillas and beans.

There was an active feud between Maria's family and another local clan. The violence had started because of disputes over landownership, but after men on both sides were killed, it morphed into a vendetta. Another of Maria's older brothers, Diego, who had lived away from the village for years but returned to try and support his siblings, was killed in an ambush by the other family. Maria's family retaliated, and in response their men terrorized women in Maria's family. As a child, alone and unprotected, Maria was an easy target. At some point in her early teens she was kidnapped for several days and repeatedly raped.

During those days, Maria's survival might very well have depended on forming a connection with one of the men who violated her. I considered again the strange logic of Maria's decision to marry Steve. Steve's abuse was familiar; so, perhaps, was her method of surviving it.[16] Likewise, I could see how sending Edward and his brother to Mexico to live with her older sister, who had a stable life in a safer part of the country, appeared to be a decision that would help her sons. Her sister was the one sent away from the family, in the hope that life elsewhere would be better. Maria was behaving according to the logic that had spared her sister violence. She understood this logic viscerally; she had experienced its consequences. This context helped me comprehend choices of hers that otherwise seemed callous and reckless toward her children. It was essential context to understanding her actions.

Without conscious knowledge of his mother's experiences, Edward had, in many ways, absorbed her trauma. Maria had a short fuse, and it was impossible for him to anticipate what would set her off. As her child, Edward tried so hard to please her yet constantly found himself failing. From our first meeting, I'd noticed in Edward a deep need to please others. It was hard to know why his trauma might have expressed itself in this way. Maybe he'd been conditioned into it through his experiences of rupture and nonroutine. Maybe he'd noticed that things were easier if he just went along with whatever others wanted. Maybe his compliance was related to his struggles with critical thinking. He was a concrete thinker—he assumed that what you said was what you meant. Nuance, including sarcasm, was often lost on him. When compliance didn't work for him, he had learned to leave the situation—to "burn off," as he put it. He spent a lot of time outside, in the sunshine. Warmth and light helped him cope. Later, he would tape colored construction paper over the light in his cell because it soothed him.

After several years of working on Edward's case, I saw how his immediate openness to me, which had at first made me feel relieved, was in fact a symptom of the traumas he had both inherited and directly lived. He so readily believed in the goodwill of those who said they cared. When I said I was there to help him, he simply accepted that statement without getting to know me at all. Of course, he had been told by his attorneys in advance of our visit that I was a member of his defense team, and that he could trust me in the same way he could trust them. Still, it struck me that his level of cooperation, from our first visit, wasn't self-protective. Even his refrain of "That's what's up" in response to my questions, before I'd learned to let patience guide me rather than hunger for answers, suggested a lack of self-protection. Edward didn't think about the potential dangers of immediately going along with me.[17] He didn't think about his own safety. It was Edward's acquiescence, even toward untrustworthy people, that had expanded the ambit of his family's trauma outward to claim another innocent life.

BY THE TIME Edward was sixteen, Steve and Maria were embroiled in a terrible separation, and Maria's abuse of Edward had become intolerable. Maria had moved Edward and his siblings to another part of Houston, far more chaotic and violent than the trailer park. It wasn't ideal, but Maria's brother Mateo had also moved to Texas and lived on that side of town. She hoped that he or his wife could pitch in to watch her children. The rent was also much less expensive, allowing her to afford a three-bedroom apartment for herself, Edward, and her other four children.

The move was a turning point for Edward. In the trailer park, he found a surrogate family who lived nearby. I located and interviewed his friend Antonio and, separately, Antonio's mother, Delia, who both remembered Edward fondly. Delia in particular recalled how she had tried to talk to Maria about the bruises she saw on Edward. It wasn't lost on her that empty beer bottles littered the front porch of their home. Maria suggested that Delia mind her business. At that point, Delia felt the most she could do was keep an open door for Edward. He spent many nights in her home, and the move suddenly took that safety away.

Edward's three teenage cousins lived in his new neighborhood. Looking for a new place to go, he started spending more time with them. These were the children of Diego, Maria's brother, who had been killed in Mexico during the feud. After their father was killed, these cousins moved to Texas with their mother, who hoped to live a quieter life. But violence found them in Houston. A couple years before Maria relocated to the three-bedroom apartment, her sister-in-law was killed, leaving Edward's cousins to raise themselves. I wanted to understand the events that led to her murder, but the available police records showed virtually no investigation into the circumstances of the crime, which remains unsolved.[18]

Edward's cousins ranged from their mid- to late teens when their mother was killed. That might have been the catalyst for their use of guns; certainly, after her death, they accumulated a small arsenal. Available court records showed that shortly after the murder of their mother, they began carrying out armed robberies of fast-food restaurants with other teenagers in the area. It wasn't clear whether they needed the money. What was clear was that before Edward essentially moved into his cousin's apartment, he hadn't acted violently toward others. During one visit, well into our relationship, I asked him why he went along with his cousins. "Blood is thicker than water. They took me in. I owed them."

About a month after Edward's eighteenth birthday, on a Friday afternoon, one of his cousins suggested they rob a gas station convenience store. This was not the first time Edward robbed a store with his cousins since moving in, but it was by far the most impetuous. One of his cousins begged off, claiming he wasn't "feeling very lucky," but suggested Edward go along with a friend. The older cousin knew about Edward's desire to please and his gullibility; likely he guessed Edward wouldn't push too hard against the idea, even if there were some obvious drawbacks. It was a busy time of day, with half a dozen witnesses around, and there was only one mask, meaning someone would have to risk being easily identified. Edward put sunglasses on, took the gun his cousin provided, and went into the store with the cousin's friend, who wore the disguise.

The original trial jury that sentenced Edward heard a statement he'd given to the police after his arrest; they learned he'd entered the store and shouted, "This is a holdup!" Witness statements confirmed that someone said, "This is a holdup, we want your money." One of the two teens then told everyone in the store to lie down. Witnesses recalled during the trial that one shot went off, and someone said, "Give me your money, motherfucker." They kept telling the guys behind the counter, "Give me your money, give me your money." The witnesses reported being terrified. One witness told the police, "One of the men came over to me and told me he wanted my wallet. I told him I didn't have one and he felt my pockets. He asked me how I was going to pay for the milk and I told him I had some change in my pocket. I reached for the change and he told me not to move. He felt for the change, then tried to take the gold nugget ring off my finger but couldn't get it off. There were several more shots, and they left."

The jury heard a tragic story that focused on the details of the robbery: the shooting, in which one man was killed, another injured, and several were terrorized. They did not learn about the context of the crime, or anything about Edward's circumstances, as they considered whether life or death was the most fitting punishment. In fact, none of what I had learned about Edward was known to the jury that sentenced him to death. This information would now be presented in a brief to a judge who would decide whether his attorney had failed to adequately represent him. Would the jury have come to a different conclusion if they had known all this? Would they have extended mercy and spared him the death penalty?

IN THE OFFICE one day, I heard Danalynn say that the decision to execute someone is a decision to take away that entire life. It is not possible to reach inside a life and pluck out the horrible moments of harm done. In Edward's case, the death sentence didn't just threaten to extinguish the teenager who had committed the crime; it also threatened the baby chained to a bed, wailing for his mother, and the child with intellectual limitations sent to live in a new country where he did not speak the language or understand the culture. The sentence condemned an adolescent who had survived Maria's abuse and Steve's violence and wanted, more than anything, a place to belong. Knowing all of that changed the seemingly simple story of Edward and another teenager committing an armed robbery in broad daylight, during which one man was killed, another wounded, and others traumatized. Context made deciding his fate much more complicated.

Chapter Two

Conduct

Growing up, I saw little of my father. He worked two to three jobs, rarely had a day off, and was often asleep or about to leave for work when I wasn't in school. Many of the conversations with him I remember from my youth are connected to his views about justice. He was born and raised in Baghdad and fully believed in an eye-for-an-eye response to crime. Someone caught stealing should have a hand cut off. A person who committed a murder should be killed. He believed this consequence to be fair and, in many ways, superior to the American system of justice, which took too much outside the crime into account.

When he stopped working in his early seventies, he spent most of his time watching television, especially CNN and Fox News. I would travel back to California for holidays or occasional visits and sit next to him on the sectional with the large-screen television blasting in the background, an experience oddly similar to those I had on almost a weekly basis as I traveled the country, connecting with witnesses in my cases. A breaking news report would flash across the screen, something involving crime, usually coverage of a terrible murder. My father's response was always the same. He took it for granted that the alleged perpetrator was guilty. Staring at the television, he would tut, then remark that the suspect was "crazy." I would agree but offer some scenarios for him to consider. What if a person was hallucinating and a voice told them to commit the crime? What if the perpetrator had some sort of contact with the victim—had been sexually abused by him, for example? What if the accused had lived a good life, served in the military, had a terrible accident, and started behaving oddly before the crime, but no one stepped in to help? Each offering softened his views of what the right outcome should be. Even my father, who held to a black-and-white view on crime and punishment, acknowledged that not every crime or convicted person is the same. The law acknowledges this as well, using the terms *aggravating factor* or *mitigating factor* to describe the context that should be provided to decision-makers. As a mitigation specialist, my job has evolved from that tradition.

THE CURRENT WAY of determining who is deserving of mercy emerged out of a moment in the United States when the death penalty effectively didn't exist: a four-year period from 1972 to 1976. The hiatus was caused by the United States Supreme Court's decision in a collection of cases commonly referred to as *Furman v. Georgia.*

Around two A.M. on an otherwise ordinary summer morning in August 1967, twenty-four-year-old William Henry Furman broke into William Joseph Micke Jr.'s Savannah home. Micke, who had served in the Coast Guard, woke to sounds coming from the kitchen. Perhaps due to his training or to the fact that he was, at twenty-nine, a young father to five children, he decided to investigate. When he entered the kitchen, Micke discovered Furman, who after a day of heavy drinking had entered the house with a pistol. Upon seeing Micke, Furman took off, firing one shot through a closed door as he fled the home. The single bullet, which

Furman said was an accidental shot caused by him tripping over the power cord of a washing machine, struck Micke in the chest, killing him instantly. Police arrested Furman quickly; they followed tracks from the home and discovered him hiding underneath his uncle's porch with the gun in his pocket.

At the time of the crime, Furman was impoverished, had a sixth-grade education, and was living with serious mental illness.[1] His mental health and functioning were such a concern prior to trial that he was sent to the state hospital in Georgia for evaluation. There, doctors concluded that he was psychotic. Nevertheless, Furman was taken to trial. The jury found him guilty and sentenced him to death.

On that day in 1968, the jury heard evidence of the crime, decided that Furman was guilty, and then were asked to determine an appropriate sentence. They did not receive any guidance regarding the sentencing—nothing to help them focus on aspects of the crime or Furman himself to justify a sentence of death. When Furman's case reached the U.S. Supreme Court in 1972 after completing his direct appeal, his attorneys argued that this lack of guidance violated the constitutional protection against cruel and unusual punishment.

Why would one person convicted of murder receive the ultimate penalty when another person convicted of a similar crime would avoid the same fate? That was the issue Furman's attorneys brought to the court. Absent such direction, the death penalty could be given for inappropriate reasons like one's race, religion, or gender, or appear as an essentially random outcome. At that time research had started to show that in this standardless system, sentencing outcomes could often be traced to defendants' traits, including factors like race, income, and mental health, supporting the growing unease around the death penalty's application.[2]

A Supreme Court majority, five of the nine justices, agreed that capital punishment needed to change to be lawful, though the five justices could not reach a consensus about *why* or *how* it needed to change. Two justices said that the death penalty was inherently unconstitutional because it was excessive. Two justices argued that the standardless system could lead to arbitrary results, making the sentence cruel and unusual in application. One of those two justices focused on how it was underused, rendering it ineffectual for deterring others from committing crimes. The fifth justice to form the majority argued that it was unconstitutional by virtue of disproportionately affecting the poor and minorities. The result from the collection of opinions was that capital punishment was suddenly no longer permitted, but without a specific agreed-upon reason it was possible for the death penalty to return.

Since the court did not outlaw capital punishment under any circumstance, states that wanted to be able to seek the death penalty went to work to craft new laws that could address the various issues raised by the justices. States took one of two approaches: find a way to guide juror decision-making, or make a sentence of death automatic upon conviction of an eligible crime. When the court heard challenges to the new post-*Furman* laws, it decreed that automatic death sentences (the eye-for-an-eye response to murder) were not lawful. I find the writing about why automatic death sentences are not allowed under our set of laws very moving. Here is a shortened version from the court's decision in the case brought against the North Carolina law that adopted automatic sentences of death for people convicted of murder:

> The respect for human dignity underlying the Eighth Amendment ... requires consideration of aspects of the character of the individual offender and the circumstances of the particular offense as a constitutionally indispensable part of the process of imposing the ultimate punishment of death. The North Carolina statute impermissibly treats all persons convicted of

a designated offense not as uniquely individual human beings, but as members of a faceless, undifferentiated mass to be sub- jected to the blind infliction of the death penalty.[3]

States that took the first approach permitted the use of capital punish- ment when there was an effort to guide the sentencing jury. This statutory method became known as "guided discretion" and sought to focus capital sentencing on specific factors without stripping jurors of their indepen- dence. Legislatures passed the laws that identified the specific sentencing factors jurors could consider. These factors, known as aggravators and mitigators, identify the kind of evidence the prosecution and the defense need to collect to support their side—death or life, respectively.

Aggravators are facts about the defendant, victim, and nature of the crime that increase the harm caused by the offense and therefore might increase eligibility for the death penalty. It could be that the victim of the crime was especially vulnerable, like a child or an elderly person. Or the defendant had already been convicted before. Perhaps the murder occurred while the defendant was in the process of committing an- other felony, like arson, burglary, or robbery. Aggravators articulate a spectrum of circumstances, creating a framework for determining why some people might face the death penalty while others might not, and do so without considering extralegal factors.

Mitigators work in the other direction, articulating a spectrum of factors that might support lessened punishment, such as the defendant having no prior criminal record or acting under significant duress. Mitigation might ask: Was the defendant coerced into the offense? Were there other, equally culpable defendants who did not receive the death penalty? Some states also included factors that specifically addressed mental illness, allowing for a lesser sentence if the illness could be shown to have played a role in the commission of the crime.

It took about two years for a case to reveal the main issue with these recently adopted guided discretion laws. In 1978 the Supreme Court heard a new case, *Lockett v. Ohio*. The defendant, twenty-year-old Sandra Lockett, the getaway driver for a robbery gone wrong, was sentenced to death under Ohio's guided discretion statute. The Ohio law specified three reasons why someone eligible for a death sentence could get a lesser sentence: the victim played a role in their own death; the defendant was coerced; or the defendant had a mental disease that accounted for their crime. None of the three reasons applied to Lockett. Her relative youth, her experiences of poverty, and other potentially relevant factors had no way to figure into the final decision.[4]

Here was the paradox: the court didn't want death sentences to be imposed in an arbitrary fashion, and states were not supposed to limit factors that could be considered in mitigation, but this meant mitigating factors could be potentially limitless. Youth, emotional disturbances, and challenges during childhood; the ability to adjust well to incarceration—truly any evidence that could aid in reaching a "reasoned moral decision" about the sentence was on the table.[5] The same was true for aggravating factors. The court allowed juries to hear hypothetical evidence of a defendant's potential future dangerousness and permitted victim impact statements to be considered in sentencing.[6] In an effort to construct a system of law that could prevent arbitrary outcomes, the court ended up making room for plenty of arbitrariness in who was allowed to live and who was sentenced to die. Justice Harry Blackmun, who had voted in favor of the guided discretion statutes, made the following statement twenty-four years later:

> From this day forward, I no longer shall tinker with the machinery of death. For more than 20 years I have endeavored—indeed, I have struggled—along with a majority of this Court,

to develop procedural and substantive rules that would lend more than the mere appearance of fairness to the death penalty endeavor. Rather than continue to coddle the Court's delusion that the desired level of fairness has been achieved and the need for regulation eviscerated, I feel morally and intellectually obligated simply to concede that the death penalty experiment has failed. It is virtually self-evident to me now that no combination of procedural rules or substantive regulations ever can save the death penalty from its inherent constitutional deficiencies.[7]

I offer this incredibly simplified piece of history to give just a glimpse of the complexity of mitigation's history and also to suggest that the effort to apply "reason," as understood by the law, to a decision like capital punishment has had, from its inception, both admirable aims—to remove bias—and, despite the gravity of the subject matter, almost comically muddled results. It's worth considering whether reason can ever be applied to what is fundamentally a moral question.

I HAD JUST wrapped up presenting to about fifty capital defense attorneys in suburban Philadelphia. A legal advocacy group had invited me to speak about the basic components of mitigation investigation. After three years of working in Texas, I had shifted into private practice so I could focus on a single case at a time while simultaneously collecting data for my doctoral thesis on the nature of mitigation evidence and the origins of the field going back to *Furman v. Georgia*.

As I was packing up my shoulder bag, one of the attorneys who had been listening came up to introduce himself. His name was Eric, and he worked as a corporate attorney at a large international law firm based in Pennsylvania. Twelve years earlier, Eric had taken on a death penalty case in the state pro bono. Pennsylvania, like many other states, struggled to provide attorneys for death row inmates during the stage of state appeals.[8] Though there were public defenders who took such cases in Pennsylvania, these defenders were also responsible for many other kinds of criminal cases in addition to those involving the death penalty. In practice, this resulted in an unmanageable and unethical number of clients per attorney.[9] To ease caseloads, public defenders reached out to the heads of pro bono departments and "pitched" specific cases. As the head of the pro bono unit, Eric was moved by the facts in one of the cases. He believed strongly in the right to effective counsel, which it seemed the man in this case, Connor, had not received.

Connor's guilt was not in question. When Eric decided to represent him for free, the aim was to obtain a lesser sentence. It took more than a decade of litigating, but Eric eventually convinced the court to hold a hearing to revisit Connor's punishment on the grounds that Connor's trial attorneys hadn't done their jobs. There were only two possible outcomes at this stage: a new death sentence or a sentence of life without the possibility of parole. We chatted and exchanged numbers.

About a week later, Eric called and asked me if I would consider joining Connor's team. I was reluctant. I was already committed to so many things and worried about stretching myself beyond usefulness. Eric suggested that much of the work was already done—after all, he had worked with Connor for over a decade and succeeded in getting a state court to grant a new sentencing hearing. He knew Connor's family well and said they would be eager to help.

Connor had been on Pennsylvania's death row for about twenty years and was now in his early forties. He was raised by his mother and father, who had been married for over forty years by that point. Connor was the middle child between two brothers. His family lived in a spacious home in rural Pennsylvania. His mother was an executive assistant for a well-known regional businessman. His father taught at an exclusive private school, which enabled the boys to attend tuition-free. The family went to church several times a week for Bible study and to services on Sundays. They did not lack for medical care or community support; their material needs were met. Eric didn't think this was the typical experience of people on death row, which was true. Most people facing capital punishment do not have an intact family or financial stability, let alone access to high-quality education, comfortable housing, adequate medical care, or sufficient nurturing.[10] I sensed something was missing and said so.

"What happened to Connor?" I asked.

Eric told me that when Connor was a child, an uncle sexually abused him. Eric didn't know the extent of the abuse or how long it had lasted. Connor's nuclear family life looked, from the outside, so well-adjusted. I wondered what had gone on in the family to accommodate such a trauma. Eric also said that Connor's older brother had recently committed suicide, though he wasn't sure of the details. I wondered why Connor's brother would end his life, and why now? It was another indication that something more pervasive was happening within the family system.

I liked Eric. I was in my early thirties and working in a male-dominated profession. Most (though not all) of the male attorneys didn't value or even take much interest in what I could contribute. I was also not an attorney, which seemed to matter to some people. Eric, on the other hand, was eager to hear my thoughts. He was inquisitive. I was curious about Connor and intrigued by Eric. By the end of the call I agreed to take the case.

ERIC EMERGED FROM Baltimore's Penn Station just as the sun was rising. He was dressed in a long beige trench coat and a wool newsboy hat evocative of a 1950s reporter ready to get the scoop. We were heading to the far western edge of Pennsylvania that morning. At the time, the state's death row was located in a small town in the southwest corner of the state. It was about a five-hour drive from Baltimore through rolling terrain, in and out of pockets of West Virginia. When I took this trip alone to see other clients incarcerated in the same prison, I'd set off around five A.M. and hope to catch the sunrise as I crested the mountains in Allegany County, Maryland. I was usually only able to pick up a couple of radio stations, and the music, Americana or hard rock from the 1990s, always seemed suited to the ride.

Eric and I pulled into the prison parking lot at eleven A.M., technically four hours before visiting hours ended, but really three and a half; this facility perpetually set its clocks to run about thirty minutes fast. When Eric and I entered the visiting booth, Connor was already there. His head was shaved, which slightly masked the bald spot at the crown. Muttonchops, overgrown and speckled brown and gray, edged close to his chin. His skin was pale. Throughout the visit, Connor had a wad of smokeless tobacco positioned between his cheek and gum. When he smiled—which was rare—I noticed brown stains on his teeth from years of using chew.

Connor was soft-spoken and nervous that first day. He glanced my way occasionally, but mainly looked at Eric, or down at the concrete slab between us that served as a table. After introducing me, Eric gave Connor an update on his case. They talked about baseball, specifically the Pittsburgh Pirates. There was an ease between them, an effortlessness that comes only from spending time together. I was grateful to be in the room with them but also looking forward to visiting Connor alone the next day. I sensed his reticence toward me.

The following morning, Connor was again already in the booth when I arrived. Though there were phones on each side of the partition, we could hear each other well through the glass and so didn't use them. We said hello and chatted about how we'd spent our evenings. We talked about Eric. Eventually I asked Connor if he had any questions for me. He said he didn't understand what my role on his legal team was, exactly, and he hadn't wanted to say so in front of Eric. Was I an attorney? Was I an expert who would testify in court about whatever he told me? What was I trying to do, exactly? I was not the first mitigation specialist he had worked with; the previous person had visited a couple of times throughout the year. At their last visit she'd given him a list of questions to answer. Connor thought she might have been trying to diagnose him with something. She hadn't returned.

As I explained what my role was and wasn't, the muscles in Connor's neck loosened a bit. He had met a lot of social workers, psychologists, psychiatrists, and counselors over the years, and he "didn't trust those people." I asked why. "Lots of the employees of a place I went were social workers or psychologists. They lied about everything." I knew from Connor's case file that his parents had sent him to a substance abuse treatment program when he was fifteen years old. Rather than asking questions, I made mental notes of areas to return to later, after we had gotten to know each other better. Since we had only just met, diving into personal questions prematurely would have made it harder to develop a trusting relationship.

We came back to the present. Connor talked about how he spent his days on death row. He enjoyed folding origami and had become very skilled at it. As I listened to Connor, I noticed his hands shaking subtly, reminding me of how my hand looked when I played the board game Operation as a child. He noticed me notice and extended his arms so I could see each hand trembling. The left was worse. As far as he could recall, the shaking started after he was sent to the treatment program as a teenager, so he attributed it to his experiences there. The shaking only abated when he folded origami.

On my way home, I called Eric to give him an update about the visit. Had he noticed the shaking?

"No. Why? Is it important?"

At that point, I wasn't sure. Tremors could be a symptom of trauma. They could also indicate a brain dysfunction, physical injury, or something else entirely. All I knew was that Connor's body was sharing information.

A CASE AS old as Connor's had volumes of information. For over twenty years, members of his team had filled dozens of Bankers Boxes with records: family photos, letters, and birthday cards provided by Connor's parents; documents related to his education as well as his medical and mental health treatment; and all the trial materials, including thousands of pages of legal research, drafted briefs, motions, and orders that needed to be organized, reviewed, and summarized. I went to Philadelphia and hunkered down in a conference room near Eric's office. As I made my way through the material, I was struck by the repetition—the same information again and again. Not a surprise, exactly, but I expected that with each iteration of investigation, from trial to state appeal, there would be some broadening or deepening of insight into Connor's life, yet there was none. For instance, the investigation hadn't expanded to understanding Connor's life before he was sexually abused—his friends, his daily activities, his dreams about the future. It also didn't zoom out to how his behavior had changed in the immediate aftermath—the changes that people around him in school or at church might have noticed, whether he continued engaging in the same social activities or started to withdraw. Connor had lived a set of facts, and here they were, looping endlessly through years of litigation.

Between the ages of thirteen and fifteen, Connor experienced sustained sexual abuse at the hands of his uncle Ron. Incest and rape were common experiences for my clients.[11] But usually there's no record. This is the rule rather than the exception: between 70 and 90 percent of childhood rapes go unreported to the police.[12] I was well accustomed to helping attorneys understand a client's behavior as evidence of abuse in the absence of a report. However, in Connor's case, investigation of his experiences had stopped because there *was* a report. The fact that Connor had been raped was taken as obviously mitigating, end of story. Why? It was essential to know how he was shaped by the assaults. That meant asking: Who was Connor before the abuse? And after? To fully grasp the impact of the experiences, I needed to understand how the abuse had altered his trajectory. *That* is where mitigation lived.

I VISITED CONNOR every three to four weeks. Together we worked methodically through a timeline of his life, starting with detailed descriptions of the places he'd lived. During each visit he walked me through what he could recall of the spaces—the rooms, the furniture, the items on the walls. When he was born, the family lived in a small apartment, moving when he was a toddler to a double-wide trailer, where he shared a room with his older brother. When he was about eight years old, the family moved into the home where his parents still lived; back then, a brand-new three-bedroom, single-bathroom rancher to which they added over the years. By the time Connor was fourteen, he'd moved into the basement, which had its own bathroom. Walking me through a typical day as a fourteen-year-old, Connor described the clothes he'd wear to school; jeans, T-shirt, Nikes. His family did their clothes shopping at outlet malls. His parents relied on coupons and regulated the amount of food he and his brothers had access to, facts that didn't quite fit with the outward appearance of the family as solidly middle class. We also did these day-in-the-life "walk-throughs" of Connor's schools, doctor's offices, places of employment, and other spaces where he'd spent time at different points in his life. It was a powerful way to learn about material things and, through them, recognize what kinds of support were present in his life or absent from it.

I never asked Connor directly about the sexual abuse. But as I got to know him better, I came to better understand the dilemma that preoccupied him during those years regarding whether to disclose the experience to his parents. He shared with me the questions he often asked himself: What would happen if he told his mom? What would she, Ron's sister, think? What if she didn't believe him? Ron would surely learn about it and be angry. What would Ron to do to him as a result? How much worse could things get?

Ron had managed to cultivate a reputation for decency, making Connor's allegations less likely to be believed. On top of that, Connor and his family belonged to an evangelical Anabaptist Christian sect. His parents subscribed to socially conservative views, including the belief that it was a sin to engage in sexual activities outside of marriage or with those of the same sex. These were the only terms in which Connor's caretakers spoke to him about sex when he was young. He was convinced that his parents would see what happened to him in that way.

Connor turned inward. His performance in school, where his father taught, began slipping. Teachers' notes in his file documented Connor's decline from a consistently average student to one who failed to turn in assignments. His once open and kindhearted demeanor became uptight, aloof, and scattered. The file mentioned his "disrupting" class and referred to calls to his parents and detentions. School administrators apparently concluded that Connor had transformed into a problem teenager, without any further inquiry. Nowhere in the academic records did I see evidence of an adult asking him what was going on or even expressing curiosity about his home life. Connor's parents were told to intervene more in his life to help their son get back on track. His parents reached out to church elders for support. And they suggested increasing prayer and taking away privileges like television and social activities.

As I worked to map the timeline of Connor's life, I could see his behavior becoming more defiant after each interaction with Ron. Connor started chewing tobacco. Then he started missing classes. Eventually he was skipping detention. His youth criminal records showed that he began stealing from neighbors and members of the church. His parents chastised him, made him stay home, and continued to mete out punishment. When his father discovered that Connor was using tobacco, he forced him to eat an entire packet of cigarettes. Connor wasn't deterred. After nearly a year of decline, his parents finally decided to send him to a therapist recommended by members of their church. The choice of mental health professional was consequential.

Though Connor had signed an authorization for me to obtain his mental health file, this provider wasn't responsive to the numerous requests I sent over several months. I finally drove to his office, about three hours from Baltimore, to request them in person. Showing up did the trick. The records arrived about two weeks later. The first thing I noticed was that Connor had rarely received individual therapy; his parents and brothers were usually in the room. Notes from the first session suggested that most of the questions were directed at the parents, with Connor and his brothers listening to their responses. There was no indication that Connor spoke at all during that session, though the therapist noted that he appeared "distrusting." It wasn't long before Connor received a diagnosis of conduct disorder.

Conduct disorder is defined as a group of behavioral and emotional problems characterized by a disregard for others and for social rules.[13] Connor was given this diagnosis about thirty years before I met him. It's still common for mental health professionals to use this label for children or adolescents who display socially unacceptable behavior or difficulty following rules, though in my experience it is uniquely suspect as a diagnosis. Here's why: Having at this point seen "conduct disorder" on many hundreds of mental health records, I've noticed that it's especially common where counselors have relied heavily or exclusively on information provided by parents (or other adults, like teachers), as in Connor's case, *and* where counselors give no or little corroborating evidence of the disorder. What's more, many of the behaviors that could support a diagnosis of conduct disorder also support symptoms of a history of trauma. It is common for youth to act out, struggle with memory, appear disconnected, have trouble with authority, or engage in self-harming behaviors when they have experienced trauma.

A mental health diagnosis sets the stage for each type of intervention to follow. Effectively, it sets the course, which means that once a person is placed in a category, it is very hard to undo. The system is additive, so even if a different diagnosis is subsequently given, treatment plans tend to layer it atop the first rather than resetting the course. A diagnosis of conduct disorder implies that something is wrong with the child, not their environment. In Connor's case, after several months of weekly therapy relying primarily on his parents' reports, his "conduct" showed no improvement. The therapist concluded that the issues were chronic and likely the result of a personality disorder.

·

IT TOOK MONTHS to get the files in Eric's office organized. I was assisted tremendously by his legal secretary and others at the law firm who pitched in. I was amazed at the comparative speed. The same work with a public defender or court-appointed attorney could easily have taken years. Part of it was the sheer access to resources like numerous well-trained staff and up-to-date technology.

When I added to these older materials the new information I'd gathered from witnesses, a picture began to emerge of Ron's impact on Connor's preadolescent and adolescent life. Though Ron lived several hours away, he was ever-present. Contained within the materials from Connor's family was a card Ron sent him for his sixteenth birthday, a few years after he had received his initial conduct disorder diagnosis:

> *Happy birthday Connor. Keeping in touch with you is something I really enjoy because you're so often in my thoughts and so much a part of my life. I'm always interested in whatever happens to be happening with you because I care about you and everything that touches your life. No matter what the coming years may bring I want us to stay just as close as we are now. That's why it's so very important to me to keep renewing those feelings that will always keep us so close. I'll always want you to know that you mean a great deal to me. You're someone who really makes a difference in my world. Connor, I want so much to see you. Our time together at the Holiday Inn was really appreciated. I'm looking forward to doing it again. I got a box of Topps baseball cards—the kind of packs you buy in the store and have the gum inside for you when you are allowed to have them. Please work hard to get back to us. I've always believed in you and always will. I'm always thinking and praying for you.*

The hair on my arms stood up straight when I read this. Ron was replaying the abuse, walking Connor back to the places where it happened and, in my reading, explicitly saying it would happen again. What an immense amount of fear, confusion, and anger Connor must have carried, with no safe place to disclose it. How understandable, even expressive, his "conduct" was in this context: his actions communicated his suffering.

CONNOR'S PARENTS HAD met a lot of people working on their son's defense team over the years. The notes in Eric's files suggested that they had spent plenty of time sharing information about their struggles with Connor but never gave a sense of who *they* were as people. It wasn't until I started working on the case that the fact that Connor's father was adopted as a child was investigated. He was removed from his biological mother due to what sounded like neglect. He'd been malnourished and living in unsafe and unhealthy housing. She was described as being unable to tend to his emotional needs. Connor's father was old enough to have vivid memories of being taken away and placed with a neighboring family whose beliefs he adopted. His new family and the religious community were his salvation. I could see how his faith and commitment to following the advice of the church elders would be central to his views on parenting. More than how his father *perceived* Connor's behavior, I wanted to understand why he decided to *address* it as he had done. As always, there was no replacement for time spent. Within a couple of weeks of my initial visit with Connor, I began visiting his parents. Connor had already spoken with them about me and reported that I was "cool." It was a helpful endorsement.

The house sat on a hill overlooking rolling fields of farmland. Our visits took place in the family room, one of the later additions, designed to take advantage of the beauty of the landscape. It was a peaceful space. As we sat in armchairs with mugs of freshly brewed Folgers coffee, I complimented Connor's mother's ability to make the space feel comfortable and warm. Family room, armchairs, Folgers. This became the routine. By the time we began talking about the period of Connor's life where he had started seeing a counselor, I was a regular presence around the house. I'd been visiting them every three to four weeks for about four months.

"We were at a loss for what to do," his mom said, looking at his dad, who was walking around the house and nodded in agreement. "Connor was lying all the time. I know I shouldn't have, but I started going through his backpack to see what he was hiding from us. And then I found some whiskey and caffeine pills. We were so scared that he was using drugs. It had to be the reason for his bad behavior." This was the mid-1980s, and their church and community were especially panicked about teenage drug addiction, reports of which saturated local news. The War on Drugs was raging. Nancy Reagan had started the Just Say No campaign, geared toward getting youth to reject recreational drugs entirely.[14] Connor's parents had been raised to view using drugs and alcohol as sinful, a tool of the devil. I learned this on one previous visit when we looked through old photographs, including those of their wedding. No alcohol or dancing had been allowed. The whiskey and caffeine pills in Connor's bag did not just fit into a national narrative; they were existentially frightening. By the time Connor's mother spoke about her discovery of the substances, during a session with the church-recommended therapist, she was already nearly convinced that her son would benefit from an inpatient stay in a mental health facility focusing on addiction. Connor said he wasn't addicted to drugs—that he hadn't even tried drugs. The pills weren't drugs, he said; they were over-the-counter medications that could be purchased at any pharmacy. But the counselor agreed with Connor's parents.

Connor's parents asked church elders for their prayers and for guidance. Some of the elders suggested a privately run substance abuse treatment center out of state. One morning, Connor's parents told him to get into the family's minivan. In secret, they had arranged his admission to the out-of-state program weeks before. At the program's recommendation, they had enlisted two large, strong men from their church to prevent him from escaping; the men sat on either side of Connor in the minivan. His parents sat in front. Some three hours later they pulled into the parking lot of a massive, warehouse-like building. The two men carried Connor into the facility, where staff stripped him naked and examined his clothing for the presence of drugs. After signing him over to the program, which included paying the enrollment fee and assuming financial responsibility for substantial out-of-pocket payments not covered by insurance, his parents were instructed by staff to leave.

When Connor spoke about his time in the program, he looked down, and the tremors in his hands became more pronounced. His voice and manner of speaking changed too; with his face obscured, I'd forget for moments that I was listening to a man of almost forty and not a teenage boy.

"They just left me there. I asked them not to do it, but Mom and Dad just walked out," he told me. After that, "I wasn't allowed to make any phone calls or write letters until I 'adjusted,' " a benchmark that wasn't made entirely clear to him or his parents. In the meantime, he'd see his family during weekly visits in a group setting.

STRAIGHT, INC., BILLED as a rehabilitation facility for youth and adolescents, opened treatment centers throughout the United States in the 1980s, during the height of the War on Drugs.[15] The program, which accepted children as young as thirteen,[16] utilized an expansive definition of drug abuse that included a single use of marijuana or alcohol. It even admitted kids who had never tried drugs or alcohol but seemed to exhibit what the program considered "druggie behavior": acting out or spending time with peers suspected of using.

Straight was structured as a peer-to-peer program, which meant that participants led therapeutic sessions, children to children. Many of the facilitators were adolescents who had recently graduated from Straight. They received almost no formal training and often used brutal techniques. "Spit therapy was the worst," Connor said. A peer leader would spit in the faces of attendees who did not share details of their alleged drug-addicted past. Since no one from Straight verified whether a participant had truly experienced drug or alcohol addiction, kids like Connor had to confess to things they'd never done or else be spat at, physically held down by larger teens or young adults, or placed in five-point restraints.

Out-of-state participants like Connor lived with the families of local participants. The program instructed Connor's hosts to have him strip down to his underwear each night. He was not allowed to wear pajamas to bed lest he hide drugs in the lining or seams of his clothes. All windows and doors were secured with additional locks. Connor, a rape survivor, was sent half naked to sleep in rooms with older boys, with no way to escape. Even using the bathroom was an exercise in control and humiliation: every time he needed to go, an older program participant had to accompany him—a measure used to prevent escape and ensure no drugs were being used—and would dispense toilet paper one square at a time.

Every week, when his parents came to visit, Connor begged them to take him home. Finally, after several months, desperate to escape the torture and humiliation, he disclosed what Ron had done to him. "I thought if they knew about what Ron did, they would get that I wasn't on drugs. It was about Ron." He hoped the information would show that his "bad behavior" wasn't drug-related—that he was reeling from an experience he hadn't been able to cope with or talk about.

"I was so relieved that they believed me," he said. "I thought I was going home."

Connor's parents viewed the disclosure as evidence that the program was working and that he was getting clean. Finally, thanks to Straight, he was being honest. Connor's attempt to get out of the program was precisely what kept him in.

OVER THE MONTHS I spent visiting with Connor and his family, I wondered about others who had taken their children to Straight. Was Connor's experience unique? I needed to locate the families of others who had attended at the same time.

I arrived at Suzie's address at nine A.M. on a Saturday morning. She lived in a single-family home in a town adjacent to Connor's parents. As always, I walked to the front door and rang the doorbell with my heart beating loudly in my ears. Cold-calling always elicits this physical response in me no matter how many times I have done it.

A petite Caucasian woman answered. She was very tan, about five foot two, and thin enough for me to notice her collarbone under her shirt. We spoke in front of her house for about half an hour. Suzie was fidgety and seemed nervous. She had been gardening at the back of the house when I arrived, so I asked if I could help her with anything. She said she planned to take care of some yard work over at her daughter's house, a few minutes down the road. I offered to tag along. We set off together, stopping at a McDonald's on the way.

We ate hash browns and Egg McMuffins on her daughter's front steps, and I confessed that I didn't know the first thing about gardening. Suzie brought me to the back shed and patiently showed me how to plant petunias in hanging containers, the kind I always saw empty outside of grocery stores in spring. I joked that my husband wouldn't know what happened to me when I returned home suddenly able to plant hanging flowers. I was grateful for her patience in teaching me something new.

Suzie adored Connor's parents and loved Connor dearly too. She had so many questions about his case but didn't want to pry. I shared what I could, which was just whatever was publicly available. As we pulled weeds and planted purple, pink, and yellow flowers in the garden, we talked about life—hers and mine. After four hours Suzie invited me back to her house. We had put in a good amount of work.

Suzie's oldest son, Matt, had been in the program with Connor. Suzie had divorced Matt's father when their son was around ten years old. Matt's father had been sent to Vietnam, where he was exposed to Agent Orange, a carcinogenic herbicide scientifically shown to cause physical and mental health disabilities.[17] Already a heavy drinker when he left, he returned from the war a damaged and volatile man. Suzie endured slaps, punches, sprains, and even a broken bone before she could not bear the abuse any longer.

The divorce wasn't amicable. Suzie, who also relied on alcohol to make it through the day, started drinking more each night to ease her stress. A couple of beers turned into a six-pack. A six-pack turned into eight or nine. Suzie went from evening drinking to drinking throughout the day, starting first thing in the morning. Matt was getting into trouble at school, which brought attention to his mother's behavior. He moved out of state to live with his father. It took Suzie a few years to get herself back on track. By the time she was able to take care of Matt again, he was a teenager, full of confusion and anger. He ping-ponged between Suzie's place and a local mental health facility for the better part of a year. At some point Suzie was given a pamphlet about Straight by one of the facility employees. Matt was drinking, and Suzie thought his issues were related to alcohol more than anything else. She was desperately afraid for him. She signed him up.

Suzie met Connor's parents through the program. Once they realized how close they lived to each other, they began carpooling down for weekly visits. The drive took about three hours one way, and it was nice to have company. Suzie got to know Connor's parents and his younger brother. They became close; she viewed them as an adopted family.

Suzie was my favorite kind of person—one who kept every single piece of paper, including everything she had received from Straight. Documents faded yellow at the corners and folded neatly in their original envelopes confirmed much of what Connor had told me about the program's admissions process and rules.

Suzie and I sat drinking coffee and combing through documents. Day turned into evening, and her son Matt joined us. It was common for people to filter in and out during visits with witnesses. I adjusted the conversation from focusing on Suzie to asking Matt general questions about his life. Before Matt arrived, Suzie had told me how he struggled after Straight.

After making small talk, Matt began describing the same history Suzie had shared a few hours before. "I was a part of the program for about eight months before I escaped. Some parents knew what was really happening at Straight, and they were trying to get it shut down. Kids escaped by something like the underground railroad. One mom would find parents to take in the kids that ran. I couldn't wait and ended up walking out with another boy during a bathroom break. We found an abandoned truck on a farm to sleep in for the night. The next day we hitchhiked to see the boy's girlfriend. She connected us to a group of Catholic priests who let me stay with them until I was able to get a flight to Oklahoma, back to my dad. I stayed with the priests for almost one month. When I arrived at the church, I was excited to finally speak with my dad. I wasn't allowed to have contact with him at the program, so nearly a year."

After escaping the program, Matt returned to Oklahoma, where he stopped going to school, struggled to maintain employment, got into trouble with the law, served about four years in prison, and eventually returned to Pennsylvania to live in Suzie's basement. He still had regular nightmares about his stint in the program.

After I'd been through all the paperwork, Suzie and I stood in the breezeway between the house and her garage and talked a little while longer. We hugged goodbye, and she thanked me for spending the day with her. I felt uneasy for her and Matt. Their future still seemed so uncertain, despite all the years that had passed.

CONNOR CHECKED HIMSELF out of the program when he turned eighteen and went back to Pennsylvania. Between the ages of fifteen and eighteen, he hadn't attended school. I found no information related to the "curriculum" provided to youth attending the Straight program in Springfield, Virginia, and no evidence of courses offered. He had gained no employable skills. His social development had halted, too. While at Straight he wasn't permitted to use a phone or write letters; there was no way to maintain any relationships that might have supported him. To his former school friends, it seemed like Connor had just disappeared one day. He was technically an adult but still very much the fifteen-year-old who had been sent away years before. The trauma Ron inflicted on him was now compounded by years of torture at the program, and Connor possessed nowhere near the coping skills he needed to be able to process it all. Still, he was expected to get on with his life, to "launch" from his parents' basement.

The relationships among the members of Connor's core family unit were also damaged in ways both visible and invisible. The eldest, Bobby, resented how Connor seemed to swallow up their parents' focus and time. Bobby's adulthood included depression, isolation, a failed marriage, an inability to maintain employment, and eventual suicide. Connor's younger brother, Sam, tried to conform his behavior to their parents' expectations, hoping for recognition. He was the only child to attend college and land steady work. On the outside, Sam looked to be doing well, but he, too, struggled with relationships. He was controlling, emotionally unavailable. His marriage ended in divorce. I showed up at his condo one afternoon to find he'd just woken up; all the curtains were drawn, and dozens of empty bottles of vodka and gin were strewn around. Even though his parents knew what was happening, it was as if all parties had silently agreed not to acknowledge his alcoholism.

When Connor returned to Pennsylvania at age eighteen, he went back to doing what he did at fifteen: stealing. His parents continued doing what they had done years earlier: seeking support from the church. The family would get Connor a job through a friend, and he would fail to keep up with the work. He would get fired. When the family kicked him out of the basement, he'd stay with various members of the congregation. Soon enough he'd steal from them and be politely asked to leave. Back to the basement. Repeat. Decades later, there was still no open dialogue within the family, just recurring patterns of silence and resentment.

CONNOR BEGAN CYCLING in and out of the local criminal legal system. He slept in unlocked cars, burgling neighboring homes for change or small trinkets. Those surrounding him now viewed him as beyond help. He was making a conscious choice not to behave better. He was damaged and unsalvageable. This point comes in nearly every one of my clients' trajectories. As children they stole from local convenience stores or bodegas, or as youths they were found sleeping under bridges or on park benches or walking the streets well into the night, looking for a place to rest. Each of these clients, like Connor, carried the weight of untreated trauma from childhood into adolescence. And each of them, like Connor, had at some point in early adulthood stopped being viewed as deserving of care and patience. These clients, like Connor, were still children in many ways, developmentally, emotionally. They might have looked grown on the outside, but inside they were still hurt children struggling to make sense of the harm they'd suffered.

By the age of twenty, Connor was a regular guest at the local jail. During one of his stays, he met Russ, a man in his seventies and a congregant of a local church who had volunteered to encourage incarcerated men to lean into their faith and trust in God. Russ was active in the community—a veteran, a small business owner, and a regular contributor to local charities. He and Connor immediately struck up a friendship, which included writing letters. Here's one from Russ:

> *I am wondering how your job is coming along. I really shouldn't wonder for I really believe in you. This is your chance to make a whole new life for yourself. You know I never, never condemned you for what you're supposed to have done, and I never asked you when or why. But from here on I will expect nothing but the best of you. As I told you many times you have a great head on your shoulders—just use it for your betterment. You know I am with you all the way. I don't have too many years on this earth, but I truly hope to be here long enough to see you turn your life toward a meaningful prosperous future. You can do it!*

Connor didn't have friends. His life was full of people—his parents, brothers, neighbors, and church members—who all communicated their disappointment. The kind of encouragement Russ offered was, to him, an unexpected gift.

Part of Connor's sentence was to engage in a work release program that allowed nonviolent offenders to hold day jobs and return to the jail at night. This was the new job to which Russ referred. Though work release was, in theory, intended to support employability by developing punctuality, consistency, and connections with local employers, in practice it met even minor failure with retribution rather than support. After one of his workdays, Connor went to meet a woman he had started dating. He lost track of time and failed to meet his curfew. This meant he was now considered an escapee. He was afraid of what might happen to him if he returned to the jail. He couldn't go home: his parents would take him back to the jail. Without money or means, the only person he could go to for help was Russ.

Here we are in the brief space between the before and after of a murder. We know that heightened stress—fear, desperation, a memory of utter powerlessness—can activate unresolved trauma. When that happens, survival responses—fight, flight, freeze, fawn—can override rational thought. After having a cup of tea and talking with Russ, seemingly out of nowhere, Connor grabbed a heavy vase from an adjacent table and struck him across the head. He took Russ's credit cards and some checks and dragged Russ into the basement, where he tied him up and placed a bag over his head. Connor was close to the Canadian border by the time Russ suffocated to death.

AS IS OFTEN the case, much of the information I gathered was never presented in open court. Eric communicated what had been learned about Connor to the prosecution, hoping it would weigh in favor of the state dropping its pursuit of the death penalty. At the same time, Eric filed a number of motions asking the judge to impose a sentence of life without the possibility of parole. The judge, who had been authorizing and tracking my mitigation work, granted one of them. It was a sudden, strangely anticlimactic but final end to twenty years of litigation.

The morning of the hearing where Connor would be formally re-sentenced by the court, I met him at the courthouse in a room where, for the first time, we could have physical contact. His attorneys were already present, speaking with him, when I entered. Connor walked over and wrapped his arms around me. I hugged him back. I was sur-prised: beneath the billowing prison jumpsuits he always wore, his build was slight. We squeezed each other so tightly. Then we stood back. We looked different standing, out from behind that glass. "I didn't know you were so short!" he said.

It was painful to sit in the gallery that day and listen to the prosecu-tor's comments about Connor, the local press's questions, all focused on how he'd behaved in one moment. It seemed so willfully incomplete. If no one now acknowledged the role that so many others had played in creating the circumstances for this crime, then when would they? Eric had arranged for the mitigation findings to be shared with Russ's surviv-ing family members and loved ones: maybe there could be something beneficial in their knowing more about the person who had caused them so much pain. Still, I felt there was an opportunity lost that day— to reckon constructively, and more publicly, with the community's role in this tragedy, rather than placing all the responsibility on one man.

About three weeks after Connor was sentenced to life without the possibility of parole, I received a text message from his mother. She wanted me to know that Suzie's son Matt had taken his own life. He was forty-two years old and left behind two sons. I wondered what kind of life he could have had if he had never been taken to Straight. There were so many other centers that claimed to rehabilitate youth but were shown to use similarly abusive and damaging techniques: Aspen Education's Outback program in Utah,[18] the Monarch School in Montana,[19] and Élan in Maine,[20] to name a few. And just like Matt and Connor, scores of children who entered those facilities left with invisible scars. Yet programs like Straight, which represent a small portion of the troubled-teen industry, remain lucrative and available to those who are desperate to help their children at any cost.[21] I thought about all the ways Matt's life might have gone. Connor's, too. All the trajectories, all the different endings.

Chapter Three

High-Rise

George was a Black man who was in his early fifties when we first met, in 2012. He was well over six feet tall, broad, and appeared to be in good physical shape, considering his age and the conditions of his confinement: he was isolated at least twenty-two hours a day in his cell, with little space to move, let alone exercise. He took pride in his appearance. Even though he wore the same orange prison jumpsuit provided to all men on Pennsylvania's death row, he had somehow managed to make it his own through the stylish way he folded the sleeves and the collar.

The legal error in his case was simple: mitigation investigation hadn't taken place in advance of George's trial, so the jury that had sentenced him to death some twenty-five years before knew next to nothing about him beyond what they had learned of the crime.[1] Now, half his lifetime later, it was my job to deepen his portrait beyond the jury's one-dimensional image of him as a murderer.

When I arrived for our visits, George was always sitting patiently on his side of the booth, ready. On the counter, a concrete slab, sat a dark-red accordion folder filled with papers, which he placed slightly off to his right, out of his immediate view. Throughout the time I visited with

George, at least once a month for two years, he never actually took out any of the papers from the folder to show me. I sometimes wondered if he forgot about the folder, but invariably, at some point in each visit, he would pick it up, fish around the bottom, and pull out a hard candy. He would suck on the sweet, a gentle wheezing sound sometimes emanating through a prominent gap in his front teeth, until at some point it dissolved, and the same loop of recollection, discovery, and enjoyment repeated.

George wasn't very talkative, a symptom, perhaps, of the mental illness and trauma he lived with, though I could tell from the nodding of his head that he was engaged in our visits. When our conversation turned to basketball or the streets he remembered in his South Philly neighborhood, he'd flash an impressive smile. His enthusiasm over small things was infectious; I looked forward to my visits with him.

George was born and raised in Philadelphia. His family lived in a neighborhood contiguous with the city center. Even though he had not set foot there for nearly thirty years by the time we met, George loved reciting the names of the streets around where he'd lived, telling me where to turn to get to certain establishments in his old neighborhood, now long shuttered. He was a spatial thinker. Having him walk me through certain spaces, days, and memories gave me an unusually clear picture. I guided this process by offering bite-size, nonjudgmental questions for him to respond to. In this way I was able to piece together a typical day in George's life at various points throughout his development.

George was the second of five children. As a toddler and into early childhood he lived with his mother, sister, and younger brother in a studio apartment on the top floor of a wood-frame house. I asked George to tour me through the unit.

"When I walk into the apartment, what is to my right?"

"A couch."

"My left?"

"A table. Two chairs."

"What is in front of me?"

"The kitchen."

We continued like this until we had mapped the whole apartment. There were few furnishings. For a bed, George, his mother, and his two siblings all shared the sleeper sofa that dominated the room. He never mentioned toys, books, or other material comforts.

One day, as we were working through his childhood, he mentioned that he'd eventually started sleeping on a foldout cot in the kitchen.

"Why did you stop sleeping on the couch?"

"I peed the bed sometimes."

I had read in medical records that George was incontinent until entering his teens.[2] Until now, it hadn't come up in conversation. Incontinence can be a sign of any number of things. I put it together with another clue in his records: he experienced unexplained blackouts throughout his teenage years. His medical and school files described George walking or running and suddenly dropping to the ground like a bag of sand. Visits to doctors didn't get to the bottom of the issue, though it wasn't clear that the physicians were trying very hard. Together, the two symptoms were strong indications of trauma and possibly another cognitive concern, maybe some kind of seizure disorder. George hadn't been evaluated by a neuropsychologist yet, but I knew that the defense team would likely take that step once we had learned more about his symptoms.

So as not to cause George shame and potentially shut down our dialogue, I asked how he felt about sleeping apart from the rest of the family.

"I didn't like it."

"Why?"

"It was hard to stay asleep."

"Why?"

"We had rats."

By this point I had spent at least a hundred hours with George. He had never mentioned rats. Earlier in my career I might have asked myself what I had failed to do to elicit this information sooner, but by then I knew that there was never a single question I could have asked to learn this information. The disclosure was the result of time, patience, trust, and the day.

In short sentences, George described a change. The apartment had been fairly comfortable if sparsely furnished when he was younger. The rat problem began as George's family was preparing to move into a larger apartment in a nearby public housing development. The reason for that eventual move became clear through my research, along with a broader picture of community degradation. At the time, much of George's neighborhood had been slated for demolition in order to build a proposed crosstown expressway, which led to scores of retail businesses and residences being abandoned.[3] The result was blight for the residents who didn't have the means to leave the area, including George and his family, along with thousands of other low-income residents. The crosstown expressway became a point of controversy between the neighborhood and city planners: the city didn't have the ability to adequately rehouse those displaced by the expressway. According to concerned residents, the designated area for the expressway also had the potential to erect a racial barrier between the city center and areas to the south, which housed majority white and Black residents respectively. Some even referred to it as the Mason-Dixon Line.[4]

Those without the means to relocate were left behind to wait for affordable housing to become available. Property records show that the building where George's family lived was sold shortly after they finally moved out. It seemed likely that the landlord had allowed the house to fall into disrepair, knowing that the destruction of adjacent homes would reduce local supply and increase the value of his property should the expressway fail to materialize. He would profit regardless. What was clear from George was that over a period of about a year the apartment rapidly deteriorated alongside the neighborhood. Drafts crept in through holes in the walls and floorboards. Waste accumulated as nearby buildings were torn down, creating a haven for rodents. Trash piled up for weeks without collection. Of course George struggled to sleep most nights. He was often startled awake by the sensation of rats scurrying over his ten-year-old body.

By 1970, when George's family finally moved, a study investigating the proposed crosstown expressway's transportation benefits to the city had concluded that it was not worth the investment relative to other improvements the project would delay. In 1974 the expressway was officially scrapped after more than a decade of steady community abandonment: the closure of businesses, the decline of housing values, the increase in crime and blight. George's family was stranded in the cramped studio apartment for the duration, watching the erasure of their community for the sake of a thoroughfare that would never even exist.

AROUND THE TIME I began working as a mitigation specialist, results from a medical study that began in the 1990s were fundamentally changing how many people thought about the forces that shape the trajectory of a life. The study had started, like many breakthroughs, out of frustration. A San Diego–based internal medicine doctor, Vincent Felitti, managed a preventive care clinic. As a part of the clinic, he ran a program aimed at addressing obesity. The program accepted patients who were moderately overweight, though it was geared toward people who needed to lose hundreds of pounds. Despite the fact that many of the patients lost weight, the clinic had an abysmal dropout rate: about 55 percent of the participants who had started successfully shedding pounds left the program, which was a serious issue.

Confused, Felitti scrutinized the files of the patients who left. He didn't find the answer in the records, but he noticed something else: many of those who had dropped out had gained the weight back quickly. He had assumed that individuals who weighed four hundred pounds or more had become progressively overweight across years. What he noticed instead was that the weight gain was often abrupt and then stabilized. If a person lost weight, it was fully regained over a very short time.

He saw a pattern in the records but didn't know its meaning without context. He decided to interview the participants who had left the program. In a 2012 interview with the health journalist Jane Stevens, Felitti recalled accidentally asking a patient, " 'How much did you weigh when you were first sexually active?' The patient answered, 'Forty pounds.' "[5] Confused, he repeated the question. The patient gave the same answer, burst into tears, and added, "It was when I was four years old, with my father." Of the 286 people whom Felitti and his colleagues interviewed, most had been sexually abused as children. Through these interviews, Felitti and his colleagues learned that, for many people, being overweight wasn't a problem—it was a fix. As one of his patients said, "Overweight is overlooked, and that's the way I need to be." Overeating might have addressed some of the anxiety, fear, or anger that came with being sexually abused. For many, gaining a lot of weight also resulted in being left alone.[6]

Sexual abuse was just one of the adverse childhood experiences—specific traumas that could take place during childhood and were connected to experiences within a family or household—that Felitti and his colleagues ended up studying in the hopes of understanding the link between early life obstacles and subsequent medical, social, and public health problems. The other factors included experiences of physical abuse, neglect, and family dynamics, such as having an incarcerated parent or parents who divorced. By the time I started working in Texas, the Adverse Childhood Experience (ACE) study had investigated early life adversity and its long-term public and private health impacts in over seventeen thousand patients.[7]

During adolescence, a majority of people will experience at least one of the adverse experiences studied by Felitti and his colleagues.[8] However, the ACE study shows that some populations are more likely to have these experiences because of social and economic factors—such as race, ethnicity, and social network—that impact where people live or work.[9]

Two key points emerged from the research. First, there was a direct correlation between the number of adverse experiences a person had during childhood and poorer individual physical and mental health outcomes. Plainly, the more trauma of the type studied, the greater the chances the child grew into an adult with heart disease, was living with obesity, or developed symptoms of severe mental illness such as suicidal ideation or hallucinations, for example.[10] Second, there was a compounding nature to adversity: more traumatic experiences often resulted in more trauma. This layering of trauma made it more difficult for an individual to emerge unscathed in adulthood.

What was happening? Nadine Burke Harris, a pediatrician who worked in a socially disadvantaged area of San Francisco, delved further into the research of childhood trauma and found that adverse experiences that take place in early life impact the delivery of key hormones in the body, which, without therapeutic interventions, can alter the brain and body of a child with lasting effect. The lasting effects include children growing up with greater odds of harming themselves or others and ending up incarcerated. The work of the doctors and researchers who investigated early-life trauma through the ACEs framework showed how being stuck inside a family system where compounding violations took place without intervention led to early death, physical and mental unwellness, and often a tendency to cope in ways that perpetrate self- or community harm.

My work showed me more. I could see additional patterns that had to do with the traumas inflicted on my clients by the social systems they interacted with throughout adolescence and into adulthood. The ACE study accounted for human mistreatment; it didn't account for the harms inflicted by the public housing system or the public school system, for example. Those of us doing mitigation work saw these social systems as a crucial part of the ACE calculus. They explained how a group of people who were already at risk of hurting others because of traumas might be channeled in a direction that narrowed their options even further and culminated in the murder of another person. So it didn't surprise me to see a 2007 study of death row inmates confirm that two thirds had experienced six or more of the eight ACEs examined by the study.[11] Inescapable intrafamilial trauma was a powerful factor in the lives of my clients, but it wasn't the only form of trauma with which they reckoned. The ACE framework articulated the effects of adversity, but it didn't go far enough.

The traumas my clients experienced didn't stop when they stepped out of their homes. Outside those walls, institutions that were purportedly designed to aid in healthy development caused further damage. There was rarely a time, a moment even, in the days of their developing lives when their brains and bodies could decompress, find peace, know safety. Such a reprieve, even if insufficient for healing, might have been just enough to keep many more people from becoming my clients.

THE HAWTHORNE SQUARE high-rise public housing development was built by the Philadelphia Housing Authority in 1960.[12] The complex consisted of 576 units in four separate buildings, including the fifteen-story high-rise where George's family relocated in 1970, the same year the development was renamed the Martin Luther King Jr. Plaza in commemoration of a visit the civil rights leader had made to the area a few years before.[13] George's mother, Teresa, hoped that the spacious new apartment, a three-bedroom on the top floor, would be an improvement. This hope quickly vanished. The plaza was engulfed in constant violence that residents likened to the Vietnam War raging half a world away: they called the complex Little Saigon.[14]

In a public housing development, tenants have to rely on budgets authorized by elected legislators to address maintenance issues and upkeep. Lawmakers routinely failed to invest in this heavily impoverished, primarily Black area. Repairs were done on the cheap when they were done at all. A 1989 report commissioned by Congress looking back on this era of public housing lamented a catalog of failures: uninhabitable conditions, inadequate and fragmented services that did not support residents, and institutional abandonment by the Department of Housing and Urban Development and other federal and state entities that were tasked with ensuring the dignity, safety, and health of low-income residents.[15] Redlining policies in the area extended back to 1937, when it was categorized as "hazardous," with "many negro families doubled up" and condemned properties marking the section's slow deterioration.[16] Investment in the community wasn't a priority then, and it wasn't in 1960 either, when the plaza was built. By

1999 nearly half of the units, 200 apartments out of 576, were vacant, and many were unlivable. The city imploded the plaza shortly after.[17]

To call day-to-day life in those towers at the plaza a nightmare doesn't cover it. Just to make it from the family apartment to the street tested George's survival skills. The elevator, which was often broken down, was commonly used as a quick place to get high or a venue for muggings. If George chose to climb the fifteen flights to his apartment, he needed to step over individuals who were passed out from heavy drug use on the stairs. There was a smell he couldn't describe, some miasma of shit, vomit, and the pungent odor of unshowered bodies. He became keenly aware of the discarded needles that could easily pierce him if he wasn't paying attention. George's blackouts began somewhere around the age of eight, before he and his family moved to the plaza around age eleven, and persisted through his teens; he might lose consciousness in the elevator or the stairwell. He knew this made him an easy target and tried to make sure he was always with someone else when coming or going.

An armed security guard walked the vestibule of the tower, but his presence didn't deter people from robbing, beating, or shooting at residents, including George and other children. During one of my visits, as George reminisced, he made a surprising remark.

"Dwayne lived there, too."

Dwayne was a friend from death row whom George would mention on occasion. I asked if they'd known each other before arriving in prison.

"Yeah. He saved my life."

It is extremely rare to end up on death row. In 2023 more than nineteen thousand murders occurred in the United States.[18] That same year, a fraction of a fraction of 1 percent of the national population—twenty-one individuals—were sentenced to death.[19] They joined the approximately two thousand people under a death sentence in America.[20] The commonalities among this small group of people defy coincidence. Edward had lived in the same zip codes, attended the same schools, and interacted with some of the same social service agencies as other residents on Texas's death row.[21] On a case out of East Baton Rouge, Louisiana, I discovered that my client was related to another death row inmate; again, he'd been raised in the same neighborhoods and attended the same schools. Before Colorado abolished the death penalty in 2020, the state's death row cohort consisted of three Black men who had all attended the same high school.[22] And of the approximately two hundred men on Pennsylvania's death row at that time,[23] as I was now learning, at least two grew up in the same housing development.

One day when they were children, thirteen and fourteen years old, Dwayne and George happened to be in the vestibule when gunfire started. George was slower to react than Dwayne, who instantly took off, grabbing George's hand and pulling him in the direction of the elevators. Dwayne got them inside before any of the bullets could find them.

"What happened after?" I asked.

"Nothing."

I didn't understand. "What do you mean?"

"I went home."

After George narrowly escaped being struck by a bullet, he went back to the apartment, shared the news with his mom and sisters, and kept living life. George's mother, Teresa, had just returned from work and would soon be on her way out again to attend night school. She was crunched for time and likely desensitized to the war zone they lived in due to their lack of options; they had no money to move, no social connections to help get them to a safer place, no access to counseling to manage George's anxiety after nearly being shot. One way or another, the residents of the plaza had to live with the fact that death lurked in the halls, inside elevators, and around every corner. It's not hard to imagine someone detaching from the environment, focusing on immediate commitments elsewhere, such as financial maintenance, and tamping down emotions that come with being fully present, like grief and joy.[24] "You cannot play, take risks, or be creative when you don't have a minimum of safety," writes Esther Perel, a psychologist who was raised in a community of Holocaust concentration camp survivors in Belgium. Survival requires limiting feelings of agony or ecstasy.

TERESA WANTED A better life for her children and strove for it. By all accounts, she was kind and generous despite how hard she had it. She died from a heart attack at sixty-three. Modern standards for Western nations would identify her as a relatively young woman when she passed. I understand her untimely death as related to the traumas she had survived, the many adverse childhood experiences she had weathered. Like Edward and Connor, she had suffered within her own family environment and never received adequate support.

Teresa was sexually abused by her stepfather, Amos. Her one surviving sister told me about the terror of victimization they each experienced at his hands. Their father had left their mother, Lucy, for another woman. Single with two children, Lucy remarried quickly. Amos, like Teresa and all her kin, was from North Carolina. Born in 1917, Amos had a fourth-grade education. His school records bore notations about farming and working in the fields as a child, which was common among sharecropping families who had come out of enslavement. Shortly after their marriage, Lucy left North Carolina and headed north to Philadelphia. She wanted better for her daughters and hoped to find work. She left the girls alone with Amos. Amos molested each girl, becoming more violent as the days passed without Lucy. He would force the girls into the kitchen, turn the gas stove on high, and hold their hands over the flame, threatening to burn them if they didn't succumb to him. Teresa was around twelve during this time. While collecting marriage certificates for the family one day, I had noticed that she married at age fifteen to a man in his twenties. Her sister did the same thing—anything to get out of that house. Teresa's husband, with whom she didn't have any children, turned out to be an abusive alcoholic; she'd traded one terrible existence for another. Eventually, Teresa divorced him, but she must have absorbed the lesson that marriage wasn't a safe haven. Though she later had long-term relationships, she never remarried.

Teresa's efforts to improve the family's financial situation—working multiple jobs, attending night school—meant she was often elsewhere. Without close supervision, George became a target for an older man who sold fish out of his car in the neighborhood and had a reputation for "messing with" children who lived in the plaza. Fishman, as he was locally known, also lived in the towers and knew when George was alone. George never told me whether Fishman had abused him, but suddenly, in his early teens, George was found in the apartment of a nearby family, fondling a much younger girl. He'd had no history of this behavior before the move to the towers, and the sudden change indicated that he might have been subjected to sexual abuse. He would have been safer if he could have stayed outside with other children, playing, but that wasn't possible without risking his own life.

There was no safety at school either. When George was a child in the 1970s, neighborhood feuds were rampant.[25] By dint of geography, George was viewed as a member of the Thirteenth Street crew. No initiation or consent was needed to join. Kids knew who lived where, and that was all it took. At school, fights regularly broke out between the crews. Teachers were overwhelmed and ill-equipped to address the mounting distress their students brought to school each day.

On a Saturday afternoon I arrived at the front door of Linda, one of George's schoolteachers, who lived in a large two-story home in a Philadelphia suburb. She answered the door in a T-shirt and shorts, her hair pulled up in a bun. It was early August, and the heat was heavy. Linda welcomed me into her home, and the two of us sat drinking sweet tea in her living room for about four hours.

As she sipped her cold tea from a tall glass, Linda told me about herself. She had taught for more than a decade at the middle school George attended and left the school in 1978. Linda was from South Philly too and understood from her own experiences the challenges the children faced each day.

Linda's middle school students were between the ages of twelve and fourteen, and they regularly came to school with weapons. With watery eyes she described how the children were "gang warring every day." She wanted to give her students a chance to feel relaxed enough to learn, a chance to absorb the lessons she had prepared. Her unconventional approach was to have a drawer where all her kids could put their weapons. She wouldn't ask questions or try to lecture students about carrying whatever it was they brought along that day. She simply insisted that they all put their guns, knives, chains, hammers, and other arms in that drawer. Linda believed this enabled the kids to focus for the hour they were with her, since each child knew no one else was holding a weapon during that time. She would hand back the items at the end of the class, and silently pray that each of her children would return alive tomorrow.

Constantly afraid for her students and raised with the belief that physical punishment could change behavior for the good, Linda practiced strict discipline in her classroom. If a student was getting out of line in her class, she'd take the child into the hallway and "whoop their ass." She used a stick on any student who was disrespectful or misbehaved.

Though decades had passed, the news of George's situation brought Linda to tears. She was saddened but not surprised; she named other former students who had been convicted of murder and sent to prison. The children she taught were not bad kids, she said. "They were trying to survive."

GEORGE STARTED CARRYING a hammer to and from school each day. There was no one to drive him—his mother started work too early. He traveled with a small group of children from the plaza. He and his friends varied their routes to avoid kids who would start fights or older kids who would try to get them involved in selling drugs. For a time he had a bike, which made it easier to get to school, until it was stolen. His mom couldn't afford to get him another one. It was back to walking and packing his hammer.

George and a friend were walking past a locked classroom one day and saw, through the window, a purse sitting on a table. Together, they broke into the classroom, grabbed the purse, and ran out of the building. They took the money and threw the purse away. Someone saw them and called an officer in the area. The kids were arrested within minutes. As a part of his sentence, George was sent to a youth facility, which noted on psychological admissions testing that "there were moments when he seemed to lose contact with what was going on around him and began talking to himself soundlessly." Though the psychologist noted that he might be exhibiting early symptoms of schizophrenia, no treatment plan appeared in the records for that possible mental health concern. Rather, he was said to be dangerous, and attempts at therapy, the main mode of support at the center, were not successful. By the time he was a young adult, he had a juvenile criminal history and mental health evaluations that labeled him with conduct disorder and oppositional defiant disorder. He moved between the plaza and bursts of incarceration for property crimes. Before turning twenty-two, he had developed a serious drinking and drug addiction.

Within months of his release after one stint in jail, George was arrested for the murder of a young woman, for which he was sentenced to death. Precious little was written about her in the case file. I gleaned that she and George had used drugs together at the plaza. She was bone-thin when she died, weighing under a hundred pounds at five feet, six inches tall. She was Black. She had been sexually assaulted and died from injuries related to the assault. There was no information at all about her family, and my efforts to trace her next of kin failed. I had so many questions about who she was, aside from George's victim, but I never found answers. All I knew was that she'd spent time living at the plaza too.

Online videos of the implosion of the MLK Jr. Plaza towers in 1999 capture cheers and applause, whoops of relief and triumph. Watching, I felt the elation of a community that had endured a generation of losses to this place. I replayed the footage. And replayed it again. Anyone who wants to understand George, Dwayne, and so many other children born with limitless potential who end up causing irreparable harm—anyone trying to understand Teresa as a mother, or searching for a scrap of information about the ravaged young woman George killed—let them start here, I thought.

I WAS THINKING of the plaza again one gray and darkening Saturday in early 2017. I had spent it at my dining room table preparing for a Monday meeting at the Department of Justice in Washington, D.C., I would attend with other members of my team to share what we had learned about the life history of one of our clients, William. Our audience was a panel of assistant U.S. attorneys, federal prosecutors, who would make a recommendation to the attorney general of the United States as to whether the department should seek the death penalty in William's case. Most of the cases I'd worked thus far had originated in state courts, so this was new for me. It was also the first time I would be part of the process whereby the United States determines whether to seek the death penalty in a specific case. A collection of binders, notepads, pens, and highlighters were splayed out on my dining room table and spilled onto the floor, forming a circle around my chair. I got up and walked around, thinking about how to verbalize what was so apparent to me about William's case—that his environment, like George's, had entrapped him. That he'd been confined long before he went to prison.

I met William in 2016, when he was sixty-one. By the time he was in his late fifties, he had spent decades living in some of the harshest prison environments in the nation. A sinewy five-foot-four Black man, he eventually found himself in a cramped sixty-square-foot cell with Martin, an inmate who had been living with severe mental illness. Martin was also Black, but young, in his midtwenties, and had recently been transferred to this maximum-security prison from a mental health unit at another facility. Martin's treating psychiatrist had spent months working with him and concluded that, should he come off his medication, he would become floridly ill, likely physically aggressive, and very difficult to manage. Martin was living with schizophrenia. A hallmark of the illness is the sufferer's profound belief that they do not, in fact, have any mental health issue.[26] This lack of insight, a symptom of the disease, means that many struggle with adherence to a medication regimen.[27] Martin had a poor track record and had to be given his medication by staff daily; he was unlikely to comply on his own.

Once he had been moved into the cell with William and cut off from his mental health support, Martin (predictably) stopped taking his medication. His condition quickly deteriorated—also predictably—spiraling into active delusions, bursts of anger, and an inability to manage basic needs. He stopped eating, ceased bathing, and starting defecating outside the toilet of their small shared cell. William repeatedly asked officers for help, but no one responded. He began to assist Martin with eating, showering, dressing, and even using the toilet. But as the days wore on, Martin slept less and less. He'd spend hours banging the bunk with his legs, hollering loudly, rambling incoherently, and moving erratically about the cell. The situation was edging toward a breaking point.

Still pacing around the dining room table, I imagined the agony of it. To be trapped in a space the size of a walk-in closet, cheek by jowl with a person you don't know, watching helplessly as he loses touch with reality, all the while experiencing the psychological detachment that comes from being sleep-deprived. Caring for Martin, wiping him after he defecated, bathing him, trying to get him to eat or sleep. I didn't think I would last a week before harming Martin or myself. William lasted fifty-nine days.

WILLIAM WAS ACCUSTOMED to being treated as less than fully human. He was born in 1955 in Washington, D.C., to Lisa, a Black mother who, much like Teresa, worked extremely hard to raise her family without any additional support. Lisa labored as the housekeeper and caretaker for a white family on the other side of town. She often left before dawn to catch the bus and would return late at night with just enough energy to put on some washing or get a bit of food with her family before catching a few hours of sleep. She had no margin, no buffer in her life.

Like many Black residents of Washington at that time, William's family lived near the Anacostia River. The neighborhood, like George's in Philadelphia, was rife with the markers of the marginalized and ostensibly discarded, and this was done by design. Black residents were not allowed to live in many parts of the city due to racial covenants—provisions in property deeds that forbade their sale to non-white residents[28]—and the segregation of public housing that lasted into the 1950s.[29] The area was dilapidated yet densely populated, and it was isolated: residents (non-Black residents specifically) outside the community could easily avoid it. They certainly never stumbled into the area. Lawmakers, who were also almost entirely non-Black and therefore not from or familiar with these communities, had compounded already difficult circumstances by allowing the neighborhood to house the city dump, which workers routinely set on fire, releasing carcinogens into the area.[30] According to the Environmental Protection Agency, the dump "burned from 1942 to 1968 ... for over 25 years. A quarter of a million tons of refuse went up in smoke every year." The fires from the city dump were the largest single contributor to air pollution in the Washington area.[31] When the wind blew, it could turn laundry drying on the line outdoors black with soot.[32] The dump was finally closed after seven-year-old Kelvin Tyrone Mock was trapped by one of the routine open fires and burned to death.[33]

William outlived many of the people who had known him best. His mother, father, and all of his siblings but one died before they turned sixty. I ended up relying almost exclusively on documents to help me understand many of the unknown or long-forgotten details of William's young life. His school records gave significant clues pointing to mental health issues related to stress and trauma: erratic attendance, highly reactive behavior, difficulty concentrating and staying in his seat, and verbal outbursts. At age ten, William was shot by police as he ran from a corner store. The police were chasing a suspect in the area, and William, imitating both the police and those fleeing the area, took off running.

For his instinctive action, he received a bullet in his leg and another at the base of his head, close to his spine.

After physically recovering from these injuries, William started engaging in self-harming behaviors, including suicide attempts. His mother, who was working around the clock, saw that he needed more than she could provide. Lisa first sent William to South Carolina to live with his biological father, who had remarried and started a new family. Within a year, for reasons unknown, his father sent William back to Washington, D.C. Lisa didn't know what to do. William's behavior was erratic, and she couldn't manage him on her own. She petitioned a court to place William in a youth facility at the age of fourteen.

William was sent initially to a pair of youth detention centers, Oak Hill and Cedar Knoll, in suburban Maryland, just outside Washington, D.C. The facilities were rodent-infested and overcrowded, housing some two hundred impoverished children in spaces built for fifty, and lacked any meaningful mental health or medical care, to say nothing of vocational development programs or rehabilitative services. A class action lawsuit raised by eight youth who were sent to the facilities in the 1980s detailed "a climate of violence" where employees "periodically assault the children who are in their care."[34] As one of the youngest and physically smallest at the facility, William found himself a constant target of horrific torture and abuse. Other residents, older boys, raped him. So did several adult staff. He ran away as often as he could, incurring even harsher, more vicious treatment.

In every state where I've carried out investigations, I've come across at least one such facility, where underfunded, untrained, and ill-equipped adults are left to manage (not assist) the impoverished children placed in their care, most often Black or from other minority groups. These children, who were exhibiting behaviors that indicated profound traumas but tended to be labeled as "defiant" and "combative," were considered uncontrollable but for the intervention provided by these state-run facilities. The result of this woefully simplified narrative: thousands of children like William were subject to the most brutal treatment. Some did not survive. William witnessed the ferocious beating of one child who was never heard from again; he was convinced that boy was killed.

By the time I began investigating William's life, other prominent and well-known reform schools had made headlines, and more have since then, for conditions similar to what William described. In 2009, an investigative report of the Dozier School for Boys released by the *Tampa Bay Times* pointed to the presence of dozens of unidentified graves on the grounds of the school, which began operating in Florida in 1900 and continued to do so until 2011. Forensic archaeologists dug up sections of the school and discovered over fifty unmarked graves.[35] At the time of the discovery, at least seven men sentenced to death in Florida had been students at Dozier.[36] These were places of excessive corporal punishment, which William experienced, and even murder, which he likely witnessed.

When William turned seventeen, he was released from the custody of the federal government. He had no education, no prospects of gainful employment, no family to return to. His siblings had gone their own ways, and his mother had severed ties with him. He was suffering from mental health issues, compounded by the time spent at Oak Hill and Cedar Knolls. He was homeless and alone.

In 1975, within two years of his release from the Maryland facilities, William was accused and convicted of the rape of a woman in her late fifties, a crime for which he maintained his innocence. The evidence against him amounted to several shaky eyewitness statements that put him in the vicinity of the crime. If the crime took place now, I wonder, with all today's advances in forensic sciences, would a jury find him guilty given the evidence available? He served nearly eighteen years of a twenty-year sentence in various Maryland state prisons. In 1994, almost two years after his release, he was arrested again, this time for the murder that landed him in federal prison. He took the stand and testified that he was innocent. He was convicted and sentenced to forty-five years in prison. All told, William had lived just eight of his sixty-one years outside of government-run facilities.

William's behavior in custody tracked what I expected to see: lots of disciplinary issues, fights, placements in solitary confinement, and struggles to connect with those around him. There were several suicide attempts in the early years of his incarceration. Yet William's records also showed a desire to grow. While serving time in Maryland, he tried several times to obtain a high school equivalency diploma, putting in over twelve hundred hours of study, but was never able to pass the exam. He turned to art, therapy, whatever was available at the institution where he lived. Eventually he was sent to a prison with a music program. There he was able to thrive. He had a beautiful voice, and the years when he could sing with other inmates were the very best of his life. For the first time he had connection, a community where he belonged.

AFTER FIFTY-NINE DAYS living in almost unfathomable conditions with Martin, William just wanted some silence. Martin had been agitated for days, banging the bunk, moving constantly. William grabbed him by the throat and choked him until he was quiet. He didn't want Martin to die. He just wanted peace. But then Martin came to and jumped on William. They fought. William choked Martin until he was still. The cycle repeated a third time, with William choking

Martin until he was unconscious but breathing. Within the hour officers found Martin on the ground and William crouching in a corner of their cell.

The prison guards placed William in a green cage, referred to as a holding cell. It was hard to make out the size of the container in the video footage I watched—a camera was trained on William, who was in what appeared to be the center of the space, curled tightly, knees to his chest, his arms wrapped around them and his head down. The cell looked to be about three feet wide and three feet deep, the height impossible to see. It looked like it was made to hold a wild animal, not a human being.

I had never seen a client so close in time to the offense, and everything about it was awful. William was whimpering. An officer approached the cage and muttered something unintelligible, to which he responded, "I have been taking care of him but he has mental issues. I told staff they needed to get him help, but they wouldn't listen to me. I have been washing him and taking care of him. He should be in a mental institution; he can't take care of himself. I was so tired of doing all of this and he has been so loud the last three nights. I have not been able to sleep; I just snapped and I killed that kid."

The footage lasted over an hour, during which time William's demeanor remained the same; the only variation came from the sounds of people and movement taking place around him. Since the camera was focused on William, I couldn't see anyone else in the room. I imagined federal corrections officers rushing around him, not stopping to look his way or ask if he was okay, though he was clearly in distress. About forty-five minutes into the footage the same officer who had spoken to him at the start of the video quietly let him know that Martin was, in fact, still alive and had been taken to a hospital. William's cries, which had been continuous, became louder, his body rocking faster. Mixed in,

I could hear William repeating, "*I didn't want to kill him. I didn't want to kill him. I didn't want to kill him.*"

Martin died from his injuries three months later.

ABOUT HALF A dozen white men and one woman of color were seated around a table, with several other attorneys joining by phone. The men appeared to know one another. Their demeanor was quite cavalier, I thought, given the reason we were gathered. Their smiles and small talk about the weekend left me with the impression that they were either indifferent to or comfortable with the idea that William should die for his crime.

My team had invited me to make some remarks about William's life. After William's lead attorney spoke briefly, it was my turn. I stayed seated. I tried to make eye contact. I made a joke about my discomfort in a room full of prosecutors. I told them what I had learned about William. I worried, as I spoke, that this room had already judged William, that judgment is the death knell of compassion, that judgment makes it impossible to listen.

When I had finished, several members of the committee asked questions about William's poor adjustment record in prison. After some discussion, one of the younger federal prosecutors said that he wasn't very concerned about William's prison record, bad as it was. He was stuck on this question: Why had William choked his cellmate more than once, if he didn't want to kill him? What had he been thinking?

I was stuck on a different question: How had William managed to live all those days—those 1,416 hours—in a six-by-ten-foot cube with an unmedicated, floridly ill stranger from whom the medical staff at the Bureau of Prisons had predicted, correctly, violence and not act out *sooner*? What could any one of us, any one of those lawyers, endure?

William was being measured against impossible standards, while the prison system had, defying any standards, blatantly failed in its responsibility to provide safe housing to all its inhabitants. To ask *any* question that didn't start there struck me as a continued abdication of that responsibility. Struggling to pull my thoughts together, I blurted out that I didn't believe William had been *thinking*. He had been trying to survive. Running on no sleep, having endured extreme stress for almost two months with no end in sight, after a lifetime of abuse, William had just reacted, done *something—anything—*to get a few moments of peace.

The federal prosecutor thanked us, and no other questions were raised. As they escorted us out of the building I wondered if I had answered the prosecutor's question. I sensed I hadn't, that somehow he and I had been speaking not to but alongside each other, about two different cases.

"WILLIAM IS GETTING life!" one of my colleagues shouted as she ran up and down the halls of our windowless Baltimore office. "HE IS GETTING LIFE!" After months of waiting to hear what the attorney general of the United States had decided, an email popped up on my screen. In exchange for William accepting a sentence of life without the possibility of parole, the government would not seek the death penalty against him. I felt a wave of relief, which was almost immediately followed by another enormous wave of sadness. William *did* deserve life—a real life—not a caged existence inside brutal institutions. He deserved more than eight years free out of the sixty-plus years he had lived. Now he would never even have the chance to contemplate such a future.

Life sentences are handed down every single day across America. More than fifty thousand people incarcerated in the United States are serving life sentences with no opportunity even to be considered for release.[37] These sentences are not in service of promoting public safety.[38] Longer sentences do not meaningfully deter crime,[39] though they cost taxpayers enormously.[40] Said differently, lengthy sentences do not reduce crime more effectively than less expensive and more humane alternatives.[41] Understanding how senseless, how purely retributive, the deal was for William made it hard to feel pleased with the result.

Sending someone to prison to die is routine in American society, but I wonder how many people really think about what it's like to live in the knowledge that freedom will only come with death. Every time I work with a client to help them see that their best outcome is to give up their freedom, to forsake the hope of ever living outside of concrete walls, I feel hollow. I know that where the death penalty is pursued, the current system rarely provides a better outcome than life without the possibility of parole. And yet every time a client agrees to accept such a sentence, I brace myself, white-knuckling through the court proceeding where he is giving up all his rights. I worry he will balk and decide to go to trial, where the best result could *only* be life without parole. I have spent enough time with men who have made this decision to know that the act of being sentenced can feel psychologically different from agreeing to accept that same sentence. That accepting a plea can feel like dispensing with all hope. I have yet to meet a single person who can live without a belief that there are better days ahead.

WILLIAM DID NOT have a close relationship with his attorney. Though they were in occasional phone contact, she had visited him in person just once in the two years she had represented him. It would now fall to her to get William to sign the stack of papers agreeing to die in prison. I worried that William might not sign the forms. If he refused, the government was likely to seek the death penalty against him. I decided at the last minute to drive from Orlando, where I was presenting at a conference, to Houston, where William was being held. His attorney could only carve out time to see him on one of two days, and if I managed to get on the road I could join her. The forms needed to be signed within a month of receiving the paperwork or else the government could rescind the "offer," such as it was. We were already down to the wire with meeting that timeline.

Less than forty-eight hours later, I was waiting in the prison parking lot for William's attorney to arrive. She drove up in a black luxury car and stepped out, impeccably dressed in pressed slacks, a fashionable blouse, and perfectly paired jewelry. Her blond hair was coiffed and her makeup flawless. I looked down at my Gap jeans and laced gray Keds and hoped I didn't have food on my face: I hadn't looked in a mirror since I left my hotel in the Florida panhandle sometime early that morning.

As we waited in the prison's visiting area for William, his attorney took out the stack of paperwork that he would need to sign. I reflected on how odd it was that a person could literally sign their life away in less time than it took to buy a car. She placed two pens on the table. An officer escorted William in. He arrived in belly chains and shackles, wearing a blue prison jumpsuit too big for his slight body. His hair was styled in uneven box braids. As he walked closer, I noticed that his eyeglasses had been pieced together with part of a shoelace and a rubber band.

I could tell he was upset. He sat down, shaking his head from side to side.

"Why are you here?" he asked his attorney.

Though he hadn't directly asked her why this was only their second in-person encounter, she began to explain her absence, alluding to difficulties in her own life—a sick family member, a move, a busy workload. It was too hard to get to the prison where he had been held before he was transferred here, much closer to where she lived. William sat and listened. After a while he decided to move on and asked some other questions. We started talking about topics unrelated to his case, and the mood lightened.

We had been with William for less than an hour when his attorney announced that she needed to get going soon and directed him to the stack of pages on the table. Awkwardly, with his hands chained to his waist, he grabbed a pen. In a calm voice, without a trace of animus, William explained that the only reason he was signing the papers was because of the relationship he had formed with people at my office, who had worked on his case and routinely visited him in person over the last year. He offered his attorney a piece of advice:

"The next case you take, try to see your client more than once before asking them to sign a plea to life."

I knew it took a lot of resolve for William to say what he was feeling in that moment. He did so in a kind but clear way. Instead of meeting his understandable pain with equal dignity, his attorney sharply replied, "I am not your mother or your friend. I am your lawyer. I did my job."

I slid my hand across the table to William and said, "I am here."

She flipped through the pages and pointed out all the rights William would give up by accepting this offer to serve out his natural life in prison. He'd given up the chance to appeal the conviction or sentence, the opportunity to sue the prison for its role in the offense, and a host of other legal avenues he could have pursued. He quietly initialed each page and told me not to worry.

When he was done, William shuffled the pages together into a neat pile, then turned to his attorney. "Have a good life," he said.

GEORGE AND WILLIAM entered prison already familiar with how to serve a life sentence. They were trapped inside homes, neighborhoods, and facilities where they had been ignored, isolated, neglected, and abused. During the most formative years of life, we left them. Society left them. We relegated these men as children to places that would be demolished to cheers and celebration. The harms we allowed to happen went unchecked for generations.

For both George and William, the same avenues available for leaving prison—extraordinary luck or death—had also been the only ones out of the MLK Jr. Plaza or the youth facilities like Cedar Knolls. This was not because there was something inherently wrong with either man but because we determined, before they were born, that they weren't worth the investment. William's words hung in my mind. *Have a good life.* His lawyer would, and so would I. We would have those lives simply because we were lucky enough to be born to parents whom society valued more. It wasn't fair.

Chapter Four

Death Qualification

During those early days in Houston, the drive from my apartment to the office took about as long as it did for me to smoke one cigarette. I was up early on this particular Wednesday, early enough to see the sunlight just starting to appear in the sky. I started the car, rolled the window down, popped a Parliament into my mouth, turned up the speakers.

But what was normal in the evening by the morning seems insane.[1]

It was November 1, 2006. Tracey was scheduled to be executed by the state of Texas at six P.M. In about twelve hours.

I had started visiting Tracey around the same time that I began working on Edward's case. I often visited Edward and Tracey on the same day. By the time November 1, 2006, arrived, I had been consistently visiting Tracey for over a year.

I did not collect records about Tracey's life or the lives of others in his family as I had done in Edward's case. I didn't spend time with any school friends, community members, family, or coworkers who had known Tracey growing up. He didn't want any investigation into his history, and he'd threatened to fire his court-appointed team if we tried to pursue such an investigation. He maintained his innocence and thought that understanding him as a person, his context, was a foolish waste of time. He'd meet me, but nothing more. My role was therefore unusually restricted to regularly visiting him.

In contrast to the ease I felt with Edward from our earliest visit, spending time with Tracey was hard. He was in his late forties, with straight salt-and-pepper hair that he wore in a slightly askew bowl cut. His eyes were a vivid blue, and his brow furrowed whenever we met. He looked permanently skeptical and maintained strong and searching eye contact, which I found intense and unsettling. I felt like he'd seen right through my good intentions and determined, before I had a chance to prove otherwise, that I was incompetent.

The rhythm of our interaction the first time we met set the tempo for all future visits. Tracey peppered me with pointed questions, much like a seasoned prosecutor, and then cut to the chase:

"What are you going to do to get me out of here?"

I was thrown off by the question, though upon reflection there was nothing strange about it. It was strange that up to that point no one else had asked it so directly. I knew that his attorneys had been working to help Tracey see the value in mitigation investigation to supporting his claims of innocence, and I had been told that if he asked me something I couldn't answer, I should just be honest: I wasn't familiar with the details of his case yet, but I could bring any questions he had back to his attorneys. It wasn't the most satisfying response. Had this conversation happened today, I'd be better prepared and respond to his question with a question: What did he think I could do to help him get out? That might have gotten the conversation moving in a direction where I could have learned more about him. Instead, this is what happened after my response:

"Did they think sending a pretty girl was going to distract me?"

Silence for what felt like an eternity. My mind swirling, I tried to think what I could say and came up blank.

Then Tracey asked, "Do you want to know what it feels like to be back here on my side of the glass?" And again, "What are you going to do to help me?"

This time his desperation was unvarnished. His speech was so pressured. I choked up, feeling stupid to have thought I could help him. Tears rolled down my cheeks. I assured Tracey that I would return better prepared and left the prison in an anxious panic.

That was how our relationship proceeded. He remained disappointed in me.

From that first visit, Tracey said he had been framed for the murder of his parents and uncle. I devoured all I could about his case in advance of each meeting, ready to have a conversation. Yet my questions frustrated him. What he wanted, during each visit, were my thoughts about the evidence against him, which he viewed as flimsy. And he wanted me to gather the proof he needed to show that he'd been set up. At some point he would prescribe tasks that, if I could carry them out successfully, would demonstrate how he had been set up: Interview a specific witness and prove they were lying. Find a document to show the same. I'd leave and diligently follow up on the requests where possible—there were other members of the team trained to do this kind of fact-based investigation into the evidence of someone's guilt (or lack thereof)—then return with the information I'd found. No matter what I discovered, if it didn't confirm Tracey's theory, he didn't believe it was true or that I had been thorough enough. On visit after visit, Tracey would express his disappointment and casually note that I wasn't much better than anyone else on his defense team. He was convinced that we were working against him.

I didn't look forward to my visits with Tracey. I slept poorly on the nights before I was scheduled to see him. After each visit, I felt like I was recovering from a marathon.

Occasionally he would discuss his declining physical health or the nasty treatment he experienced from other inmates and officers. He spoke of the wrongs he'd suffered throughout his life. The blame for missteps or misunderstandings, I noticed, was assigned to others. I wanted to understand the world from his perspective, but he dismissed my attempts as pointless. His world was black and white. If I didn't agree with his views, I was just like everyone else he had known in his life. Regardless of how I tried to keep the context of these interactions in mind—the man was on death row, in solitary confinement, and clearly in distress—I found myself judging him as self-centered. Why couldn't he see that I was trying my hardest to help him?

I wasn't the first person to experience Tracey this way; the jurors who convicted and sentenced him to death had too. There was little physical evidence connecting Tracey to the crime—hiring three men to murder his parents and an uncle. Of what evidence did exist, the strongest was provided by two of his codefendants, who had actually carried out the murders and received lesser sentences in exchange for their testimony against him. They described Tracey as manipulative, cold, violent, and controlling. And so did a chorus of witnesses, including exes, his children, extended family, and acquaintances. I thought there must be more to him, but I wondered.

AS PART OF my education in the signs and symptoms of mental illness and trauma, I often debriefed my client and witness visits with psychologists and psychiatrists who routinely consulted on death penalty cases, almost all of which are also complex mental health cases.

One such expert, Dr. B, didn't fit the stereotypical image I had of a psychiatrist. Dr. B was over six feet tall, with a bodybuilder's physique. He was kind, direct, and extremely intelligent. During one exchange about Tracey, Dr. B asked me a question:

"Do you think all of your clients are people living with mental illness?"

Sheepishly, I revealed that I hadn't thought about it.

"Who do you think provides most mental health support to people experiencing a crisis?"

"Hospitals. Probably emergency rooms."

Dr. B nodded. "And hospitals have very limited capacity. Once the hospital determines the person in crisis is not a threat to themselves or others, they are released." He paused. Though his exterior was tough, he had a gentle, unhurried way of making his point. "Does that mean they have addressed the issue?"

"No, of course not."

"Right, so now the person is out of the hospital. What happens?"

"They might do something that gets them in trouble."

"Like what?"

"Get drunk or high and steal a car. Break into a building. Maybe they don't have a place to go and so end up sleeping outside on the street. And probably they get arrested."

"Yes. And then who has to treat them?"

Dr. B pointed out that the Los Angeles County Jail was the largest mental health provider in the country. Research bears this out: a report by the Treatment Advocacy Center, a nonprofit that supports reforms aimed at serving the unique needs of those with severe mental illness,[2] shows that more people with mental illness are incarcerated than are being treated in hospitals.[3] More than half of those incarcerated in the United States have received a diagnosis for a mental health disease, illness, or disorder.[4] The numbers are likely even greater for people sentenced to death.[5] Carceral facilities are truly America's mental health asylums.

Unsurprisingly, many symptoms of mental illness also undergird unlawful behaviors, as well as those behaviors deemed antisocial. The conclusions we draw about a person interpersonally—that they are cold, lazy, weird, an asshole—can point to potential symptoms. I thought about how Tracey made me feel. The way he'd tasked me with finding the key to his exoneration, and his scorn when I couldn't. I thought of how other people had described him.

Dr. B continued. "What else might cause such 'manipulative' behavior? What about someone who is 'cold' or 'violent'?"

I didn't know, so he filled in the blanks for me. "Paranoia. Mental inflexibility. Delusions. An inability to assimilate new impressions." All could indicate a history of trauma or damage to the brain. "A person who is controlling could be masking a bad memory or other cognitive disability or displaying an adaptive response to traumatic experiences—or all of the above." A multigenerational history could provide valuable context for the behavior. Absent such collateral information, as in Tracey's case, a person with complicated behaviors, especially ones that caused alienation, might never be accurately understood.

Talking to Dr. B helped me reframe Tracey's behavior into what it was: evidence of both his cognitive functioning and his history responding to his environment. I thought of Edward's pliability when I'd first met him, which had put me at ease. This wasn't so different. My feelings about Tracey's behavior—acting controlling or manipulative—were irrelevant. At best, they were data points. What mattered was what the behavior indicated about how Tracey viewed the world around him. I could see how easy it would be to conclude that Tracey was acting with bad intentions when his actions were in fact automatic. Automatic in the way that all behavior becomes at a certain point, unless and until there is effort given to changing it.

The more time I spent with Tracey, the more I came to see his stand-offishness and obsessional dialogue as indicating something more complex. He maintained unshakable false beliefs about the evidence in his case, an unyielding commitment in the face of reasonable information. ACE studies showed that early childhood trauma led to greater incidences of both paranoid and delusional behavior, as did studies around early childhood abuse and neglect.[6] To better understand what was animating Tracey's internal world, I needed more information about his social and biological history, which we never obtained.

DESPITE THE OBSTACLES, Tracey came to trust me—as much as he could trust anyone: with limits and reservations. I learned to stop trying to convince him to see things my way and instead listened to what he believed.

The day of Tracey's scheduled execution, he spent hours visiting with pen pals from Europe who had traveled thousands of miles to support him. These visits were conducted behind glass and could not, per the rules of the prison, involve physical contact. Visiting hours ended around four P.M., when Tracey was taken to a transportation van and driven about forty-five minutes away from death row to Huntsville, where executions took place. There, Tracey was only allowed contact with his legal team and a spiritual adviser.

The office phone rang periodically, each time raising the hope that Tracey's execution had been stayed by one of the various courts reviewing pending legal claims. But often it was Tracey calling for an update. His attorneys were filing briefs and responses with various courts; they didn't have time to speak with him. So I did. Between calls, I stood outside on the front porch of the office, smoking cigarettes and guzzling whatever forms of caffeine I could find. I'd come to understand Danalynn's relationship with Diet Coke.

Around eight P.M., two hours after Tracey was supposed to die, the phone rang again. I was sitting cross-legged on the floor in my office, surrounded by secondhand bookshelves stacked with bound trial transcripts. I kept looking up at the shelves, feeling as if the contents might topple over on me.

It was Tracey, still alive, calling for another update. There were still some pending legal issues, so it wasn't clear whether the execution would go forward or not. Tracey asked me to hold on. I hung my head and closed my eyes, holding the cordless phone tight against my ear. No one had prepared me for this day, for how to talk to someone who at any moment could be taken away to be killed. On the other end of the line, someone was talking to Tracey; through the muffled conversation, I heard "That's it" and "It's okay." Tracey's time was up. All the remaining legal arguments had been dismissed. The path was now clear for the state of Texas to kill him.

I expected him to return to the phone angry. I thought he would yell at me, tell me that I was the reason he was going to be dead in a few minutes. But when Tracey returned to the phone, he sounded calm. "They are taking me now," he said. "Just do what you can with the time you have. Keep fighting for people. And don't worry about me. Don't worry about this. You listened. You were honest. Just do good."

"I'm sorry, Tracey," I said. "I'm sorry things are ending this way." Before I could get another word out, the line went dead.

I held the cordless phone in my hand, feeling numb. I didn't know what to do or where to go. I didn't feel like talking or crying. I felt stuck. How could I get up from the floor and walk out of this office right then? But at some point I did. I grabbed my bag and what remained of my cigarettes and walked a couple blocks to a small, dark bar. I drank with some other people from the office. Local news outlets pronounced Tracey dead at nine sixteen P.M. There was little national media attention for another routine execution in Texas. One of his pen pals had been allowed to visit his body after the execution and had taken a picture of him, which she sent to me by email. I regretted opening the attachment as soon as I saw him.

Tracey did not want to be buried in the United States. Another pen pal had arranged for his final resting place to be in Italy, a country that had long since abolished the death penalty. Tracey's pen pals had clearly been sympathetic to his plight. A colleague at the office navigated the bureaucratic process of getting Tracey's corpse sent overseas. I had to get back to work on another case, a client with an upcoming hearing. Texas had executed more than twenty people that year already, and the state would put a total of twenty-five people to death before the new year. There wasn't much time to reflect. I wasn't sleeping well. I hadn't always liked Tracey. A lot of people hadn't liked him. His jurors hadn't liked him. The thought kept intruding as I opened another Bankers Box stuffed with documents: Do we kill people we don't connect with?

TRACEY'S DEATH COINCIDED with a wake-up call. I was putting in ten-, sometimes twelve-hour days of emotionally flaying exchanges with clients and witnesses who handed over one shattering memory after another. I would follow this up with several hours of drinking with colleagues to soften the intensity and fall asleep. The pattern couldn't continue. I started seeing a therapist.

Within the criminal defense community, seeking mental health support wasn't discussed. This remains true, though it is starting to change. I could see the collateral damage all around me. Shortly after

Tracey's execution, a well-known capital defense attorney died from a heart attack induced by a drug overdose. Suicide wasn't uncommon. Neither was a shorter lifespan.[7] I suspected that, like some other high-stress professions—think homicide detectives[8] and surgeons[9]—defense attorneys and other advocates in criminal defense experienced higher levels of substance use, mental health concerns, and other challenges like broken marriages and strained relationships with their families.[10] From my perspective, it seemed like there was a resistance to acknowledging the personal cost of the constant exposure to other people's trauma. There was a fear that doing so might result in people leaving the profession. I guess that attitude makes a certain kind of sense, coming from a team of people fighting against impossible odds to chip away at the huge forces of state power arrayed against them. What good would it do to dwell on the Sisyphean effort? But pushing down the emotional toll wasn't working for me. I wanted to keep doing mitigation investigation, and I knew there was no way to do it without help.

My earliest experiences of therapy quelled some of the anxiety I struggled to shake. It was the first time that I really interrogated my choice to be a mitigation specialist, which was in and of itself a valuable exercise. But while I appreciated being pushed to think about my own choices, the way my therapist kept asking that question—why did I do this work?—week after week, started to bother me. Would she have asked an emergency room surgeon the same thing? Was she somehow implying that I should stop? During one session, I snapped:

"What's wrong with feeling called to stand between the full weight of the government and a poor and marginalized person who is in danger of being cast out of the human community?"

She didn't immediately respond. I interpreted her hesitation as proof that she thought my energy and time would be better spent on more deserving people. I got that feedback often in Texas. If I was out at a bar or meeting someone outside the defense community who asked me what I did for work, I had learned to say I was in the legal field. I had learned to try and figure out their views first before saying more. Outside of Texas, my family didn't agree with my choice to work as a mitigation specialist either: they were in favor of the death penalty and other harsh laws like three strikes, which mandated lengthy sentences for those convicted of certain crimes three times.[11] I couldn't talk to them about my job in any great detail. Even with more sympathetic friends, there was an awkwardness. No one really knew how to respond to the things I noticed about the histories of my clients. I felt frustrated with the therapist and often left her office annoyed. What might she say, I thought, about Edward and Tracey? Each man had apparent mental health issues that had animated their behaviors. Wasn't that fact alone enough of a reason to spare them the death penalty? And then I thought of the people who deliberate in these cases, who make these decisions: the jurors.

When I carry out a mitigation investigation with a client who has already been convicted and sentenced to death, I visit the jurors who heard the evidence, deliberated about my client's guilt, decided he was responsible, and eventually determined that he should be sentenced to death. I approach jurors the same way I do anyone else, showing up without advance notice in hopes of learning something about their experience. If they open the door to me, I always make clear that I'm part of my client's defense team. And I always bring a colleague along to observe, in case a dispute arises later about what was said. These conditions—my status as a defense team member and the presence of a third party—unavoidably limit the former juror's sense that they can speak freely. They often assume I'm trying to catch them in some mistake that will help overturn my client's conviction. True, if they didn't follow the law—if, for example, they used the internet to look up information about the case during the trial—a court would need to determine whether that had impacted the fairness of the process and needed to be corrected. But when I meet with jurors, I'm not hunting for errors to correct. I want to know about the fullness of their lives and experiences. I want to learn from each person. It can be hard to reach that level of trust when they see my visit as the continuation of an adversarial process.

Nearly all the jurors I have spoken with as a mitigation specialist decided to sentence someone to death. There has been no occasion in my work to connect with jurors who listened to the evidence at a capital trial, found the defendant guilty of murder, and decided they should not be sentenced to death. Those jurors, in an adversarial system, awarded a win to the defendant. Very rarely would there have been an appeal. The case was over. I wondered what I might learn from those jurors. What, for them, tipped the balance in the direction of life? Was it the evidence presented? Or something else entirely?

Since 1976, when the death penalty was repackaged and reinstated, researchers have uncovered a great deal about how capital jurors make their decisions, and the findings are bleak. Results show that capital jurors fail to follow the most basic tenets of the law.[12] Even the most desirable, law-abiding juror often struggles to understand exactly what the court wants of them.[13] And who can blame them? Most of the instructions jurors are given were written for someone with an advanced degree. Consider this language instructing jurors on the matter of mitigating evidence:

> [The jury shall decide] whether, taking into consideration all
> of the evidence, including the circumstances of the offense, the
> defendant's character and background, and the personal moral

culpability of the defendant, there is a sufficient mitigating circumstance or circumstances to warrant that a sentence of life imprisonment without parole rather than a death sentence be imposed. The jury shall answer the issue "yes" or "no"; may not answer the issue "no" unless it agrees unanimously and may not answer the issue "yes" unless 10 or more jurors agree; need not agree on what particular evidence supports an affirmative finding on the issue; and shall consider mitigating evidence to be evidence that a juror might regard as reducing the defendant's moral blameworthiness.[14]

I once interviewed a juror who *was* an attorney. He had no idea what these instructions meant.

Another wrinkle is that only people who can, in theory, support a sentence of death are allowed to serve as jurors in capital cases because the law requires them to be open to the full range of potential punishments.[15] Anyone who says during jury selection that they couldn't sentence someone to death is therefore removed from the pool of potential jurors. This process is called death qualification. Perhaps unsurprisingly, the research has indicated that "death-qualified" jurors are more likely to assign guilt to an accused person.[16] They're also more likely to assign guilt to a defendant who doesn't take the witness stand and more likely to believe law enforcement witness testimony.[17] These same jurors, who tend to support harsher penalties, also tend to be hostile toward mental health defenses such as not guilty by reason of insanity.[18] On the other hand, those jurors disqualified *because of* death qualification tend to be more critical of evidence, more likely to engage in thorough deliberations, and less retributive.[19] In sum, the capital jury is tilted toward conviction and death, even before any evidence is presented.[20]

In 2007 I joined a consortium of university-based researchers working collectively on the Capital Jury Project. Launched in the early 1990s, the Capital Jury Project is the largest nationwide study into capital juror decision-making.[21] At that time they needed a researcher to focus on juror receptivity to mitigation evidence in Texas, which was, fortuitously, exactly what I wanted to investigate.[22]

My instinct that I could learn something about my work from jury members was right. The lessons came in phases. Many of the people who participated in the study did not have prior experience with the criminal legal system other than serving on a jury in a capital murder trial. Many remarked that they'd been surprised by how vastly different a real trial turns out to be from the ones portrayed on *Law & Order* or *CSI*. The presentation of evidence was often boring, the arguments on both sides far less engaging. Most jurors, even those who ultimately sentenced their defendant to life without parole instead of death, were entirely confused by the concept of mitigation. They often believed that the defense was presenting the perpetrator's biography as some sort of moral justification for the crime in question, which left them with a murky and contorted sense of how to engage with the contextual information.

The jurors I spoke to offered, through their accounts, so much insight into the American criminal legal system.

Especially those who voted for a sentence of death.

Especially one juror, Roger.

It was already ninety degrees when I pulled up to Roger's house at nine A.M.—a typical sticky East Texas summer morning. He lived outside the Harris County line, in a partially constructed and expanding subdivision. A white man answered the door almost immediately after I rang. He looked to be in his late fifties, dressed neatly but plainly in khaki pants and a short-sleeved polo shirt. I introduced myself, and he welcomed me in. We sat in the living room with the drapes closed and ceiling fans churning. Other than a few breaks for the restroom and an interlude outside for some fresh air, we stayed in the same spot for the ten hours I spent with him.

Roger worked as a music teacher at a local public school. He was divorced and estranged from his two children. As part of his church ministry he had at one point taught music in a prison. One of the incarcerated men he taught had been convicted of multiple murders; Roger referred to him as a "serial killer." This man made a deep impression on him. Before meeting Roger, I reviewed the public records for the case he had juried, including the trial transcript. He had also mentioned his connection to this inmate during jury selection. Roger had been quite taken by what struck him as the inmate's deeply humane, even soulful qualities—concern, intelligence, musical talent. These shows of humanity crystallized something for him. He saw them as firsthand proof that evil existed in the world disguised as decency. The inmate's good qualities weren't real; they were a ruse designed to hide his true, wicked nature.

As a result of his relationship with this inmate, Roger believed he could tell if a person was a killer by simply looking at their face. He believed that Willie, the defendant in the capital case that brought me to him that day, was a fine example of what evil looked like. Willie was accused, and eventually convicted, of killing two people in what the prosecutor framed as a drug deal turned massacre. Willie's team mounted a self-defense argument. Crime scene investigators found that the victims had guns. Dozens of shell casings from the various weapons told a chaotic story. It seemed impossible to determine with any certainty who shot first.

Over the course of the trial, the jury heard from various witnesses about Willie's childhood. According to Roger, Willie was "not a brilliant scholar" and Willie's mother was a "street whore." I was struck by how

Roger adopted the exact words used by Willie's own attorney during the trial when questioning Willie's mother. Roger recounted a story that I had also read in the transcript: Willie, as a ten-year-old child, was often in the position of looking for his mother, who would disappear for days. Sometimes, he would find her in the cars of strange men, where she was engaged in sex work to support her powerful heroin addiction. Other times, finding her passed out in vacant houses, Willie would not know whether she was alive or dead. He would have to slap her back to consciousness or failing that, run out to find an adult to help him drag her limp body home.

Roger remembered that Willie's father was also addicted to drugs. Witnesses testified that Willie's father had given him PCP when Willie was twelve years old. There was one person in Willie's life who, in Roger's estimation, seemed decent. This man, Brian, had been in a relationship with Willie's mom during a rare and brief period of sobriety. Brian—Roger referred to him as "the good-guy stepfather"—lived with Willie and his mom for about a year. Willie's mother became pregnant and, shortly after delivering a son, started using drugs again. When Brian realized what was happening, he tried to get her help, but she refused. He moved out with Willie's baby brother, intending to return for Willie, he said. Brian's testimony during the trial suggested his devastation at leaving Willie behind. He said he wished he could have removed Willie from his family, from that life. Brian felt like maybe then Willie would have had a chance. Willie wasn't a bad kid, Brian said. His future could have been different.

Roger thought it was a shame that Willie hadn't been able to live with Brian, but he dismissed the significance of the fact that Willie had been left many times in his life without a capable adult to raise him. "One of the points that the defense had attempted . . . was that this child who had grown into an adult was a product of his environment. The problem with that argument was he *did* have a good influence in his former stepfather who kind of semi-raised him." Roger thought that Willie, at age eleven or twelve, could have gone to live with Brian, could have sought out the benefits of having a positive role model in his life, but chose to revel in bad influences. Roger spoke of young Willie as if he viewed him not as a child but as a person failing to make the right decisions for himself. Viewing Black children as adults within American culture is not uncommon.[23]

As the day wore on, Roger became more animated and descriptive about the witnesses from Willie's family who testified at trial. One uncle was "the visual representation of Shaft from the seventies. A pimp with the purple suit with a feather coming out of the hat." Roger recalled all the witnesses saying nearly everyone in Willie's family sold street drugs. Willie's cousin who testified about their hard upbringing and who was also incarcerated was a "loser." Roger role-played the testimonies of some of Willie's family members, mimicking their accents and speech patterns. Willie and his family were caricatures of human beings to Roger—individuals who looked like people but were somehow inherently different from him.

To Roger, Willie's past *had* been determinative of who he became, *had* played a part in his ultimate path in life, but not in a way that mitigated a sentence of death. Roger didn't think Willie was capable of rehabilitation because he was from a family and community that could not be saved: he was "unsalvageable." As far as Roger was concerned, there was simply no reason to keep Willie alive.

> I don't think we have a perfect world, resources aren't unlimited and because resources aren't unlimited I think you have to make decisions for the good of the total group. Some people just need killing. Whether you call it murder or you call it execution or simply elimination . . . those are people who have lost all dignity and respect for anything. They can't exist with the rest of us and

I wonder why it is we have to support them . . . I think we go to too much trouble to execute them. Too much money is spent on losers. Eliminate the ceremony and move on.

He strongly supported a death sentence, which is what Willie ultimately received.

Getting into my car after the day spent with Roger, I tried to piece together his reasoning. Willie was a product of his environment—his family, who dealt drugs—or he wasn't because he'd had someone like Brian, however briefly, in his life. He was because his community, like him, was "unsalvageable," or he wasn't because young Willie could have made different decisions and had simply chosen not to. Willie seemed to be, in Roger's view, both a pure product of his environment *and* a self-created individual at the same time. And yet when Roger spoke about his own setbacks, his children's, or those of the students he taught in the suburban public school where he worked, he accepted that a life wasn't lived in isolation. He agreed that support and care were essential to grow into a healthy, thriving adult. Viewing Willie as someone who had "lost all dignity and respect for anything" made it simple, even logical, to put him out of his misery and sentence him to death. In a twisted way, Roger seemed to feel that what he was doing was morally right: "simply elimination."

Before the day I spent with Roger, I hadn't connected how essential dehumanization is to the retributive quality of the death penalty and, more broadly, to both the American legal system and to American culture. I considered the death penalty and other severe punishments as mechanisms of social control, which they are. But Roger helped me understand that control more clearly: it works against communities that are already devalued. As another juror I interviewed from Willie's case said, "I am not in that world. I wished I had never learned of a life like his."

Undergirding Roger's views, dissonant though they were, was the unmistakable dominant American cultural narrative of individual success: hard work and ingenuity are all it takes to make something of yourself. Another juror from the same trial commented, "Minorities in this country have a better shot of going to college than anybody. Where you grow up is no excuse in my book because there are so many more opportunities to get grants and money to go to college. As a white male over the age of forty I have less opportunity than a Black man in his twenties." Failing to live a better life in America is a personal problem, not a social one. I saw in Roger's perspective the awesome power of this narrative. It's powerful enough to trump, and thereby silence, the testimony of over a dozen witnesses to the truth about how Willie lived as a child. Powerful enough to accommodate the cognitive dissonance I saw in Roger, who did see early life experiences as determinative but then blamed Willie as if he had chosen his early life experiences or could somehow have counteracted them but had decided not to. Powerful enough to obscure the fact that adversity is not equally distributed, that it falls disproportionately on already marginalized, ignored, or isolated people, such that those in need of the most support are the least likely to have it. Powerful enough to justify retributive sentences as morally right.

WHO DO WE spare? Who is given mercy? Or a second chance? I hoped to hear answers from the jurors who had chosen life rather than death.

Diana was a small white woman with curly light-blond hair cut in a bob. Though she was just over five feet tall and probably weighed less than one hundred pounds, her presence was commanding. A mother to sons, she was a tough, no-nonsense communicator. Diana believed in capital punishment, and her service in John Miguel's case hadn't altered her view on the topic.

I visited Diana at her home, in another suburb of Houston. We sat outside for most of the six-hour visit, interrupted occasionally by phone calls from her grandchildren. We were speaking about five months after her jury service had occurred. She had learned a lot about John Miguel over the course of the trial. As in Willie's case, members of John Miguel's family had testified about his early life. John Miguel grew up in a relatively stable family; his parents expected that each child would work hard in school and become a professional. People around John Miguel cared about him even though he appeared to be the black sheep of the family, ended up using drugs and alcohol, and could never live up to his parents' hopes for him. They still loved him despite the crime he had committed.

A nun from the village where John Miguel was raised testified about the religious community to which the family belonged. Diana found this testimony especially helpful because it revealed John Miguel's exposure to a moral foundation. Diana believed that John Miguel was a "foxhole Christian"—someone who finds God again when they are afraid of being killed. Even so, Diana valued his religious background; she felt that foundation would help him with the rest of his life.

Like Roger, Diana also studied John Miguel's appearance during the trial for a sense of who he was at his core. Diana recalled that John Miguel "had no reaction to anything" until he started crying when his younger brother testified. "It made me feel like he was a person," she said plainly.

John Miguel did experience hardships, which Diana learned about during the witness testimony; he had had a brain injury as a young child, experienced physical and emotional abuse from his parents, and was an alcoholic. Yet, when pushed for the reason she had spared his life, she pointed to his work ethic, saying simply, "He wasn't a deadbeat." And there it was: we save people who are like us, or people who demonstrate qualities that we want to be associated with. To Diana, John Miguel was human. She saw in him the potential to become a hardworking Christian, much like herself.

It struck me that perhaps we were asking the wrong questions of jurors. Rather than asking what punishment someone deserved—such an impossible question to extract from our own cultural biases—why not ask: What would it take to return this person successfully to the community? Is there enough support in place for them to live good lives if given the chance? If not, what role do we need to play in finding that support?

And why not ask jurors to consider mitigating evidence in the same spirit? Instead of: Why should this person's punishment be mitigated? we might ask: What attributes does this person have that indicate their potential for growth, if they are given appropriate support?

Imagine that.

Chapter Five

Cruelty

#BREAKING #SCOTUS has denied all of Inmate Ledell Lee's
motions for execution #ARexecutions #arpx

On April 20, 2017, the attorney general of Arkansas, Leslie Rutledge,
tweeted to her twenty thousand followers that the way was clear:
the U.S. Supreme Court would allow the execution of Ledell Lee after
twenty-one years on death row. I had not heard of Ledell until a few weeks
beforehand, when I received a phone call from a capital defense attorney.

"Liz, you probably know what is happening in Arkansas right now.
Do you have any time to help out?"

On February 27, 2017, the state had scheduled eight executions to
be carried out in the span of eleven days, starting April 17, because its
supply of midazolam, one of the three lethal injection drugs used to
put people to death, was set to expire on April 30.[1] Up until that point,
Arkansas had gone more than eleven years (since November 2005)
without an execution.[2] At the time, few states that had gone more than
a decade without an execution returned to carrying out the sentence.
Equally startling was that, to accommodate the number of killings, the

state had set two executions to occur on one day. Arkansas had a history of carrying out multiple executions in a single day, as many as three people; Paul Ruiz, Earl Van Denton, and Kirt Douglas Wainwright were all put to death on January 8, 1997.[3] Yet twenty years had passed since then. Such a spectacle as a double execution felt like a relic from other times. Public support for the death penalty had waned significantly over those two decades. By the time Arkansas announced its intention to execute Ledell in 2017, Americans were almost equally split, with roughly half favoring life-without-parole sentences over execution for murder convictions.[4]

Arkansas's execution protocol relied on a combination of three drugs: midazolam, a sedative intended to render the individual unconscious; vecuronium bromide, a muscle relaxer that causes paralysis; and potassium chloride, which causes cardiac arrest. There was concern over the use of midazolam, which had a track record of failing to cause unconsciousness in other executions. None of these drugs was originally intended to be used this way: they had been created to improve patient outcomes and control pain, not for euthanasia. A number of the pharmaceutical companies producing the drugs were located in European countries that had long abandoned capital punishment and were committed to seeing the abolition of the death penalty worldwide.[5] In 2010 the United Kingdom placed restrictions on the export of these drugs. In 2011 the European Commission followed suit. These restrictions meant that about two thirds of the thirty-four states that still allowed capital punishment back in 2010 could not get the drugs needed.[6]

But to fully understand the situation Arkansas now found itself in, it was essential to go back even further. When lethal injection became the primary method of execution in the 1980s,[7] departments of corrections, the agencies responsible for carrying out executions, created regulations, or protocols, that specified which drugs were permitted for use in the procedure (often a two- or three-drug mixture, depending on the state). As pharmaceutical companies learned that their medications were being used to execute people, many either explicitly banned their products from being used for executions or stopped producing them entirely.[8] The short supply halted or slowed departments of corrections from carrying out state killings.

Impatient for a solution, many of these departments turned to what are known as compounding pharmacies. These operate as boutique medicine providers, able to mix very specific types of drugs. They tend to serve people for whom mass-produced medication isn't an option—due to allergies to commonly used ingredients, for example. The Food and Drug Administration does not approve the drugs produced, meaning that the quality and effectiveness of the compounded drugs is unknown.[9] There is no way for departments of corrections to ensure that drugs provided by compounding pharmacies will work as intended. But that made no difference to state actors eager to use the drugs in executions.[10]

In 2010 the Arizona Department of Corrections worked with the compounding pharmacy Dream Pharma, operating out of a driving school in London, to procure lethal injection drugs that were used in at least two executions.[11] In 2012 Idaho officials chartered a plane for $2,448 to fly the state department of corrections director and chief of prisons round-trip to Tacoma, Washington, to purchase compounded lethal injection drugs. The two brought along a suitcase with $15,000 in cash. They met the head of the compounding pharmacy in a Walmart parking lot, where the exchange took place.[12] Mississippi officials explored obtaining sedatives from a veterinary school.[13] States with a surplus of any particular drug swapped with other states for the supplies they needed. California traded some of its muscle relaxant for vials of

Arizona's sodium thiopental, an anesthetic used in lethal injection. In what was classified as a secret mission by the head of San Quentin State Prison,[14] a team of California corrections officers picked up the drugs from Arizona and handed them off to a second team for transport all the way to San Quentin's death row. Public records requests found emails from a California prison executive at the time hailing the mission's success: "You guys in AZ are life savers. By [*sic*] you a beer next time I get that way."

IN 2014, THEN Arkansas attorney general Dustin McDaniel lamented, "I've done everything I can do to carry out the executions that have been ordered in my state, and if somebody has an idea of how we can do that, I'd like to hear it."[15] In addition to the shortage of necessary medications, pending lawsuits that focused on the state's execution protocol had halted killings.

The protocols mattered insofar as there was a commitment to ensuring that inmates were not tortured during the procedure. There had been many botched executions, perhaps none as notorious as Clayton Lockett's in Oklahoma in 2014. Oklahoma had been struggling to obtain one of its drugs, pentobarbital, which it used as the sedative in executions.[16] In response to the challenges, Oklahoma changed its protocol to allow the warden of the prison overseeing executions sole discretion in selecting the drugs used from a list of several possible drug combinations.[17] The warden wasn't a medical professional, but it was an election year and the state's attorney general and governor, both back on the ballot, were applying pressure to get executions moving again. Even though the protocol bestowed on the warden this decision, somehow it was general counsel for the Department of Corrections, Michael Oakley, who ultimately revised the state's execution protocol to allow for the use of midazolam as the new sedative in the procedure. Mr. Oakley testified in the aftermath of the death of Mr. Lockett that he had carried out online research before approving midazolam, which was known for failing to render people fully unconscious during executions. As it turned out, midazolam was never intended to be used as an anesthetic, according to the Food and Drug Administration's website. Regardless, none of the other approved protocols were available.[18] The protocol was updated less than one month before Mr. Lockett's execution date.[19]

It took forty-three minutes for Mr. Lockett to die. Mr. Lockett was awake as officers who had failed to get the IV into the correct spot carried out a cutdown procedure, slicing into his body to make it easier to see where to place the line. The drugs leaked into his muscle tissue. Even after he was declared unconscious, Mr. Lockett was awake, attempting to get off the gurney. He groaned, spoke, and eventually died, though not from the chemicals the officers had attempted to administer, but from a heart attack.[20] He had been tortured to death.

Quietly, between 2014 and 2017, the Arkansas Department of Corrections obtained the necessary drugs by telling pharmaceutical companies that their products would be used only for medical purposes. When the lawsuits concluded, Arkansas had about a month before its supply of midazolam expired. Officials decided to set eight executions to make sure the precious supplies wouldn't go to waste.[21] It was a very short window in which to kill eight people.

A government killing is a highly orchestrated event that requires planning and coordination. The setting of an execution date sets off a chain reaction of tasks. Prison staff need to coordinate with witnesses attending the execution: loved ones invited by the person who is to be killed, and family members of the murder victim, who can also choose to be present.[22] Members of the media need to be present so there can be a contemporaneous account of the condemned person's final moments of life. A medical professional must be engaged to oversee the event. Most doctors will not perform the actual execution because it runs counter to the Hippocratic oath's principle of doing no harm, so states find volunteers to talk the execution team through the homicide. Each potential attendee needs to have a background check.

The prison must set up a waiting area where the attendees can go in the event of a delay. This area must be close enough to the execution chamber so that spectators can get into place quickly whenever the final legal challenges conclude and the road is clear. This can take hours; the prison must provide refreshments and snacks in case there is a long wait.

Executions need to be practiced, which means roles must be rehearsed. The execution team, usually corrections officers employed by the prison, prepares for various scenarios. What to do, for example, if the inmate victim refuses to walk to the death chamber? They must know how to tie down limbs when the victim is unwilling to participate. Practice also helps the officers prepare emotionally; the more practice, the more mechanical the proceedings can become before the execution date.[23] The officer designated to administer the drugs must practice finding a vein and placing the needle inside. In some cases, they're unable to do so during an initial execution attempt, and the victim has to be brought into a room for vein mapping, a procedure that aims to ensure the needle finds a home during the next attempt.[24]

The inmate also makes his preparations. The last meal request must be lodged, belongings cleared out. He may send his worldly effects to people of his choosing. Visits between the inmate and his legal team, family, friends, and a spiritual adviser will often occupy much of the preceding day. Coordinating these last visits, the prison will often limit calls or visits for the other inmates. If there is going to be an autopsy, a medical examiner needs to be ready. Arrangements for the body need to be coordinated with a funeral home and burial site. Someone has to clean the death chamber afterward.

Setting an execution date also triggers further litigation on behalf of the inmate, much of which can *only* be raised at this late date. Legally, the question of whether someone is "competent to be executed" can only be addressed when the killing is imminent; indeed, "competency" at this stage is contingent on the inmate's understanding that they are soon to be killed for the murder for which they were sentenced to death.[25] Other late-stage appeals seek to correct legal wrongs before it's too late. The two most common errors in death penalty cases are, first, trial attorneys not providing effective representation and, second, prosecutors withholding evidence that should have been turned over to the defense before trial.[26] Death penalty cases have a shockingly high error rate, an average of about 50 percent nationwide, with some states reaching outrageous levels: Wyoming saw 77 percent reversal rates; Louisiana clocked in at 74 percent; Mississippi came in third, with about 70 percent of its capital cases being reversed.[27] Only 18 percent of all the nationwide reversals have generated a death sentence again, and a full 4 percent of the cases that went back to trial resulted in acquittals, meaning there had never even been enough evidence to *convict*, let alone impose a death sentence.[28] In 2001, two Supreme Court justices commented on the growing body of empirical evidence of errors in death penalty cases, with Justice Sandra O'Connor stating, "If statistics are any indication, the system may well be allowing some innocent defendants to be executed."[29] She was joined by Justice Ruth Bader Ginsburg, who noted that in dozens of instances where she has reviewed requests for stays of executions on the high court, she had yet to see one "in which the defendant was well represented at trial."[30] I can't think of another instance of public safety where such high levels of error are permitted to continue.

BACK TO THAT phone call in April of 2017: "Liz, you probably know what is happening in Arkansas right now. Do you have any time to help out?"

I really didn't have the time to help. In 2014, I'd founded a nonprofit organization, Advancing Real Change, which I hoped would become a place where people who wanted to learn how to do mitigation investigation could do so. Teaching the work—as I had been taught a decade before—made me realize that so much of how I carried out an investigation was automatic. By that time I no longer thought about *how* I performed the job; I just did it. This unconscious engagement was partly in response to the raw emotions of my early days of working in Texas. Gone were the uncontrollable tears I once shed, the unchecked anxiety. I did not reflect as much as I had at the start. I just got on with the work. But my staff members were new to this field. They needed to talk about the emotional challenges involved. I wasn't sure how to shepherd them through and continue to perform without dwelling on the heaviness.

We operated out of the basement of my East Baltimore row house for more than a year. There wasn't money for an office space. Once we could, we moved into a small office above a pawnshop. Less than six months in, the pawnshop caught fire. My health was also suffering. I had been in a car accident and was now on a slow path to recovery from a concussion. The future of the organization was uncertain. I knew if I quit I would not attempt it again. I was determined to keep going because I'd seen the unmatched power of mitigation investigation, how integral it was to justice. I knew how few people were properly trained and qualified to carry it out. If I did decide to help in Ledell's case, I could be putting my inexperienced staff through an execution. I listened to the attorney's voice on the other end of the phone as all of these thoughts ran through my mind.

"Liz, Ledell might be innocent, but even if he is not, the case is a mess. He has been writing anyone and everyone for over twenty years, begging for help."

Ledell had been tried twice. In the lead-up to his first trial he asked for new attorneys because he believed the attorneys assigned to his case were not working to secure his freedom. He didn't get new ones. Despite his concerns, the first trial ended when the jury couldn't reach a decision about whether he was, in fact, guilty. Before the second trial started, Ledell filed new motions to remove his attorneys, citing, among other reasons, a conversation in which one of them told him, "Well, technically, I think you should have got the death penalty. The next time you will get the death penalty."[31] In response to the filing, the trial lawyers described Ledell as challenging and hard to communicate with. The client-attorney relationship was obviously strained, but Ledell didn't have the financial resources to hire his own lawyers. Like most people facing sentences of death, he was left to accept the representation he'd been provided.[32] As his attorney had predicted, the second trial ended in a conviction and sentence of death.

It was common for my clients to be represented at trial by attorneys who did not provide the zealous representation to which they were entitled. Many lawyers were not equipped—they didn't have the training or experience needed—to provide strong representation, and courts were too often willing to allow blatantly inappropriate legal representation for people facing the most severe penalties. One of Danalynn's clients, Calvin Burdine, had originally been represented by a court-appointed attorney who fell asleep for periods of up to ten minutes throughout the trial.[33] Calvin came within hours of execution, receiving a stay before the sentence could be carried out, which allowed him the chance to litigate the issue of his sleeping lawyer.

"I'll help," I heard myself say. "I can help. I'll do it." Maybe it was Ledell's desperation over all these years. Maybe feeling so out of my depth running Advancing Real Change made me crave the kind of challenge I already knew I could manage. Maybe the exact reason didn't matter. I was heading to Arkansas.

THE PASSENGER TO my right looked slightly annoyed. I was balancing a laptop, a notepad, copies of Ledell's trial transcript, highlighters, and pens on my tray table on the flight to Little Rock. After just two hours of review, I was more than a little confused by the jury's decision to convict Ledell, let alone sentence him to death.

The victim was a young woman named Debra Reese, killed in her home on February 9, 1993. According to the transcript, Debra and her husband, Billy, woke at around eight thirty that morning. Billy worked as a truck driver and set off at ten thirty A.M. Twenty minutes later, Debra called her mother, who lived a block away, and told her that a Black man had just stopped by the house, asking to borrow tools, which she didn't give him. Debra planned to head to her mom's place after doing her hair, but she never arrived. Over an hour went by. Without checking in on Debra herself, her mom called the police. They arrived at Debra's place around one thirty P.M. Her body was in the bedroom. She had been beaten to death with a small tire iron that her husband left by the bed for her safety when he traveled.

Ledell was arrested two miles away at his mother's house ninety minutes after the police found Debra. He'd had been there all day with various other family members, except for about an hour when he went to run errands.

The police claimed that the hour that Ledell wasn't at home was when he went to the house of Debra, a woman he did not know, and beat her to death. The crime scene was awash with blood, but when Ledell was arrested there wasn't anything on his clothes, just a pinhead-size speck of blood on his shoe. After Ledell was arrested, the police tied several unsolved murders and rapes to him, though no DNA connected him to the crimes, and his fingerprints did not match any that had been found at those crime scenes.[34]

I had never met a client for the first time so close to the day of their scheduled death. Since there had been no meaningful investigation into Ledell's life, it was hard to know what legal issues, beyond his potential innocence, needed to be addressed. It was possible, for example, that he was a person with an intellectual developmental disability and so not eligible for the death penalty. He had been held back in school, his grades were poor, and he'd eventually dropped out. Perhaps I would uncover something else that might be useful for executive clemency, something about his case or his personal background that might be important to the governor, who could, in theory, commute his sentence to something less than death.[35] I dove in to see what I could learn.

I had also never met witnesses—a client's parents, siblings, children, and community members—under such time pressure. It would be impossible to build the kind of long-term foundation necessary to elicit difficult memories. With just over a week left before Ledell's execution date, I knew I'd have to probe into areas of his past I hadn't earned the right to ask about. But there was no other option. There was no time to tread carefully, as I'd learned to do, no time to consider how much each witness had been through over the years, to observe evidence of the personal baggage they carried. There was no time even to ease into a relationship by focusing on the present: What was happening with them on the day of my visit? Maybe they'd fought with a loved one or had a difficult time at work; maybe they were struggling to navigate everyday life. The legal system wasn't concerned about the well-being of anyone connected to the man counting down the hours he had left on earth.

I fumbled my way through the visits. The best thing I could do was apologize and apologize often. I was sorry for the loss each person faced, sorry that the case had languished for twenty-four years only to be compressed into a matter of days, sorry for dropping into their lives and pressing ahead without knowing them at all. I could feel moments when witnesses pulled back, unsure that they could really confide in me. There is simply no shortcut to establishing trust; it takes the time it takes. I wondered what I wasn't learning because of people's understandable reticence. Ledell was running out of time, which meant I was too.

I spent part of each day with Ledell. We sat in a cell encased by steel bars, exposed to the officers circling us throughout the visit. I felt like an animal in a zoo. It was hard to share personal information within earshot of the men whose job it was to keep Ledell confined and alive long enough for the state to kill him. We hunched toward each other, speaking in low voices. Sometimes I asked Ledell to write down answers to ensure privacy. I apologized. I was sure he would rather spend these hours with his loved ones and not with me.

I left the prison each day angry, eager, and afraid. Angry that, after all these years, there was precious little time to do work that should have been done decades before. Eager to do everything I could to help, eager not to waste a minute. Stopping to eat felt like an indulgence: I was afraid that I would miss a critical piece of information, which would mean that, because of my mistake, Ledell was going to die. I hadn't known this feeling in years. It was the fear my staff at Advancing Real Change had been bringing to me and which I didn't know how to meet.

When I wasn't with Ledell, I was out knocking on the doors of anyone connected to him or to his case. Although most people I attempted
to visit were sympathetic, a few were quick to say they didn't want to
be involved: If Ledell could be railroaded like this, how could they
speak safely? Even interacting with government employees while I attempted to collect records was illuminating. One young clerk, seeing
Ledell's name on a private records authorization, wished me good luck.
Another man at the courthouse, helping me sort through various files,
commented that the executions were an embarrassment to him and his
state. There didn't seem to be a person in Little Rock who hadn't heard
of Ledell. When all the offices were closed and it was too late to keep
knocking on doors, I'd make my way to Ledell's mother's house.

Ms. Young's body told the story of the nightmare she had been living. She had dark, heavy circles under her eyes. She hadn't had a good
night's sleep since Ledell was arrested for this crime. Her gait was slow
and lumbering, and she walked slightly hunched over, as if there was an
invisible load on her back. She looked at least ten years older than her
age. Trying to have a conversation with Ms. Young was almost impossible because she was perpetually distracted, her mind focused on all the
ways Ledell had been set up, on the callousness of the people responsible for taking her son away. During one visit the smoke alarm went
off. She had become so absorbed in recounting these wrongs to me that
she'd forgotten she'd left the stove on. She repeated herself often—not
in a frantic way, but in a way that suggested she had learned to air her
grievances succinctly, like she might have just a couple of minutes to
make her case before a listener's sympathy for her plight ended and they
continued on their way.

Ledell wasn't a perfect person. Ms. Young knew that he had stolen
from people, used drugs, and gotten into trouble now and again, but
he wasn't a rapist or a murderer. The day of his arrest, Ledell had been

at home with her and the rest of the family since morning, minus the hour-long period during which the police claimed Ledell had gone to another part of town, broken into an unfamiliar woman's house, and beaten her to death with a small tire iron he couldn't have known was there. Nothing about the timeline made sense to Ms. Young. "A mother knows her children," she said. She knew he was innocent of this crime.

Ms. Young kept two large wheelable suitcases packed with every news clipping about Ledell's case she could find, paperwork from various courts, and letters—dozens of letters seeking help that Ledell had written to notable people and organizations. These she had copied and mailed out at her son's request. I went through each suitcase, taking pictures with my cell phone, page by page.

I left Little Rock a few days before Ledell's execution date. Another wave of attorneys and investigators had come to town to carry on the work, making it possible for me to return home and support the team from Baltimore.

In a compressed period of time, I had learned much more about Ledell then others knew about him up to that point. He had endured real struggle and hardship, stemming from the environmental trauma he and his family for generations had experienced. He had been exposed to unsafe levels of toxins in water, soil, and paint during infancy; he had learning difficulties, which went unaddressed by underresourced schools, and struggled to acquire basic skills that would have ensured him a better chance at success. Ledell found it hard to maintain steady employment. Some of his limitations, such as difficulty following instructions and a poor memory, made it hard for him to get to work on time and carry out important tasks consistently. He struggled with substance abuse, and he sometimes stole to get the funds for drugs. He was in jail on occasion. I have observed similar dynamics in other clients' lives. As it turns out, many people found to be innocent share vulnerabilities with those who are found guilty.[36]

Other similarities exist between the experiences of the families of the innocent and the guilty. Even after an acquittal or exoneration, for example, an association with the accusations remains, tainting the wrongfully convicted as well as their families, leaving a mark. The news media portrays the worst parts of a crime, sensationalizing the most disturbing aspects of a murder, as if trying to convey that the person who has killed is not entirely human, paving a diverging path between us and them that remains even after an acquittal.

I heard something similar from family members who had lost loved ones to murder: people didn't look at them the same. No one knew what to say. A distance developed between them and their friends and communities, engulfing the bonds they had previously shared. In this bizarre way, all the people touched by murder were dumped on an island of experience where few people came to visit. In many ways, the families of the accused and the families of the murdered had more in common with each other than with anyone else.

LEDELL'S EXECUTION WAS scheduled for Wednesday, April 20, at eight P.M. Central time. His attorneys were litigating various issues that had not been raised before because no one in the twenty-four-year history of the case had looked for the breadth of mitigation evidence involved or presented it to any court. Every few hours I would get a phone call, text, or email with an update from one of his lawyers so I could update his family. Journalists and state officials were also giving updates on Twitter. I stayed glued to social media, hoping to see some sign that the execution had been called off. As the clock approached midnight, hours after the scheduled time of the execution, I began to feel more hopeful that Ledell would live and we would be able to continue the investigation into the murder of Debra Reese. It was common

for executions to take place after the original time set on the death warrant. Still, making it to midnight mattered because the legal instrument
that allowed the state to kill Ledell—the death warrant—expired when
the clock struck twelve.

I was sitting in my bedroom when my cell phone rang, about thirty
minutes to midnight. It was the attorney who had asked me to help in
Ledell's case a few weeks before. She was crying. All of Ledell's appeals
had been denied, and the execution would be allowed to go forward in
a few minutes. We needed to share the news with his family. I sat on the
edge of my bed, frozen. How does someone tell a mother, brother, sister,
or child that their loved one is about to be killed?

WHILE I MADE calls, journalists and state officials began tweeting that
the road was clear to kill Ledell. I shouldn't have looked but couldn't
stop reading the messages, some of which were jubilant at the thought
that he was going to be dead soon. I hadn't realized how much hatred
could be contained in 140 characters. It was surreal to read the virtual
celebrations, gut-wrenching to know how much he was loved and to
anticipate the pain in so many people. I wanted to believe that human
beings were more parts love than hate, but in this moment of what felt
like a virtual lynching, I didn't know how.

Ledell was pronounced dead at eleven fifty-six P.M., four minutes before
the death warrant was set to expire. Four minutes. The length of a song.
That was the space between Ledell surviving and being killed. All that effort
and money spent to kill him, to ensure that no one who loved him would
ever be able to hear his voice during weekly phone calls or to visit with
him in person. I had come to know a kindhearted and faithful man during
the short time I worked with Ledell. His last few hours on earth reflected
the quality of his character. He gave away his food to others on death row

who had less than he did. He refused his last meal for the same reason, opting instead for holy communion and prayer. The last minutes of his life were flooded with fear, not because he was about to die, but because he had an intense aversion to needles.

Ledell was tired. Tired of screaming into the void about his innocence. Tired of being pursued so aggressively by the state and its insatiable, ceaseless efforts to ruin him. An endless reserve existed to secure the destruction of so many lives. Where was the same commitment or desire to invest in a person to flourish? I didn't see the same persistence in keeping my clients, as children, safe, healthy, and secure. What I saw time and time again was cruelty for cruelty's sake.

WHEN I WAS a child, I marveled at how my father drank his tea. On weekends, my mother started work before the sun came up, opening the diner where she waitressed at five A.M. It fell to me, as the daughter in the household, to make sure my father's tea was ready. I knew by the color and smell whether it was right. He took it black, in a small teacup, with two heaping spoons full of sugar. He would slurp a quick taste; finding it acceptable, he would pour it from the teacup into a saucer so it would cool faster. I'd stand beside him quietly, like a waitress myself, to take his empty cup and saucer to the sink after he drank the rest.

My father generally worked two jobs at a time, three when he was able. He was always concerned about money. Life could change at any moment. He stockpiled resources of all kinds—cash, but also toilet paper, bags of chips, ramen noodles, chocolates, medication. It was a constant and insatiable insecurity, which I absorbed like a sponge.

The memory of preparing my father's morning tea flickered in my mind as I struggled to keep my hand steady. I was spoon-feeding him tea, which kept dribbling down his chin. I gently dabbed his face with a tissue. We were in the intensive care unit of a hospital in Northern California. He had been there for three days after suffering a series of small strokes and a heart attack. *Tea* and *banana* were the last words that I could make out before he lost his ability to speak entirely.

My father was born in Baghdad in 1944 and raised there. His parents were ethnic Armenians who had fled their homeland during a genocide between 1915 and 1917. I knew virtually nothing about my father's family. What little I learned trickled in by accident. My grandfather was at least a decade older than his wife, my grandmother. He died somewhat unexpectedly when my father was around eight years old. The few accounts of my grandfather I heard portrayed him as brutal toward his wife and his four sons. There didn't appear to be love between my grandfather and the rest of the family, just obligation. I don't recall my father sharing any stories of laughter or lightness from his childhood.

As an adult, I began to notice that my father was constantly at the doctor. He volunteered for invasive screening exams of cancers, though there was no known history in his family. He pressured doctors for unnecessary surgeries. He was intense in this pursuit and ended up on the operating table several times because doctors yielded to his persistence, even against their own medical judgment. His medicine cabinet was full to overflowing, with dozens of additional prescription bottles lining his bathroom sink. If I ever mentioned not feeling well, he would disappear into his personal pharmacy, emerging with a cornucopia of options for me to choose from. He took dozens of pills each day, many for phantom ailments.

Even though we lived in the same house when I was growing up, he worked so much that days would go by without my seeing him. When I did see him, I was never sure what to talk about. As I got older, we argued, and in the fallout sometimes went months without speaking. We loved each other, but we didn't know each other as people or how to connect. I was constantly groping in the dark—a desperate wish to get someplace with him that I could never find.

In hindsight I see how a deep anxiety about death loomed over my household. My father's behavior—using work to avoid social interactions, hoarding, compulsively seeking medical care—created an anxiety in me that I didn't understand. The thought of dying made me panic. I could not even contemplate it without feeling my entire body brace and a wave of sickness fall over me. Working in an environment thick with death and loss gave me permission to contemplate death's inevitability even as it also distracted me from my own mortality.

My work life meant that I often went long stretches of time without speaking to family or friends. I mostly communicated with loved ones through text messages. So when my brother called several times in a row on a Tuesday morning, five days after Ledell was executed, I knew I had to answer.

"Elizabeth, I think you need to get out here. Dad isn't doing well."

I was in an airport hotel room in Dallas, preparing for a presentation about how trauma manifested in the lives of my clients. I told my brother I would get there as soon as I could. I hung up the phone and kept working on my PowerPoint on autopilot. It took me the better part of an hour to realize that I needed to shift gears. I sent my apologies to the conference planners and landed in California that evening.

When I arrived at the hospital, my father was lucid. We greeted each other and made small talk about the flight. He was sorry that I had interrupted my work to come all this way. He didn't think he needed to be in the hospital. After a lifetime of hypochondria and phantom ailments, now he needed real care; he'd had a series of strokes. But he wanted to go home. He pleaded his case with his trademark insistence, explaining that he was fine and would come back in a few days if he wasn't feeling better. I tried to reason with him, but he wanted to be in his own bed, surrounded by familiar sounds and smells. Shortly after I arrived, he had another cluster of strokes and lost the ability to see clearly. He called my name and my brother's name. He wanted his children. I held his hand. He said he was scared.

"I know you are. I am here, Dad."

I was in a physical space with my father and at the same time in a memory space with my clients, but especially with Ledell. All my clients were scared. Some were scared of death, others scared of life. I had learned to hear a person's fears without pushing those fears aside. Our own discomfort makes us try to reassure people who are fearful, which isn't always helpful. It's a way to minimize the true emotion of a moment. My father grabbed my hand tighter, while other people in my family came in and out of the room, struggling, as people often do, to be in a space where death was obviously so close.

"Elizabeth, I don't want to die."

"I know, Dad. I don't want you to die either. Try to breathe."

Another stroke, and he could no longer speak, his efforts producing only loud moans. The sound cut through me. As a child I never knew what would anger my father, so I learned to just stay away. I'd pretend to be asleep sometimes when he was home, to avoid interacting with him. But now his anguish pierced through the decades of hardening I had perfected. Without knowing why, I climbed onto his hospital bed, still holding his hand. There was no way I was going to leave his side.

"I am here. I love you."

I kissed his palm. The beeping of the machines kept time. A steady drip pumped morphine into his body, relieving his pain. A few hours later the beeps slowed to a single tone. Then the final rise and fall of his chest. I was sorry we'd never found each other. But creating a space of love and comfort for him at the end was something I could do. I needed to carry that with me as my life continued and his did not. He wouldn't remember the care I'd provided, but I would.

I had spent my entire life feeling ill-equipped to be his child, but the last two days we had together resolved that for me. Seeing my father fully at the end allowed me to grieve without regret. I hadn't been the kind of daughter he knew how to connect with, but I was able to let that go. At the end of his life, I'd been near him. He died on April 27, 2017, exactly one week after Ledell.

DURING AN EXECUTION, the family of the person about to die cannot be in the room. They must sit and watch from behind glass, alongside the loved ones of the victim. Mothers wail as they watch their children die.[37] In Texas, the witnessing room is split into two adjacent rooms so that neither group has to observe the other.[38] The mother of a murder victim does not have to watch another mother become the parent of a murder victim too. Texas doesn't allow any physical contact between the condemned and family the day of an execution. I have been in the visiting area on the day of an execution and listened to the piercing sounds of children screaming for their father's embrace.

Ledell didn't want members of his family to be present if they could not hold his hand while he died. It's a devastating unfairness, this denial of touch. A double loss, this separation at the end. Ledell couldn't spare his parents, daughters, siblings, and others who loved him the decades of suffering that had come before, but he could spare them this: the memory of seeing him die from behind glass. None of Ledell's family attended his execution.

The urge I had to curl up next to my father while he lay dying was automatic, visceral. I tried to imagine what it would be like for a daughter to sit calmly in a room of others, supervised by prison guards, and watch through a window as her father was killed. Keeping a child from their parent at the end of life, no matter how that end unfolds, is a punishment not only for the parent but also for the child. If each of us were made to observe not just the execution but also the pain of these witnesses, whether present or absent, denied closeness at the end, would we still put people to death? Killing a murderer is comparatively easy. Killing a loving father is something else.

Several months after Ledell died, I returned to Little Rock with attorneys from the Innocence Project and the American Civil Liberties Union who remained committed to investigating Ledell's role in the crime. It was the last time I saw Ms. Young. From the outside, it didn't look like anything had changed at her house. I knocked on the security door and Ms. Young appeared. Her eyes were bloodshot. She had lost considerable weight. She mustered a limp embrace, her body much frailer than before. In the living room a large posterboard with Ledell's picture on it, from his funeral, sat on an easel. Others told me that they often heard her speaking to the picture as if she were carrying on a conversation with her son.

Ms. Young seemed tired and disoriented. A few minutes into our conversation, she seemed to disconnect from what we were discussing and began describing a state of fear. She feared for her own life and those of her other children. She'd stopped sleeping at night, opting to stay awake with a gun in hand, sitting by the window.

"How heartless does someone have to be to have taken my son that way?" I had no answer. All the cruelty dispensed to destroy and ruin lives until the final breath was undeniable.

Four years after Ledell was executed, the posthumous investigation would confirm, as much as possible, that Ledell wasn't responsible for the murder of Debra Reese: evidence that Ledell wasn't given access to (though he asked) before his execution was finally made available. Biological samples were taken from the murder weapon itself and from a bloody shirt wrapped around it. Both samples belonged to an unknown male, not Ledell.[39]

Chapter Six

Public Safety

I slowed the car down so I could make out the numbers on the mailboxes that dotted the winding road. I had traveled over a hundred miles to find this house. Tall green sugarcane stretched out into the endless horizon. I reluctantly pulled into the driveway. It felt aggressive to park on the property of a person I didn't know, but there was no other place—no curbs or side streets. Three cement steps led up to the front door. I knocked, waited a few seconds, knocked again. I reminded myself to keep breathing. I eased closer to the door, listening carefully for the shuffling of feet, signs of movement, but I couldn't hear anything. The front curtains were drawn and still. No one was home. My shoulder muscles relaxed, and my racing heart instantly began beating slower.

I bounced down the steps, relieved that I wouldn't have to visit with Carlos yet. I knew I would have to return in a few hours, but I was grateful for the reprieve. This wasn't just any witness visit; Carlos was a victim of my client, Raymond. About thirty years had passed. Carlos had clearly found some peace in this life. The area was tranquil, the house a light blue that blended into the landscape and the crisp, cloudless Texas sky. I wondered what me being here would do to him, to this peace, but there was no doubt that someone would contact Carlos—that fact had been determined as soon as the county prosecutor made the decision to pursue resentencing of my client after his death sentence was vacated. It was just a question of who would contact him first and when.

I was getting into my car when a gray minivan pulled into the driveway behind me. A man was in the driver's seat, a woman in the passenger seat, and behind them three children who all looked to be under the age of ten. I had spent hours envisioning various ways this interaction could unfold, but I hadn't considered this particular scenario. My stomach tightened.

Carlos was in his forties. Raymond had murdered Carlos's younger sibling Michael decades before. Raymond wasn't a stranger. He lived in what was described as a freestanding apartment on the same lot as Carlos's family home. The landlord, looking to make more money, had rented Raymond a converted garage without running water, a bath-room, or a kitchen. In exchange for a reduction in her own rent, Carlos's mother, Denise, agreed with the landlord to allow Raymond access to her house for these necessities. For Denise, struggling financially to provide for her three children, the lower rent felt like a life raft.

A couple of months after Raymond moved in, Michael disappeared one night while Denise was out with a friend. An initial police search failed to find him. The second day that he was missing, officers accessed Raymond's apartment and discovered the little boy's body stuffed be-tween the box spring and mattress of Raymond's bed. Michael was badly beaten. He had been strangled to death. Later, an autopsy showed signs that Michael had also been sexually abused.

During the investigation, detectives learned that Carlos was also one of Raymond's victims. Carlos had endured and survived weeks of sex-ual violence before his brother's death. During the trial, Carlos testified and was a critical witness. Before driving out to meet Carlos, I'd read the transcript of his testimony. I imagined ten-year-old Carlos walking to the front of the courtroom and raising his right hand, with his left placed on the Bible, and promising to tell the truth. Carlos detailed the experience of being raped by Raymond and talked about how much he missed his brother. I suspected Carlos's testimony had a considerable impact on the jury's decision to sentence Raymond to death.

Then, about thirty years later, Raymond's death sentence was vacated. After the Texas Court of Criminal Appeals (the state's highest court for criminal cases) determined that an error existed in his case, it was sent back to the trial court. At that stage, the prosecutor had two choices: do nothing, and Raymond would be automatically resentenced to life; or try to secure a new death sentence. The prosecutor decided to move forward with the prosecution.

Carlos had been a significant witness for the state during the original trial, and Raymond's defense team knew he would be called again to testify; it was standard practice in such situations for all trial witnesses to be interviewed anew. That was how I found myself standing in front of Carlos and his family on an otherwise peaceful day.

I had met with people whom my clients had harmed before visiting Carlos, but I had never felt so keenly how invasive mitigation investigation could be. Mitigation investigation is anchored in the need for reliability; knowing who you are speaking with, being able to see that person face-to-face, is crucial. Knowing they are not speaking in front of others is essential. The logic was to obtain an unvarnished recollection by the witness with the opportunity to observe the witness's demeanor. So much communication is nonverbal and requires direct contact because mitigation investigation is relational. It cannot be conducted over the phone. And so someone, whether it was me or someone else, was going to show up at Carlos's home. Right now, I hated that fact. I knew what had happened to Carlos at age ten. I knew a lifetime had passed between when he had testified and this moment, standing in his driveway. I knew the case in question was about to be broken open again, its facts reviewed and reverified, its witnesses reinterviewed. I wanted to let the man keep living without being forced to return to the memories again, but I knew that wasn't my choice.

Carlos hopped out of the van with a welcoming smile. "Can I help you, ma'am?"

I inched my body toward him to try and limit what his family could hear. I leaned in a little and said, "I am not sure if I'm in the right place, but my name is Liz and I'm here to visit with Carlos."

"That's me."

I leaned in a bit more and said, "I'm here to visit with you about Raymond."

Carlos asked me to wait while he took his family inside. I stood by my car feeling small and guilty. When Carlos returned I felt the urge to apologize but waited for him to speak first. He asked me to explain how I was connected to Raymond. I said I was a member of his defense team. He nodded and then said, "I am not going to do anything to help that man. I don't care if he lives or dies. I don't want to have anything to do with him or his case. I have moved on, and I will not be involved."

That seemed fair. I mustered a "Thank you for letting me know." That would have been enough for the trip, a basic understanding of where he stood, but Carlos continued. "Look, I think he is a piece of shit and deserves whatever he has coming. But I'm sure coming out here wasn't easy, and I want to thank you." Carlos invited me to sit with him on the cement steps of his house.

A few weeks before, Carlos told me, his wife had answered a phone call from the county prosecutor's office, which was retrying Raymond's case. The man introduced himself as an assistant district attorney and asked to speak with Carlos. His wife explained that he wasn't home and offered to take a message. The prosecutor asked her to let Carlos know that they would need him to testify again against "Raymond, the man who had raped him," because his death sentence had been vacated. The prosecutor casually noted that the sentencing hearing would probably occur in about six months and requested that her husband call him back as soon as possible to discuss it. Carlos had never shared the full story of what had happened to him, or to his brother, with his wife. She hung up the phone, stunned.

Sitting on the steps of his home, Carlos and I spoke for the next two hours. He shared details about his life in the aftermath of what he had lost. His experiences in the military. How he had come to understand that violence and tragedy were integral to the human experience and his view that how one coped with it was a choice. Controlling the narrative around what he had endured and survived helped him integrate the losses he had lived through at such a young age.

What Carlos experienced occurred at a time before the internet would have made it easier for someone to search his name and learn what happened. That degree of privacy was a gift. For Carlos, there could be no space in his life for the man who had taken so much from him already. He wanted there to be a part of him untouched by Raymond. This control over information had been essential for Carlos. It helped him reclaim the pieces of himself that had been stolen. The single exchange that the prosecutor had with Carlos's wife, a call that lasted less time than it took to microwave a bag of popcorn, also stole that control from him.

I don't know why the prosecutor decided to reach Carlos by phone that day. I can think of some reasons, such as having limited time to make the long drive out to the house, having a large caseload, or maybe simply not considering the shattering impact such a call could have on the life of another person. Maybe the prosecutor was just going through the motions, the checklist of the case, without thinking about much else. I'd seen such box-ticking happen on both sides—the defense and the prosecution. Maybe it was a mistake.

What became clear to me, though, in connecting with Carlos, was that no one had actually asked him what he wanted. And what he wanted was not to be involved. In the system's attempts to address the harm against his brother and him, it had made no provisions for this need. By the end of our visit Carlos wanted to know what he could do to express his ambivalence about Raymond's sentence and his commitment not to participate in any further legal proceedings. I said he could provide a statement to that effect. And he did. Carlos explained in the statement that the state could do what it wanted, but it would have to do so without him. It seemed possible, at least in this instance, for Carlos to get what he needed without harming Raymond, even though Carlos was not motivated to aid Raymond in the slightest. I didn't have contact with Carlos after that day, so I don't know if there was any effort to convince him to engage in the process, but the district attorney some months later decided to let the case conclude with a life sentence. That decision ensured Raymond would die in prison; no further appeals or court dates would occur, and Carlos would not have to endure another trial.

I drove back to Houston that night with a racing mind. I'd hated the feeling of showing up at Carlos's door. But in hindsight it had been the most humane way to communicate with him, given the circumstances. It was uncomfortable for me—calling would have been personally easier—but he deserved the chance to drive the conversation, to tell me whatever he wanted in person, face-to-face. The outreach was going to happen no matter what, but going to him directly was, I realized, a show of respect, of the recognition that *he* should get to determine how he wanted to engage in the process. It wasn't just that mitigation evidence was most reliable when collected this way. It was also that there needed to be a steward of dignity in a system designed to strip that from every person involved. Including victims.

"WHAT ABOUT THE victims?" That is often all it takes to shut down a conversation about alternatives to capital punishment, life-without-parole sentences, or other extreme penalties. Even I knew this at the tender age of fifteen when I won my first debate trophy for speaking in support of the death penalty. I only needed to describe in graphic detail the rape and murder of a young girl for those in the audience to become closed off to other thoughts. When I was in high school I attended a summer program where I took classes on constitutional law and public speaking. I learned that the law and the podium are both driven by emotions.

Those who lose a loved one to violence are also victims, and I am often asked about them as well, as if I do not contemplate the hellscapes they have lived in the aftermath without people who cannot be replaced. Each human life is a unique one, and when that life is gone, it leaves a gaping hole that is never filled. I think about how it took me seven years before I did not spontaneously cry at my father's grave, or how I still have conversations in my head with him. I imagine that will never stop. And he lived a full and complete life before his death.

My image of who a victim is has changed dramatically since I started working as a mitigation specialist. So have my ideas about how the system handles victims and what it tries to give them. Before I started investigating the histories of people who have killed, I had a view in my mind that all victims and their loved ones are largely kept abreast of the status of an investigation. I assumed they all wanted retribution. I thought that law enforcement would seek the same redress for *any* person who lost their life to murder.

Most of my clients are men of color or poor white men, both groups that are held in little value within American culture. And because of this, the vast majority of witnesses whose homes I spend time in share their own experiences of harm—including losing a loved one to murder.

I could share many stories. But here is one. I met Ms. D at her row house in Philadelphia. She was active in the neighborhood where my client was raised, often taking him in for meals and shelter. She was heartbroken to learn that my client was on death row and rattled off a list of names of the boys she knew from the surrounding area who had been killed or were now incarcerated. An anchor for the kids in the neighborhood, Ms. D ended up moving away because she was attending too many funerals. "I felt like I was going to a funeral once a week," she said. All the death was too much for her to take.

I didn't know it when I arrived at Ms. D's home, but it was an especially hard day for her. Exactly seventeen years prior, her nephew had been beaten by Philadelphia police officers. He was picked up because they thought he had stolen a car. The officers placed him in the back seat of the vehicle with his hands cuffed behind his back and decided to leave his safety belt off. Officers slammed the brakes repeatedly, smashing her nephew's body against the safety partition. Of the many injuries he suffered, the break to his spinal cord is what resulted in lifetime paralysis. He was bedridden.[1] Almost like she was trying to convince herself too, Ms. D said I shouldn't feel too bad for him because he still has a good life: "He is able to use a phone and has a lot of girlfriends. He is very handsome." I'd been told of this practice—the "rough ride"—by witnesses in other cities. People who didn't live in communities where this was done learned about it from the killing of Freddie Gray in 2015 in Baltimore.[2]

Ms. D was a witness to far more cruelty. She was an archivist of brutality. There had been so much death in the neighborhood. "Why do we need to talk about all the death that happened?" she asked rhetorically. "No one cared about all the young Black men who had been slaughtered in the streets." Someone needed to care, to memorialize the tragedy. She knew that to fail to do so was to cede all hope that life could improve. She brought out a list of boys with whom my client was raised who had been killed from about 1995 to 2005.[3]

- Maurice: Killed because of mistaken identity. The boys who killed him thought he was a witness to another crime. It wasn't him.
- Malcolm: Killed in the Tasker Homes.
- Carl: Killed when he was about 20 years old.
- Kwame: He was about 15–16 years old when he was killed in 1999.
- Jeff
- Ed
- Don: He was playing ball when he was shot dead.
- Jamar
- Lamont
- Khali: Killed when he was 14–15 years old.
- Ramon
- Pinky: Killed the day after he got out of jail because people were concerned he would snitch.
- Jab
- Benny: He was shot at Walnut & Logan on 13th Street in broad daylight.
- Porky: Another mistaken identification. The person who killed him was trying to get his brother.
- Ramel
- Lionel: Shot on Garage Street.

- Leonard: He was doing good for himself. He was making money through cell phones. He was killed in 2001. He was shot in his car on the train tracks one morning. His car was then lit on fire. He wasn't killed for any reason except people in the neighborhood didn't like seeing someone do better.
- Harvey: He was the check-cashing guy. He was hogtied and killed. Ms. D mentioned that Harvey was Hispanic but included him in the list because "every death mattered" to her.
- David: His death may have been a suicide but it wasn't clear.
- Boobie: He was just 13 when he was shot. He was killed doing community service in the Tasker Homes.
- Two boys killed at the Triple Seven: Shot execution-style, lying down on the ground and shot in the back of the head. People thought they had witnessed a murder. The younger of the two wanted to be a firefighter. Ms. D shook her head and said, "These boys had dreams. They were people."
- Jab's brother: The streets say Boo did it.
- Kev: Killed coming out of Audenried High School after a basketball game. He was brilliant and was heading to the Wharton School at the University of Pennsylvania.
- Jamal

Jamal's was the last name on the list. It was his murder that broke her. Jamal was killed around ten P.M. His body lay out in the street until the following day. "The police said that the coroner couldn't come by any sooner to take away his body. That boy laid out there for hours before someone even put a sheet over him." His mom screamed and hollered when she saw her son. "It was wrong that the police left him out there like that." Ms. D was convinced that law enforcement didn't care at all about the people in her community.

IN 2012, I participated as a researcher in a study with family members who had lost loved ones to murder. It was a multisite project, with researchers in Indiana and New York carrying out focus groups to learn more about the experiences of family members in the aftermath of murder. I had met so many family members like Ms. D as a mitigation specialist. I wanted to know more about their experiences of the legal process, the paths traveled after the harm.

We researchers arrived before the participants did to set up the room. We made sure tissues were within easy reach of each chair. Soon the mothers who had volunteered to talk about the experience of losing a child to murder would be there. The six ladies who signed up came into the room. They were all white.

Black people account for over 50 percent of murder victims annually, even though the population of individuals who identify as Black is just 14 percent in the United States.[4] In addition to race, people with low incomes, people living with disabilities, those who are unhoused, and people with previous interaction with the criminal legal system are significantly more vulnerable to becoming victims of violent crime.[5] I thought about mirrors: the lives that were not valued enough to invest in, the people who became my clients, reflected the same lives that were not valued enough to be thought of as victims. The people that were forgotten stayed forgotten. The people we had communally failed were still failed.

And yet, even within this homogenous group, the mothers all had vastly different experiences, needs, and paths from their losses to the present. There is no universal victim. Joanne had lost her daughter decades earlier. She was missing for months before she was found dead. When it was Joanne's turn to share, she described the knock on the door from the police to let her know they'd found her daughter's body. The gentle rocking started. Her right hand twisting a small corner of her button-down shirt. Her eyes, which had been locked on members of the group, began to roam vacantly, landing on no one, nothing in particular.

Nicole was next in the circle. Nicole's daughter's boyfriend had stabbed her to death about five years prior. She said that often as she went about her day, her mind would suddenly jump to contemplate the last few moments of her daughter's life. Most recently it had happened at work, when Nicole got a painful paper cut. She imagined how much her daughter must have suffered when her body was slashed. The thoughts looped; she couldn't focus. She told her supervisor she had a migraine and went home. Nicole felt ashamed for still feeling the rawness of her loss five years later. It seemed like everyone around her thought she would have "moved on" by now. People in her life didn't talk about her daughter, as if the very mention would cause Nicole pain. It was the reverse. Not speaking about her daughter was agonizing. She was all Nicole thought about. But the world wouldn't speak her name.

The murder itself had taken place in Nicole's home. After the body had been removed and the police had finished collecting evidence from the crime scene, Nicole was left alone to clean up in the silence of the house. Someone had handed her a piece of paper with contact information for local hazmat companies that would come and remove her daughter's blood from the floor. The police had dusted copiously for fingerprints; Pledge furniture polish would clean that right up, she was told. There were pamphlets about funeral homes, burial costs, and victim family member funds that might help cover the unexpected expense. It was both too much information and not enough, coming so impersonally. She wanted to know how she could live without her daughter. Would she be able to see her grandchildren? The man responsible for Nicole's death was also their father. Would he maintain parental rights? Could she raise them? Would he be able to keep the children from her? The thought of losing them as well was unbearable. She wanted to know what would happen to him.

Like many of the mothers in that room, Nicole received updates about the progress of the case inconsistently at best. Some mothers received no contact at all from the prosecutor assigned to the case. Some got information from the nightly news, the morning newspaper, or when a reporter reached out for a comment about a new development. For these mothers, learning about the status of the case through the media was yet another violation.

Many felt infuriated by the court hearings they attended, because no one was there to explain the proceedings or give context for the disorienting and opaque activities of the court. "I was there listening to the attorneys argue about something that had nothing to do with what happened to my daughter," Nicole said. The state could help her remove her daughter's blood from the carpet but offered nothing to help her understand the legal process designed to redress it. She wanted to know: Why did the court appear to be more focused on the rights of the man who murdered her daughter than on what he had done?

Nicole carried vengeance toward the man who had murdered her daughter, and what she saw of the legal process only deepened it. She knew she shouldn't wish for retribution because he was the father of her grandchildren, but she did. I wondered if the confusion and abandonment she felt in the wake of her daughter's murder contributed to this desire: at least retribution might provide *some* way of making meaning out of the experience. At a minimum, it would create a kind of public remembering of her daughter, a conversation that others could engage with. She'd noticed that while people avoided mentioning her daughter's name, they seemed more at ease with discussing the trial and sentence in the context of punishing her killer. It struck me that Nicole felt that she, the victim's own mother, was being erased from the proceedings but that an eye-for-an-eye rallying cry made her feel heard, unignorable.

A national survey of victims, defined as those who have been directly victimized as well as those who have lost loved ones, published in 2022 highlighted this deep disconnect between their needs and what the criminal legal system provided. According to the Alliance for Safety and Justice, a national organization that engages in criminal justice policy reforms centered on crime prevention and support for crime victims, seven in ten victims report experiencing significant challenges healing from the ordeal and continue to experience at least one symptom of trauma. Less than one in ten victims say the criminal legal system was very helpful in providing information from recovering from crime or in offering referrals for support. Nearly 50 percent of victims who did not get the help they wanted were confused about what services are available or where to find support.[6]

The vast majority of criminal cases that are not dismissed—roughly 98 percent, including homicides—conclude in a plea agreement and so don't go to trial.[7] Obtaining a conviction and sentence through a plea agreement is usually the fastest way to end a criminal case because the defendant agrees not to appeal.[8] And speed is the goal. Avoiding as many resource-intense trials as possible is essential to enabling the United States to process the high volume of criminal cases that enter the system annually. In 2023 alone, the Federal Bureau of Investigation reported about nineteen thousand homicides nationwide. Rates of burglary, robbery, larceny, and other types of crimes totaled around eleven million, though the data was incomplete, suggesting that the actual number was higher.[9] Expediency is key to keeping the legal process humming, and victims are a casualty of that expediency. Much as defendants are.

MITIGATION INVESTIGATION REVEALS the hidden cost of valuing some lives over others. I was surprised to observe that many victims and their loved ones had experienced the same cultural devaluing that my clients and their families had. More, the victims I connected with described feeling unacknowledged, overlooked, and, worse sometimes, used, as if the law had a use for their suffering but not for them. Though I have learned that speaking about victims with a singular brush is damaging to the constellation of their experiences, those who have shared their time and experiences with me have all agreed on one thing: not one of them was better for having gone through the legal process.

Chapter Seven

Spirit

I watched Sugar, a seven-month-old brindle puppy with velvet ears, zigzag gracefully through orange traffic cones and then come to a prompt heel next to Tony's legs. Tony was teaching Sugar's obedience class. They were completely in sync with each other, the way good dance partners are, moving as if one body. Sitting at attention at Tony's side, Sugar seemed pleased. Though I could not see Tony's face due to the camera angle, his body wore its own expression: straight and alert, engaged and confident.

Sugar was one of several dogs sent to live with and be trained by men serving life sentences without the possibility of parole at a maximum-security prison in the upper peninsula of Michigan. Tony had worked with Sugar for the better part of a year. The animal shelter that partnered with the prison had arranged for this graduation to be recorded, providing a rare opportunity for myself and Tony's loved ones: documentation of something meaningful that he had achieved while incarcerated.

The local animal shelter stood to benefit from the program too, if it meant a chance at reforming their more challenging dogs. Sugar was one of these cases. She'd been identified as less likely to be adopted due to aggressive behavior, and no one at the shelter had been able to train her. As a very young puppy, Sugar was left inside a cage in a large warehouse for days at a time with nothing to eat. When food was available, it was scarce, and it would be thrown into a large area of the warehouse, where she'd have to scrap with other puppies just to get a morsel. She learned early on that to survive meant staying in attack mode and being singularly focused on taking what nourishment she could.

Once out of the warehouse, Sugar's behavior remained. She would growl and attempt to bite any hand that came near her, even if it was offering food. Her behavior resulted in more isolation from dogs and people whenever food was involved. As a last resort, Sugar was sent to live with Tony and his cellmate. These two men who had learned to live together in a cell not much larger than a closet became responsible for convincing Sugar that she was safe and secure.

Tony knew something about Sugar's behavior. He had been raised in a small trailer home near Lake Huron in Michigan with his mother, father, and two older brothers. The cramped quarters might not have been an issue had Tony's parents been mild-mannered and gentle, but they were not. Tony's father, John, drank daily. Eyes open until he blacked out. Once the drinking got to a certain point, John became violent, punching his wife in the face, dragging her through the trailer by her hair, and pounding her head into the ground. These drag-down knockouts happened most days, even when Tony was an infant. No "Twinkle, Twinkle Little Star": the soundtrack of his development, a consistent presence in his environment, was flesh pounding flesh.

I met Tony as an adult, but he was fourteen years old when he committed murder, one of the youngest people I had ever met who had been sentenced to life without the possibility of parole. A life-without-parole sentence is, of course, a sentence to die in prison. Like other clients I had worked with who had killed at a young age, including Edward and Connor, there was no explanation for what Tony had done, even from his perspective. Tony wasn't thinking very far into the future when he hopped on his bicycle that night with a shotgun and set off from the trailer. He was thinking about escape. The hours leading up to his departure included many of the same challenges and frustrations that marked every day of his life. He went to school, hung out with his girlfriend, went home, tried to ignore his parents, who were drunk and fighting, started drinking himself, and waited in his room until the trailer fell silent, an indication that his parents had passed out for the night.

Tony thought if he could find and steal a car, he could drive away from his current situation. He hadn't thought about where he would go, where he would sleep, how he would eat, or any of the practical considerations an adult or someone who was preparing for a new life might contemplate. He was in survival mode. The prefrontal cortex, which plays a crucial role in judgment and impulse control, remains undeveloped until well into one's twenties.[1] This fact is one of the biggest hurdles for judges or victims to understand; adults who have forgotten the impetuousness of youth tend to map their current capacity for reasoning onto the behavior of a child.

With some change he found in his mom's purse, left over from the alcohol purchased earlier that day, Tony rode off into the dark. He approached a house and thought he might be able to steal a car, but he could see lights and hear music. He kept pedaling on and ended up at the home of an older couple. Everyone knew this couple, including Tony. He remembered they had a few cars, and he had an idea about where to look for the keys. He laid his bike down in front of their home. I wonder if he was dreaming of another life. A different life. Maybe one that could include a childhood.

Using the butt of the shotgun, Tony broke a small window and entered the house. He went room to room looking for car keys, coming up empty each time. I try to imagine what was happening in the mind of Tony, a child wandering through a home so different from his own, late at night, desperately disconnected from himself as a means of surviving. The family photos framed and placed in full view. The knickknacks he would have touched. These artifacts of another life literally within hand's distance but completely out of reach.

Tony walked down the hallway and came to a room, the bedroom of the couple, though he didn't know this until he turned on the light. Seeing the husband startled Tony, who lifted his shotgun and fired. Tony then shot the wife, looked in the dresser for car keys, and walked out of the room. He returned to the kitchen, the first room he had searched, and spotted a pair of car keys sitting on the counter, which he had initially missed. If only he had looked in that particular spot, he would have left the house. He never would have walked down that hallway.

Tony got into the stolen car and drove away. He didn't know if the couple was alive, if they had called the police, or if anyone else had heard the sound of the shotgun and attempted to figure out what had happened. Even though he had an unusual amount of experience driving for a child—he often picked his father up from various bars in town—he'd been drinking earlier. Tony ran the car off the road and into a ditch, where he was arrested by police officers.

All these years later, Tony wished there had been more of a reason for his actions. Maybe it would be easier for people to understand if there had been. It is hard to hold the truth of the developing mind in balance with the act perpetrated, but it is a fact that at that young age a person hasn't developed the brain capacity to engage in critical thinking under pressure or stress. The cognition available is influenced by experiences, especially of trauma, which alter the degree to which there is any opportunity for slowing down and considering alternatives. In other words, behavior that appears nonsensical is a physiological expression of the fight, flight, freeze, or fawn responses that a body experiences when under threat—and Tony was in flight.[2]

IN 1996, JUST four months before Tony's crime, Michigan changed its laws and permitted youth as young as fourteen to be tried and sentenced as adults. Once Tony was found guilty of double murder, he was, like an adult, automatically sentenced to life without parole.[3]

I went to meet Tony for the first time one winter morning twenty-four years after the crime. I walked a cement path lined with snowbanks that rose taller than my five feet, four inches. There wasn't a cloud in the sky. The sunlight bounced off the snow, reflecting like a mirror. I entered the front of the prison, which was empty, and waited. There was no way to call for someone, so I tried to position myself near the ceiling cameras, in the hope that an officer working the control booth would alert someone to my presence. Half an hour later, an officer appeared.

After being processed through security, I was escorted to a legal room where Tony was waiting. We were allowed to have contact and shook hands. Tony was average height, thin, and dressed in the prison uniform of blue pants and a short-sleeved button-down top with red stripes down the sides. His face was delicate, with a defined jawline, buzz-cut brown hair, and a nascent goatee that conjured up the image of a teenager who wanted to grow facial hair but couldn't. Tony looked much younger than his thirty-eight years. He was soft-spoken, articulate, engaged. I sensed he was working hard not to be nervous. I noticed his leg shaking for the first few hours we sat together, his hesitant speech, and his difficulty holding eye contact when the conversation turned toward topics he wasn't ready to discuss. His body was positioned sideways for a while, almost like he was hiding, before he relaxed enough to turn fully in my direction.

Since Tony was tried and sentenced as an adult, he was sent to an adult prison. He arrived at an adult penitentiary at the age of fifteen. Before meeting Tony, his attorneys gave me a copy of his prison records, which included reports regarding Tony's behavior from the beginning of his incarceration to the present. The information contained in those pages sketched an initial picture of Tony getting into trouble, including a significant number of fights in the early years of his incarceration, a typical adjustment for youth who are incarcerated.[4] Within months of arriving at prison, Tony was trapped in the laundry room with an older inmate who attempted to rape him. He only escaped because another inmate broke the door down and intervened. Though Tony had dodged the sexual violation, he'd suffered a horrific beating before his escape.

Glancing my way and then shifting his gaze, Tony explained how, after that experience, a few inmates coached him on surviving prison. As a scrawny kid, Tony's best chance at protecting himself meant carrying and using weapons. "The older guys took me under their wings and taught me how to use weapons to defend myself. After that, I started to get into situations. My outlook was to stand up for myself." Other inmates needed to believe that Tony wasn't going to wait for something to happen to him. He would attack first. He needed to find the biggest guy around and go after him unprompted and often.

Tony hadn't behaved aggressively toward others before committing a double murder. Nothing in his school records or other files I collected indicated such behavior. Yet, his prison records showed that within months of arriving, he was mouthing off to officers and getting into fights. Tony explained he acted that way to demonstrate that he wasn't afraid, though in reality he was terrified. "Prison was scary."

Often in trouble, Tony was frequently punished by having whatever passed for privileges taken away or restricted. This could include the loss of visits with loved ones, suspending access to the prison commissary, or "store," where he could purchase additional food or toiletries, or being placed in solitary confinement, often called the hole, for a period. All these punishments were imposed on Tony with little impact on his behavior. It was the lesser of two sufferings—institutional beatdowns or physical beatdowns from other inmates—and really the only way to survive. The institution wouldn't kill him, but another inmate might.

I KNEW FROM interviews carried out with community members years before that Tony had tried to protect his mother from the violence at home, often placing his small body between his parents to try and absorb the blows for her. His grades and attendance at school acted as a barometer for when things in the trailer were especially dangerous; both plummeted when the situation became extreme. I knew he had been in trouble for thefts and trespassing. He was often, he told me, looking for either a quiet place to go or something to steal that he could sell. Household money was spent on alcohol, and Tony was often hungry. I knew he had started drinking when he was nine years old. I knew he was isolated in that trailer and in that town, suffocated by the relentlessness of each day. And I knew that by the time he committed murder at age fourteen, he had already survived more than many people endure in a lifetime.

I also knew that Tony had a strong desire to help others and have a positive impact on those around him. As I continued to review his prison file, I observed his growth through notes from officers and medical staff and letters from administrators. I saw Tony develop into a leader. As he went from being an adolescent to a young adult and then to a grown man, Tony's behavior changed. He was elected block representative and became responsible for bringing concerns from inmates to prison administrators, including the warden. He volunteered to be a peer support officer, sitting at the bedside of other inmates who had attempted suicide or were in hospice care. During our visit Tony talked about the reasons he sat with inmates in the infirmary:

> I can relate to being in the hole and being really down like that. I remember how I felt. Sometimes, the guys I watch want to talk, and I can be there for that. The last guy who I was on watch for had been gassed. The officers gas you if you are not cooperating. That is horrible. The gas is really bad because it sticks around. If you get gassed, you will be feeling it for days. Sometimes it will even make you throw up blood. And it goes everywhere. There's no ventilation down there, so even if somebody else got gassed and you are in the cell next door, you can feel it. This guy was given, like, five cans of gas too. When I got down there, they still had him hog-tied. It was terrible.

As he entered adulthood, Tony found ways to contribute to his immediate environment and community. He was eager to learn. Yet, because he had been sentenced to life without the possibility of parole, the prison provided almost no programming.[5] Instead of being able to take advantage of education, work programs, therapy, or other opportunities for personal growth, Tony had to rely on friends and family to help him find and pay for correspondence courses. A lucky turn of events connected Tony with a history professor at a liberal arts college with whom he struck up a pen pal relationship. The professor would send Tony books and invite him to share his thoughts on the materials. In fact, this exercise resembled assignments that the professor designed for her students. Such relationships, which Tony sought out as best he could, structured the kinds of opportunities for betterment that help many incarcerated people thrive.

TONY LEARNED ABOUT the importance of deep connection to developing lasting personal change. When I met Tony for the first time in 2018, he had recently started working with Sugar, his "most challenging dog," he told me, so far. Tony had gained a reputation as an excellent handler and was given Sugar because she was a challenge. Watching Tony's face express pride, with open eyes and a broad smile, it was clear how much he loved sharing his experiences with Sugar. It was a safe topic and seemed to give him insights into himself.

As I continued working on Tony's case, Sugar became the way to help Tony explore his trauma and articulate what he would have needed as a child to have lived a different life. Seeing how much Sugar relied on his consistent presence and assurances, even when she reverted back to her fear and tried to bite him, helped Tony grasp the profound need for stability that humans have in early development. He was able to stop torturing himself about the harm he had caused and instead examine his behavior and reflect on it, working toward personal growth.

A core lesson Tony learned by working with dogs was that the most aggressive dogs turned out to have been the most fearful. He understood that they had been conditioned to act in ways that could be harmful but that, with patience and unconditional love, trust could be rebuilt between dog and human. The reconfiguring of that relationship through repeated acts of care and gentleness allowed Sugar and the other dogs that Tony worked with to slowly reframe humans as not all bad. The love that Tony showed allowed Sugar to grow and become the tender dog she always had the capacity to be. As Sugar began to relax and trust, so did Tony. He began to see himself as capable of cultivating loving relationships. Through his work with Sugar, he saw how love and acceptance could reshape the responses he had learned in early life. After they had worked together nearly a year, Sugar was adopted by a family with small children. Tony received pictures of her living her new life—head out of the car window with her tongue hanging out sideways, lying on her back on the grass with little kids on top of her, sitting obediently next to her food bowl full of kibble, waiting calmly to be told it was time to eat. A whole new life with joy and connection.

MOST PEOPLE WHO are incarcerated and serving sentences of death or life without the possibility of parole do not have access to rehabilitative programming such as education or employment that could assist in their development.[6] At the time Tony went to prison, Michigan had the second greatest number of youths in the country who had been sentenced to life without the opportunity for parole after being convicted of murder.[7] Politicians who decided state budgets and administrators within departments of corrections concluded that investing in such programming was futile since those inmates would only leave prison in a casket.[8] The lack of investment in the human beings sent to prison created a problem when in 2012 the U.S. Supreme Court ruled that people under the age of eighteen could no longer be automatically sentenced to life without parole.[9] States like Michigan could still sentence youth to the penitentiary for their natural lives, but that sentence could be imposed only after consideration of mitigating evidence, much as in a death penalty case. Hundreds of people in Michigan—and over two thousand others around the country who had, like Tony, gone to prison as children—were now given a chance to have their sentences reconsidered.

Michigan, like many other states with juvenile life without parole, asked judges to consider demonstrations of rehabilitation. The new law attempted to determine which youth were irredeemable and those who could change.[10] However, without access to programming, it was difficult for people like Tony, who had been incarcerated for decades and now needed to show a judge how he had grown, to quantify the change they had experienced during incarceration. There were no classes to point to or programs to highlight how they had been able to learn new skills over time. Only after a successful lawsuit forced the Michigan Department of Corrections to provide juvenile lifers with programming opportunities so they could work toward successful reentry into society did the agency allow them to participate in the dog training program.

TONY'S ENTHUSIASM AS he spoke of his work with Sugar left an impression on me. I was reminded of how critical engaging in meaningful work is to the human spirit and how devastating it is to be considered by society as unworthy of investment. By denying programming to those serving life without parole, American society communicated how little it valued the incarcerated. The idea that lives lived in prison are unworthy fuels budget cuts to carceral facilities. It also fuels the rise of privatization, where lives lived behind cement walls drive private profits.[11] On the other hand, spending money for programming leads to safer prisons and less recidivism for the 95 percent of people who will be released to a free society. It's also the humane thing to do. As a society, we will not save money or enhance public safety by keeping programming out of prisons.[12]

DURING FORMATIVE PERIODS in their lives, there were scant resources available to my clients, and now, as inmates, they find the same to be largely true. It isn't only the lack of education or opportunity for meaningful work but also the design of carceral facilities that confirms to the imprisoned that their lives don't matter. The inside of a standard American prison cell is purposefully cold. A steel-frame bed with a four-inch-thick mattress is flanked by a steel toilet bowl with no lid. The toilet is near a small metal sink and often placed inches from the bed. A cell might have a small steel stool bolted to the floor as the only other place in the space to sit. If an inmate is fortunate, the stool is fixed to a spot where a small metal tray is bolted to the wall, acting as a desk or table. Cells have virtually no natural light. The walls are made of concrete and painted in dull colors. Anything more than one bedsheet or state-issued blanket, thinner than the kind sometimes provided on an airplane, is considered contraband and subjects the incarcerated person to disciplinary action.

There is no way to regulate temperature within cells, and many prison facilities were built before air-conditioning was available. During the summer of 2011 in Texas, where more than four-fifths of the state's prisons lack air-conditioning in cell blocks, at least ten prisoners, and likely more, died of heatstroke.[13] Heat-related deaths in Texas prisons have led to staff shortages and millions of taxpayer dollars in lawsuits.[14] As of 2023, needless deaths, understaffing, and egregious waste—not to mention a $32.7 billion budget surplus—had not been enough to convince the Texas state legislature to fully address the issue.[15] Money that could be spent on putting air-conditioning in before people die goes instead to settle expensive lawsuits from the bereaved families.

The prison conditions that my clients experience stunt healthy development. Most of these environments don't allow, let alone provide, basic opportunities to stimulate one's mind. For example, Edward, whose case I was still working on in 2018 when I first met Tony, was nineteen years old when he arrived on death row. Like Tony, he often got into trouble early in his incarceration. Living in isolation, Edward had few opportunities for direct contact with other people. His cell was the size of a parking spot, all white except for the steel toilet bowl next to his metal bed. Bright fluorescent light flooded this cement box and drove him to the brink of madness.[16] "I knew for myself it was what was inside of me; my spirit. I needed to have something to make the space mine. Sometimes I feel so caged in here. I just want to yell or scream or something. I know that I can't lose myself, I won't let it happen." A wide breadth of research confirms that extreme restrictive housing—barren and harsh—has a psychologically damaging impact on the person attempting to exist in it.[17] This is especially true of those, like Edward, who enter prison living with mental illness and histories of trauma. Craving softer colors, Edward taped pink, yellow, or orange pieces of construction paper over the light in his cell to make it more bearable. As a consequence, he lost privileges, but he returned to the same behavior regardless of the outcome.

Edward's adjustment was a mix of acclimating and shutting down. Although he began to be able to differentiate between the officers who would immediately write him up for violating a rule and those who left him alone, the mental strain of living without any sustained contact was corrosive to his abilities and mental health. His mind dulled. I noticed that it became harder for him to retain information or to provide detail when describing events or activities; he struggled to find words. He wasn't yet forty, but sometimes it felt as if I were speaking to someone twice his age. I was a witness to his mind fading.

During the pandemic, when I couldn't travel to visit clients due to safety concerns, I began to have frequent and regular legal phone calls with Edward. Under normal circumstances, I rarely spoke with clients on the phone. Even though prisons allowed for confidential legal phone calls to be arranged, in a number of instances these communications have been recorded without consent and turned over to prosecutors,[18]

so I have never felt entirely comfortable discussing anything of substance outside of being face-to-face with a client.

The legal calls took place in a small space where, if Edward had put
both his arms out at the same time, he could have touched the sides.
Inside the booth there was no access to water or a toilet. Just a metal stool
and the handset of the phone for him to use. Though our calls were nor-
mally scheduled for one hour, the officers often left Edward in the booth
for several hours at a time. I hated the thought of Edward sitting there
alone if he was not on a call, unable to do anything but sit and stare. He
assured me that it wasn't a problem. In the booth, he could at least watch
people walking by on occasion. If he was taken back to his cell, he would
be more isolated. Even so, I made a personal commitment to staying on
the phone with him as long as the officers left him in the booth.

During one call, we had been on the phone for close to three hours,
and Edward needed to use the bathroom. A corrections officer was
walking by. Edward told me to hold on. Though he had placed the
handset to his chest, I could hear his muffled voice asking to use the
bathroom. Then I could hear him asking for a water bottle. There was
a crackling sound, and a few seconds later Edward returned to the
phone. I asked if he was okay. "Yeah. I didn't want to piss in the room.
The officer gave me an empty water bottle to go in." I didn't understand
why the officer didn't just take him to the bathroom. "I don't know. He
said he couldn't. But he got me a bottle, so it's all good." He'd had to use
the bathroom for at least an hour, and he didn't want to get in trouble
for urinating in the booth. He had no way to know how long he would
be out there and was becoming concerned that he might wet himself.
Other inmates who had been left alone after a legal call and were desperate for the bathroom ended up defecating in the closet. I imagined
the humiliation of being an adult in that booth, squatting down, without privacy or dignity, defecating in a corner of the small, unventilated

space. I imagined the shame and sadness that would follow. I thought about the anger that would accompany getting disciplined for the mess.

I WASN'T THERE when it happened, but I imagine the blood streaming from the face of the officer who escorted Edward to the shower, and the terror she must have felt as she realized he had a razor blade. I know she screamed because the reports I read afterward provided some details about how other officers knew to come to her aid. This officer, who was a mother and in her early fifties, had been consistently disciplining Edward for taping paper over the fluorescent light inside his cell. For months, Edward complained about her during our visits, shaking his head, confused about why she wouldn't leave him alone about it like the other officers did. "It was just color paper on my light. No other officer made an issue of it, and then it would be over with, but she kept constantly harassing me about my cell, about shaving and my haircut. This has been going on for about two months. That was around the time of the first write-up. I sent a complaint to the major." Edward asked other officers to intervene. He wrote to the lieutenant, the major, and the warden. But rules were rules, regardless of whether some officers didn't enforce them. "They said they weren't investigating the cases."

My mind raced after I learned of what Edward had done. Driving to the prison two days after the attack, I thought: How did I miss it? He'd talked about the lights and the paper for months. My understanding of trauma's imprint should have been enough to know that Edward describing the interactions with the officer multiple times *was* his plea for help. I prayed for the officer. I worried about what her colleagues had done to Edward immediately afterward. I felt panicked because I didn't know what I would find when I arrived.

I had stopped to get quarters in case I was allowed to buy Edward something to eat and drink. The officers at the front of the prison knew what had happened and knew who I was there to visit. I wanted to tell them I was so sorry, but I was afraid to say anything. There was little conversation with my escort as we walked the long halls to the visiting area. I was assigned one of the two legal booths for our visit, which provided the greatest privacy. I waited eagerly for Edward to arrive.

I heard the metal doors clanging before I saw Edward. He was escorted by twice as many officers as usual. When the door on his side of the booth opened, I quickly scanned his face and arms, the only parts of his skin that I could see. There were no bruises or cuts. Yet his eyes, dark brown and wide, were bloodshot and puffy. Facing me, he genuflected, bending low enough for his wrists to be reached by one of the escorting officers. He wasn't wearing a shirt underneath the billowing white jumpsuit. He looked exhausted and on the verge of tears as he wiped the phone down before sitting on the metal stool fixed to the floor.

"Are you okay?" The question felt idiotic, given where we were and what had just happened.

"I don't know, Liz. I don't know."

I wasn't sure what to ask, so I sat there silently. All the questions I could think of seemed accusatory: Why hadn't he told me he was at the breaking point? Didn't he understand that assaulting an officer meant he was placing his own life in further jeopardy? Had he thought about the pain he was causing the officer and the people who loved her? I watched Edward blink and tears slowly roll down his cheeks. "I don't know," he kept saying.

Between tears he tried to explain.

"What I am trying to get across is that I feel like this lady made this issue personal with me. She'd constantly come after me, saying she was going to write me up. I asked her if we had problems when I was out on recreation. I said, 'I would just like to know if that's the case if we have problems.' She didn't answer me. These people did me, Liz. They knew that I was the dude who was calm and collected. That's how I tried to be the whole time here. A lot of these officers hated that lady because she'd write people up for no reason. I tried talking to her in an educated and civilized way. I won't allow myself to take nothing like that. I won't and I can't. I know I did wrong.

"I stay in this cell, in this box, twenty-four hours a day, seven days a week. I am not able to walk around and roam. You keep messing with me, what do you want me to do? Sometimes I wish my door could open and I could run out there and just run back in. If I couldn't stay at my house even when there weren't problems, how can I stay here? I'm not used to being closed in. I was never grounded. I'd get a spanking, a beating, but then I could go outside, and then I could go back to the house."

Immediately after the attack, officers stormed the shower in riot gear, liberally applying pepper spray, which burned Edward's eyes and choked his throat. He was kicked in the stomach, stomped by feet wearing steel-toed boots, and dragged to a cell, where he was left to sit naked for hours. Edward wasn't the same after the attack. He was treated differently and in some ways better. Because he was flagged as a security risk, officers spent more time explaining things to him. They were less aggressive. His circumstances shouldn't have improved because of the concern that he might harm someone else, but they did.

The officer he'd attacked was rushed to a local hospital and treated for the gash across her face. Though she survived, I imagined she was also never the same. After a leave of recovery, the officer returned to the prison; she was now stationed at the front of the unit screening visitors rather than working directly among the inmates. I knew who she was immediately when I visited the prison a few months after the incident. A large scar ran from the top of her cheekbone to her chin, visible underneath the makeup she'd used to conceal it. I felt shame, sadness, and anger all at once when she asked who I was there to see and I replied, "Edward." Walking the corridor, I carried out a full conversation with her in my mind. I expressed my sorrow and frustration. She described her fear.

GIVING A PERSON in prison access to what they need to grow isn't just better for that person; it's better for everyone. Other nations accept this because they realize that "people inside" are still part of society. More than part; they reflect the society and its views on what individual community members deserve. In Germany, Denmark, Norway, and Sweden, prisons are designed to emphasize rehabilitation and encourage meaningful personal growth with the goal of giving an incarcerated person their best chance at a successful existence outside.[19] We can look closer to home, to Canada, for similar models, or closer still to one prison in Pennsylvania.[20]

Inside the State Correctional Institution–Chester in Pennsylvania, a unit within the prison has been designated as Little Scandinavia. In partnership with corrections officials in Denmark, Sweden, and Norway, researchers and Pennsylvania Department of Corrections staff have changed the physical environment in the unit to include single cells as opposed to shared cells or, worse, dorms with dozens of men living in the same room; a full commercial kitchen and a grocery program; a designated green space; and an interior design meant to encourage interaction and collaboration. Most importantly, the staff-to-resident ratio has been increased, and all officers have received additional training that enables them to engage more actively in residents' rehabilitation and reentry. The officers sit with inmates, eat with them, talk to them. The expectation is to connect and see each other as fully human in a way that permits conversation and space to express views and needs. Remember, it is harder to hurt someone you know—and that extends to both inmates and the officers. Connection is the antidote to moral disengagement.[21]

The Scandinavian model also allows incarcerated persons to wear their own clothes, work in jobs that prepare them for employment after incarceration, and cook their own meals, with fresh and nutritious ingredients. In most instances, the incarcerated in these countries also continue to have access to education and social services, including medical and mental health care, that they could utilize as free citizens. In contrast, American culture considers inhumane treatment part of the punishment. We take freedom, but we also take a person's humanity. And by allowing ourselves to treat others as something less than human, we take the humanity of *everyone* involved in the enterprise of housing the incarcerated.

In my interviews with jurors, I remember one saying: "The cost to the juror is too great. It's not dollars and cents. It is the emotional stuff that goes on forever. And it is not just the jurors. Every time a prosecutor or defense attorney tries one of these cases, they lose a little bit of their humanity too. We all did."

And another asked this question: "How do you protect society from the people who belong to it?"

The question revealed the problem. By the time we were talking about protection, it was too late. What we needed to ask ourselves was: How do we create conditions as a society where each person can thrive? It isn't about taking things away, treating human beings like animals, or demonizing others. It is about love.

Chapter Eight

The Torrent

The walk from the entrance of the U.S. Penitentiary at Terre Haute to the Secured Housing Unit, where the institution's federal death row inmates are incarcerated, takes visitors through much of the prison. After filling out paperwork, showing identification, being photographed, and then proceeding through a full-body scanner, I was escorted to the visiting area by one of the officers who worked on death row. The walk was familiar. I had done many of them since my first trip to meet Edward more than a decade earlier. I nodded toward incarcerated men and staff waiting outside a barbershop and infirmary. The smell of cooked food wafted in our direction as we approached a metal elevator. Without the officer calling for the lift, the doors to the steel cage opened. Video cameras trained on the occupants from all directions let the staff members in some unseen space operate the elevator. There were no buttons to press. The doors closed. We floated up.

When the elevator arrived on our floor, the escorting officer took out a set of large skeleton keys reminiscent of the Victorian era and unlocked a heavy metal door. The door shut loudly behind us. We were standing inside a small vestibule with two half-empty vending

machines. Nearby was a small table. On top of it was a green logbook
that needed to be signed and a stack of waiver forms ready for each
visitor to complete. The form relinquished the Bureau of Prisons from
any liability in the event I was attacked by my new client, Wes Purkey,
during the visit. I had been told that Wes had a sweet tooth and to
bring quarters to purchase items. I selected Pepsi and Mountain Dew
and a couple of handheld apple pies. After making my selections and
hoping they would meet with Wes's approval, I headed to the visiting room.

Wes was standing behind a rectangular metal table that ran across
the middle of the room. He was carrying a brown accordion folder,
and had shackles around his waist, ankles, and wrists. It was hard to ignore his size and build. Having celebrated his sixty-third birthday two
weeks before, Wes stood tall, over six feet, with broad shoulders and
an expansive chest. Though he was dressed in a loose-fitting thermal
shirt, I could still make out the muscular outline of his upper body. He
was missing several teeth, and what he did have appeared mainly to be
dentures. There was a bump the size of a small golfball on the left side
of his forehead. A scar marked his neck, a reminder of a stabbing he'd
survived inside a different prison some thirty years before. Though the
long-sleeved shirt he wore hid most of his tattoos, he could not hide the
ink on the tops of his hands. Crooked black vines covered other prison
tattoos, which I learned later indicated an old affiliation to a white na-
tionalist prison gang.

Before any words were exchanged, I knew I was facing deep-rooted
patterns of behavior Wes had honed to survive. His attorney, who had
asked me to join the team, had described Wes's early life. His mother
drank throughout her pregnancy. She was twice married to Wes's father,
with another marriage sandwiched in between. All her relationships
were chaotic, violent, and fueled by alcohol. Wes was beaten by his

father with a fury driven by self-hatred and despair, which culminated in his father's suicide.

Wes didn't start talking until he was close to six years old. When he did, it was with a significant stutter. His speech was at times slow and slurred as he worked to avoid stammering. Rather than holding Wes's hand and patiently encouraging him to take his time speaking, Wes's mother would throw alcohol in his face or slap him. This particular type of developmental trauma is especially insidious; it can strip a person of their ability to communicate their needs, even to someone on their side, someone who is in a position to help. I had seen this before: a kind of prison of silence.

Wes's mother forced him to engage in sex with her from about the age of nine until around age twenty-two. His grandmother, in whose care he was often left, was known to force him to shower with her. I wondered if he'd known a time in his life when his body was truly his own. Each violation against Wes had confirmed for him the worst parts of humanity, leaving him with a profound sense of loneliness and no self-worth. The attorney who asked me to join the team understood how his "especially challenging" and "difficult" behavior reflected this early life suffering. Others who had worked on Wes's case before had trouble viewing Wes as anything but an "asshole." I understood immediately that Wes was probably very misunderstood and alone, and I anticipated that what was known about his life was the tip of an iceberg, that he had lived through a crucible that mirrored the contours of his most challenging behaviors as well as the intensity of his crime.

Wes's attorney believed that he needed the support of someone who could manage the challenges that his history created by building trust, and she believed I could do it. I had never worked directly with someone who had endured as much as Wes. Before any words were exchanged, I sensed that showing warmth toward Wes would unsettle

him. I knew this too from previous team members' notes. I could not
rely on openness and kindness. I worried that even my practice of letting
silence linger, of not directing the conversation, would be disastrous with
Wes. But that meant my primary tools for establishing a connection were
off-limits. They would not create the intended trust. Wes was unnerved
by a quiet demeanor; he required far more direct engagement.

We shook hands. I watched as Wes took out items from the accordion folder and laid out legal materials, issues of *Compassion*, an inmate
magazine to which he was a regular contributor,[1] and a family photo
album. Once he finished placing the items where he wanted them on
the table, Wes began questioning me.

"What are you doing on my case?" he asked.

"I am a member of your legal team."

"No one asked me if you could be on my team."

"I didn't know. I am sorry."

"What are you going to do?"

"Whatever I can to help you."

"Are you a lawyer?"

"No."

"So how can you help me?"

"I'm not sure yet. Right now, I'm just getting to know you."

We went on like this for several minutes. Having reviewed the materials of Wes's case, I was aware of some immediate obstacles, based on
his experiences with legal teams. His trial attorney, Frederick Duchardt,
was single-handedly responsible for about 7 percent of federal death
row, an astonishing number given that federal death row in 2015 com-
prised fifty-eight men and one woman. Like inhumane housing, violent youth homes, and sexual violence, poor representation at trial was
another common experience shared by people on death row and those
serving life sentences.

In preparation for trial, Mr. Duchardt didn't hire a mitigation specialist to help him understand Wes's life, though it is the professional standard of care in a death penalty case. Failing to do so is akin to failing to hire an investigator to look into the government's evidence; it's an immediate indication that an attorney isn't equipped to handle a complex case. Rather than obtaining someone qualified to develop the generational history needed to give context to Wes's behaviors, Mr. Duchardt utilized a collection of untrained associates, including a private investigator with a reputation for threatening behavior who had been terminated from his previous job due to dishonesty and incompetence.

"I don't like bullshit," Wes flatly stated.

"Me neither."

Maybe that affinity was what did it on that first meeting. He didn't think that there was anything I could do to help him, but he said he would give it a chance. I had passed the first test and could return for a second visit. But I knew that my standing with Wes could change at any moment.

CONSISTENCY BECAME CRITICAL to establishing trust. Wes's memory was poor due to years of drug abuse, numerous brain injuries, trauma, and the effects of aging. He was prone to thinking that his attorneys were lying to him. The team made sure that someone from the defense saw him each week; none of us lived close by, so this required flights and overnight stays. As the team member tasked with understanding the totality of Wes's life, I was up in the rotation more than the attorneys. I flew to see Wes an average of every three weeks, our visits lasting four to five hours.

Our visits were hard. Wes was easily frustrated, and I never knew what would set him off. He wanted to know what I was doing. Why was it taking so long? Why wasn't I done yet? I would offer an explanation, such as that I needed to review all the files in his case before setting out to speak with anyone, and there was a lot to go through. Often this only made him angrier. His voice would become louder; he'd shout. I'd sit there and try to make space for him to move through the frustration, but it would sometimes take hours before he could return to a place of ease. I was always prepared for him to instruct me not to visit him again. He'd made that clear from the beginning: his agreement to allow me to work on his team was precarious.

About four months into my work on the case, during a legal call, he did just that, shouting that he would refuse a visit I had planned for the following week. I went anyway. If he refused the visit, I hoped that the escorting officer would tell him I had brought along a family tree that I had spent months building. It was finally developed enough for me to show it to Wes. He agreed to see me.

During the visit, Wes was silent as I mapped out the branches of his maternal and paternal lines. There were birth and death dates, obituaries, funeral announcements, and newspaper articles about people he hadn't thought about in decades—and some he had never heard about at all. I wasn't sure how he was processing the information. He didn't understand why any of this mattered to his legal case, but he wasn't upset. Then, for the first time since I'd known him, Wes started talking about his mom. When we got to his mother's parents, he told me that she had been raped by her father. It was a heavy visit.

I returned the next day, uncertain how I would find Wes. To my surprise, he entered the room, set up his paperwork, and said he was "bedazzled" by what I had showed him the day before. "I didn't know what depth of investigation you would do. Now I understand that the investigation didn't have a specific aim in mind, but that it could find a lot of different and useful things. I see that once you found whatever you found, then it would be possible to decide what claims could be presented based on what evidence was uncovered. I am impressed, young lady. It doesn't happen that often that I can really be surprised, but this was really surprising."

Wes thought it was incredible that he had Mexican relatives. I had found records showing where they had crossed over into the United States in the early 1900s. "There was a Mexican in the bushes of my family tree!" Wes was learning Spanish and was thrilled that he had Spanish-speaking family members. He couldn't wait to tell his Spanish-speaking friend on death row, who had taught him to crochet, and his spiritual adviser, a Buddhist monk fluent in Spanish who was helping Wes to hone his language skills. He seemed to soften at the fact of the tree, the effort it represented, how it was designed to help me and, by extension, others to understand him.

I sustained a concussion and had to stop flying for a while, which meant I had to suspend my visits with Wes for several months. I shared the news during a legal call. Wes was upset, and I worried that the break in our routine would tank the progress we had made. If he had started to rely on me, would the interruption seem like evidence that I was just another person who wouldn't stick with him? I wondered if I would hear from Wes again.

A week later, I received a small package from him with the following note, accompanied by a book on meditation:

> *Here, young lady, your circumstances actually bring to bear one of the essential tenants of Buddhist practice and that is that, " 'no bad situation is all bad and no good situation is all good,' whereas they both present unique learning opportunities when embraced . . . There are certain things in life that we cannot change, ultimately they change us."*[2]

People around me were quick to disengage when I had to pull back from work. I understood: our field was stressful, and there wasn't time to linger over a team member who was sitting out a round. And it was also a hard space to sit in. I was touched by Wes's words of encouragement. I was in a "bad situation," and he showed up when others didn't. It helped me glimpse something about who he was at his core.

It was a roller-coaster relationship. When I returned to seeing Wes in person and we became closer, he still yelled, cursed, and raged at me. Just when I felt he was on the brink of trusting me, he would do all he could to keep a distance between us. Trusting someone was painful and too unfamiliar. He seemed to be triggered by connection or the prospect of connection; it would send him into demonstrations of anger. Maybe he was afraid. For me, it felt like standing outside during a tornado—over in a flash, but brutal nonetheless.

One visit, he became so angry that I had to leave, the only time in my career I had ever left a client visit before being asked. I told him that I didn't think it was a good idea for me to stay just then because we weren't getting anywhere but that I would be back in the morning. I didn't think he could get more upset, but somehow he found a reservoir of rage.

"Don't fucking come here again with this bullshit!" He nearly tripped over his shackles as he shuffled toward the door.

I think I was calm in the room, but once I was outside, I shook uncontrollably. I returned as promised the next morning.

Wes appeared. "I wasn't sure if you would come back today," he said.

"I said I would."

"Well, I'm sorry about yesterday."

"Thanks. I know you are. If you get that upset, and I think we can't talk, I am going to let you know and end the visit, but I will come back. I promise."

That was how we worked our way to trust. It was so hard, but we both grew. About two years into his case, Wes asked each of the members of his team to take a picture with him. That was significant. He hadn't gotten a picture taken with anyone in years.

His character seeped out. One visit he shared a story about how he loved spending time at the Humane Society because he adored dogs. Another visit he talked about how he would give his dogs a little beer at night and suggested I do the same for my pug. He thought it was nice to let them relax after a long day too. Wes mentioned in passing during another visit how sometimes he would suddenly start weeping in his cell. "I tell myself to shut up and stop it," he said, "but I can't." We talked about techniques to manage sudden waves of emotion.

Wes wrote. Often he wrote about how he viewed himself, about the experiences he'd had, the pain he'd caused, how sorry he was for all of it. As trust between us grew, he told me that he had been raped by a priest at his Catholic school. Shortly after that he wrote a piece called "A Throw-Away Kid Once Said":

> Some stories are best left untold, a throw-away kid once said, and
>   then added—I have no place to go, no one to confide in, no
>   one who gives a damn anywhere! His everyday he said was
>   filled with dread and despair, he faced each and every day
>   with a heavy heart and cold silent stare.
>
> Hiding his misery and shame through a futile act of silence,
>   fooling himself
> Believing that silence would help him escape the excruciating
>   pain and shame,
> Despite the unadorned and unadulterated truth that no one gave
>   a damn—

*About the abominable things a priest did to a throw-away kid at
    the side of the church's rectory—*
*Where the continuing abuse so dreadfully lived the throw-away
    kid so poignantly said!*

*Sad, but true no one gave a damn about the abominable acts
    committed, when*
*The abuser is a priest, and the accuser just another throw-
    away kid—*
*And when dire pleas for help, and protest made, the throw-away
    kid was told,*
*Put aside your pitiful qualms and accusations and let the
    unfortunate circumstances rest!*
*O'yes, the priestly cowards always found refuge under the church's
    domain, and the throw-away kid—*
Tossed out—like a bag of trash at the back of the church!

*How many victims have there been, and how many more must
    there be before*
*Someone will actually take note of the child cruelties and the
    desperate pleas—*
*To stop the unconscionable acts of abuse taking place in the
    basement of the church's rectory,*
The throw-away kid so painfully asked me!

It is unfathomable and insanity at its best that—
Twisted the throw-away kid thought he had something to blame—
*For the depraved vile abuses that left him in crippling
    despair, and*

With hate and shame permeating every facet of his little life—
   how unfathomable it was!
Not even drugs and alcohol could give rest beyond temporary
   suppress the unspeakable pain—
That no matter what the throw-away kid did always remained
   the same!

In a quite "as a matter of fact" way the despondent throw-away
   kid said—
The years of silence to escape and hide the deep-rooted pain and
   shame inside—
Will finally find eternal rest when he is lain in that ever so
   welcome cold brown ground—
Where ultimate peace will be found—this is what "a throw-away
   kid once said"!

Over a four-year period, Wes's team carried out the investigation he should have had access to in advance of his trial. We drafted a petition, which included information related to his experiences of sexual abuse. The team thought I was best positioned to discuss the materials with him. I anticipated that Wes would be angry about the information we included; it was always a hard place for Wes to go. I braced myself for a tough exchange.

Wes walked into the room shackled at the waist, ankles, and wrists, like always. His body was tight, and he started talking before he sat down. He was so angry, but not about the information related to the sexual abuse. He was upset about descriptions from his childhood friends regarding his stuttering in class and the way the nuns at his Catholic school had humiliated him.

"Why was that fucking bullshit in there? What does it have to do with anything?"

I sat quietly, keeping eye contact with him, but he grew angrier by the moment. He raised his voice, stammered, and yelled. The officer who sat right outside the room stood up and approached the door. I shook my head no, hoping that the officer would understand I didn't want him to walk in.

I wanted to explain that, taken with everything else we had learned about Wes, these early life experiences would be crucial to helping understand why Wes's life had gone in the direction it had. The law implicitly asks: If other people experience incest and don't commit murder, why did he? Other people may have had a form of safety at school, a break in the torment experienced at home, enough of a reprieve to help them through the violence. Wes had no such place. Even as a seemingly small example of humiliation and heartlessness, it would have conveyed to his child self that the world was hostile and uncaring. And that mattered.

I wanted to share all these thoughts with Wes, but instead my throat closed and I cried. I extended my hand across the metal table. He didn't take it, so I left it there, close to him.

"Why can't you see how resilient you are?" I asked.

Wes didn't answer.

"Why don't you love yourself enough to want to try and live? Why can't you see what I see?"

Wes didn't respond, but his face was no longer angry. His body had relaxed, his rage abated. He seemed stumped by someone who knew all about him, knew some things he himself couldn't even remember, and cared for him anyway. I think he felt my love, and it tempered his rage.

•

ONE NIGHT, DURING the period when I was visiting Wes, I woke from a dream that was so vivid that I immediately rolled over to write down the details. In the dream, I watched Wes pick up Jennifer, his victim, as she was walking down the street. This seemed odd to me, him being in his forties and she being sixteen, but not dangerous. She was looking for a place to go, and he was looking for a person to lose time with. She got into his truck. I watched them talk. It seemed unforced, easy, given the strangeness of the situation. They were both calm as they stopped for alcohol and headed toward his house. The mood took a turn as they walked toward the door. Once inside the house, I felt something in her switch on, and she was suddenly afraid.

Until that point I had been disembodied, watching. Then Wes left the room, and I appeared in the house. I told Jennifer to run. I gave her the keys to Wes's truck and told her to drive away. Jennifer was confused, but there wasn't time to explain. I took her hand in mine and looked her in the eyes. I told her to get out of the house, get in the car, and drive as fast as she could. I watched her make it to the blue truck and speed away. I felt such a huge sense of relief. She was safe. Jennifer would get to live, and Wes would never know the darkest parts of himself. He came back into the room, disoriented but unfazed. It was as if I'd created one of the many moments in his life when love could have made a difference.

Prior to the crime for which he received his death sentence, Wes spent decades incarcerated before being released on parole. The transition was jarring. Computers were ubiquitous. Gas could be paid at the pump. Cells phones were common. He went to his probation officer and said he was having a hard time, but since he was working and not an immediate threat to anyone, nothing was done. So many moments in a life when, had the focus been genuine care and concern, the scales might have balanced differently. That wasn't something I knew until I started working with people who had killed; how grace and love did more to transform a person than anything. Genuine human connection—authentic, messy, hard—is the most powerful and restorative force in human existence.

I BECAME PREGNANT with my first child just weeks before the Trump administration scheduled an execution date for Wes: December 13, 2019. He would die when most people were preparing for time with family, planning holiday celebrations. His attorneys and I were with him within a few days of receiving the news.

As we were being escorted to the secured housing unit of the prison, I noticed the landscape, the building, how everything around me felt different, even though I had made the walk to see Wes dozens of times. The escorting officer tried to make small talk. He knew we were there to see someone we cared about whose death had been scheduled. I wanted him to acknowledge what was happening, but he didn't.

I brought along about twenty dollars in quarters so I could purchase snacks and sodas for Wes. His craving for sweets only seemed to be getting more intense as he aged. I could hear Wes's voice down the sterile corridor as he talked to the escorting officer. I chose an orange Fanta and a Coke. All the honeybuns were gone, and those were his favorites.

I looked Wes in his pale-blue eyes and placed the sodas on the metal table between us. His shackled hand stuck out slightly, inviting a handshake. I placed my hand in his and held his gaze. "Don't look so sad." His eyes started to water. Before I could respond, his attorneys entered the room and his demeanor changed. A full-throttled verbal assault followed. This was our fault, Wes insisted. He stammered and became red. His voice rose, which caused the officer watching us through a window to come to the door and signal that he was ready to enter and end the visit.

My heart was pounding hard as I watched Wes's chest muscles twitch. The tendons in his neck were bulging and tight. I looked at the scar left by an inmate who'd tried to kill Wes, and I felt like I was going to pass out. He was off-loading. I didn't know how to make the situation better. It was a terrible road that we would travel together, I thought, until he either received a stay of execution or was killed.

WES, ALONG WITH three others who had been given execution dates, received stays due to issues around the drugs the federal government had planned to use.[3] The weeks after Wes's first execution date passed were weightless. He was able to make sure that his daughter and grandchildren had a good Christmas with presents. He felt overwhelming gratitude that they wouldn't have to associate the holidays with him being killed. In the New Year, he was looking forward to the Super Bowl. He was a lifelong fan of the Kansas City Chiefs and had waited decades to see them win the championship. He turned sixty-eight around the time they took the title. I shared the news of my pregnancy. He was so happy for me.

Wes began knitting gifts for my daughter. He had become very skilled at crochet and made a green-and-pink monkey hat for the winter. I brought along the twenty-week ultrasound image to show him. He'd been incarcerated when his daughter was born and when his grandchildren were born. He had never seen an image of a life so new. He gripped the picture tightly, like it was the key to something he didn't know he needed. I let him keep it.

Then, in March 2020, the world shut down due to Covid-19, a highly contagious respiratory disease that was rapidly spreading throughout the United States and world, killing thousands of people by the day. The prison ceased all in-person visits with inmates. Our regular visits turned into legal calls. Wes was concerned for me and the baby and was relieved that I wasn't traveling or leaving the house much at all. No one knew what the virus could do to a fetus. "She is precious cargo," he said.

I didn't think that any executions would go forward during the first year of the pandemic. Carceral facilitates were highly vulnerable to the virus. Unlike other settings, prisons are like self-contained cities within which the housed cannot engage in protective practices like social distancing or have access to things like hand sanitizer, which is considered contraband. Numerous prisons charged inmates for soap and other hygiene products, and many inmates were too poor to afford these essential items. Limiting access to these spaces was the most effective way to prevent Covid from spreading through the prison population. The federal government hadn't executed anyone in close to twenty years. It seemed so risky for the health of everyone inside and outside the prison when so little was known about the virus.[4] I was shocked and dismayed when the Trump administration set a new execution date for Wes on July 15, 2020. Unlike the first time around, where we were given five months' notice, this second warrant was issued a tight thirty days before the event.

We were in the relatively early days of the pandemic, totally unprepared for how to do our jobs safely inside prisons. I had been listed as one of the four witnesses to Wes's execution. We hadn't talked about it, but if that was what Wes wanted, I planned to attend. I felt that I didn't need to tell him I would be there: he would know I saw it as a commitment.

As the days ticked forward, I did all I could to research the safest way to get to the prison. Would a twelve-hour drive at eight and a half months pregnant be better than a short flight? I searched various websites for maternity hazmat suits. There was no vaccine, there were no widely available tests, and the most effective masks were still being reserved for medical personnel because there was a shortage. Members of my team tried to talk me out of attending. One of the attorneys called me, crying, and asked me not to go to the prison. I didn't know how to make this decision.[5] No one had showed up for Wes when it could have changed the outcome of his life. I couldn't bear the thought of failing to be there for him at the end.

Kids have a funny way of making decisions for parents. At least, my daughter did when my water broke at four A.M. on July 1, four weeks before my due date. Though I'll never know, I wondered if the stress I felt about the decision caused her to arrive early. I knew Wes would be concerned about me and the baby. Members of the team let him know what was happening, and I hoped that the news would bring him some small bit of joy despite the circumstances.

I joined one of the team calls with Wes when I got home with my daughter. She started cooing loudly, and I apologized for the disruption. Wes said it was the best sound he'd ever heard and cooed back. He never asked me if I was coming to be with him, and I never said I wasn't going to be there. We both knew.

Each day that brought the execution closer ushered in new panic and dread, especially for his daughter. It was also a strain on Jennifer's mother, who wanted to attend the execution but couldn't either. I spoke with her as the date drew nearer, and I felt deep sadness for her during the call. Like the other mothers I had met who'd lost children to murder, she lived with it daily—not just the horror of what had happened but the recurring attempts to imagine it, the repeated self-questioning: Was there anything she could have done? Something she could have done differently, and her daughter would be alive? She carried the singular pain of a guilt that wasn't hers to bear.

Jennifer's mother spoke to no one from the Department of Justice before it set the execution date in July to see if she could be present. If someone had reached her, they would have learned how important it was to her to attend the execution, her presence an act in honor of her daughter's life. But she could not attend during the pandemic, given her many health problems. She couldn't risk contracting the coronavirus. And yet the attorney general of the United States, William Barr, had made comments about the need for these executions to go ahead at such a dangerous time because the victims needed closure.[6] Jennifer's mom did want the litigation to end, for the case to be over, one way or another. And if Wes was going to be executed, she believed she needed to be there. Her inability to make it became, in her mind, another example of how she couldn't show up for Jennifer.

I WOKE UP on July 15 and stood over my five-pound daughter. It was a surreal feeling, thinking about how to dress this twelve-day-old baby on the morning of Wes's scheduled execution. I selected a Wonder Woman T-shirt. I wrapped her against my chest. I had become the default point of contact with Wes. One of his attorneys and another investigator were at the prison to serve as his witnesses if the execution proceeded. I worried about their safety and that of everyone else who was on the way to Terre Haute. The other members of his defense team were busy responding to court orders and requests. Wes and I spoke for a few minutes each hour so I could provide him updates about the status of the execution. He cooed back and forth with my daughter when she was awake and active.

A valid death warrant is essential for an execution to take place because without one there isn't anything to stop the government from deciding to execute someone whenever it wants to, without notice. The warrant needs to have some kind of time limit too; most expire at midnight. If the execution isn't completed by the time limit, a new warrant must be issued. I felt relieved when Wes was still alive at midnight. The death warrant had expired, and he still had orders in different courts pausing the execution on legal grounds. Though his execution hadn't been called off, it was just a matter of time before the prison told witnesses to go home and sent Wes back to his cell. I reached out to his daughter and told her as much. She was also panicked about the fact that she wasn't able to be with Wes in person. She had young kids and could not risk catching the virus. I was relieved she wouldn't carry guilt for deciding not to risk her own life to witness her dad being killed.

I didn't feel comfortable going to bed until the official word calling off the execution had been issued. Around two A.M., while I was on the phone with Wes, my daughter sleeping on me, an email came across, indicating that the U.S. Supreme Court had made the unprecedented move of lifting all the stays of execution pending in lower courts. The decision occurred in a five-to-four vote of the court, which fell along ideological lines. I was very confused: Did this mean the government would try to kill him? How could it without a new warrant? And then there were other filings that the attorneys had prepared: Would these create new stays of execution? I didn't want to alarm Wes without talking to his attorneys. I told Wes that it seemed like something was happening, and I would call him right back. He stammered. I asked Wes to check with the officer who was with him, the same officer who had escorted me to our legal visits for the previous five years, that I would be able to call right back after connecting with one of his lawyers. The officer assured me I would be able to. I told Wes not to worry, though I sensed things had suddenly become very dangerous. I hung up and reached out to the attorneys.

After speaking with the attorneys, I called the direct line on which Wes had been speaking with me. The phone rang and rang. I thought I must have dialed a wrong number and tried again. A wave of panic hit me. Could they have taken him from this room to the execution chamber already? Impossible. It had been less than five minutes. The officer knew I was going to call back. I hung up and tried again. No answer. I triple-checked the numbers and dialed back. The line was disconnected.

I DIDN'T KNOW the exact moment that Wes's life ended. I wasn't there when he was killed. It happened sometime on the morning of July 16, 2020, many hours after the warrant for his execution had expired. Rather than get a new execution warrant, the federal government sent an email to Wes's attorneys, saying they were going forward with the execution. This erasure of the government's obligation to give appropriate notice was sickening. So now the government just needed to send an email before executing someone at any time? If the government could do this, it could do anything. Wes's death made it clear to me that we kill people in America because we can. It is the absolute exercise of power over the powerless, designed to remind the poor, marginalized, minority, and cast-off or throwaway human beings in our society that their bodies could be taken at any moment, that the rules meant to ensure fairness were not there for them but only for others with the privilege of having been born into a life that society values. It was a vivid display of cruelty for cruelty's sake. I didn't just lose Wes that morning. I lost my belief that ours is a system capable of dispensing justice.

It cost the federal government about a million dollars to execute Wes. I think about how that money could have been spent earlier in his life to get him the help he needed. Why didn't we make that investment? No one showed up for him when it would have mattered. Now, at the end, as he was deteriorating from dementia, during a global pandemic when not even the victim's mother—invoked to justify the execution's timeline— could attend, taxpayers spent one million dollars for him to die.[7]

I think about Wes every day. When my daughter is screaming for no reason that I can ascertain, having a tantrum, or being a typical boundary-testing toddler, I cannot help but think about her good fortune. She will never know what it feels like to be hit for showing emotion, to be afraid of her parents, to hear the thud of my head going through a wall or see me dragged by my hair, screaming for intervention. She won't know the unmistakable sound of fists hitting flesh. She will not know chaos in her home or the isolation that neglect fosters. She is full of the joy and confidence that all human beings come into the world possessing. I am relieved for her. I am equally angry that Wes didn't have the same environment to harness his capacity in life. None of my clients did.

The day after Wes was killed, a black-and-white knitted panda arrived at my office. There was no note, but I knew Wes had spent the final days of his life making something beautiful for my daughter. This is common with those who are executed.[8] They spend their final hours showing love, because that is what they carry into the end—just as we all imagine and hope to live our last moments surrounded by and offering love. I am reminded of this whenever I read a letter written by another client who was also executed. It hangs on my office wall next to pictures of my incarcerated friends, including one of me and Wes.

I hope that my letter finds all of you in good health and the best of spirits. I want to take a moment and tell you thank you. Each and every one of you are appreciated. I don't know how my appeal process will end, but no matter the outcome, I am confident you all gave it your best effort, and for that I am most grateful. I couldn't afford your services . . . and sadly, I can't repay your kindness, compassion, generosity, and dedication, so either in this life or the hereafter, I will pay it forward. Thank you so much for your hard work and professionalism. Most of all thank you for respecting mine, and my family's lives and feelings. "There's a difference between interest and commitment. When you're interested in doing something, you do it only when it is convenient. When you are committed to something, you accept no excuses, only results" (Kenneth Blanchard). Thank you all for your commitment to my legal defense. Everyone take care of yourselves and others.

The handmade black-and-white knitted panda that Wes spent his final days weaving with his arthritic hands is a part of our nighttime ritual where my daughter says good night to each of her animal friends before we read books and she falls asleep.

I talk to her about Wes. I tell her that Mommy's friend made that bear for her because he was so excited for her to be born. I will tell her the rest of the story when she is older, because I want her to know that people are complicated but possess the ability to be loving and kind no matter the harms they may have caused. Wes caused a great deal of suffering. He also gave a tremendous amount of love. When we take a life, we take the whole life, including the good, which exists in every single human being and just needs the right conditions to emerge.

Getting close to Wes was never without struggle, but it gave me the opportunity to witness Wes reimagine himself. In return, Wes helped me see how messy and complex a genuine relationship can be with someone so traumatized. My relationship with Wes was evidence that love, patience, and acceptance can serve as a catalyst for positive change. Many people had concluded that Wes was too broken or damaged to salvage, but I saw a man who was working hard to be a better version of himself every day. Sometimes he succeeded. That he never stopped trying to improve or atone was a testament to his humanity. It was evidence that growth and change are always possible, especially when love and support feed the effort.

Epilogue

Choices

I am sitting on a brown pleather love seat in the living room of a client's childhood home. I am spending time with his mother, who is in her nineties, though she looks younger than her age. The home is quintessential Baltimore—a two-story brick row house with a small front yard and a parking pad in the back. Alleyways are where the kids play. The row house has three bedrooms, one full bathroom, and a partially finished basement, which serves as the bedroom for my client's older brother, now in his sixties. My client was one of six children raised in this house, which the family purchased in the 1970s when the neighborhood was a vibrant Black community. Now many of the homes on the block are vacant and have fallen into disrepair.

Inside, his mother and I are sitting in a cramped living room with wall-to-wall recliners and a large-screen television that is anchored at the top by a metal chain to ensure it doesn't fall over. My client's mother is sitting directly next to the television, which is loud enough that I can't hear much of anything else. The news is on no matter the time of day I stop by to visit. Right now she is watching CNN, but she will switch to the local news when the evening reports begin.

It is March 2025. Federal layoffs, executive orders equating justice with retribution, hostility toward people who are attempting to immigrate to the United States. Then the mass shootings, murders, and other types of everyday American tragedy. The mother of my client sighs. She raises her voice, exasperated.

"It is crazy out there. People have lost their minds."

To her, people seem far more unpredictable, scarier, and harder to comprehend these days. She is afraid. I see the impact of her fear in the new video cameras trained on the entrance of her home, the enhanced security door with bars and reinforced glass that obscures the bright-red front door behind it. She tells me about the monitor she has in her bedroom, which allows her to view live footage from the cameras at the front, sides, and back of the house. She watches it in the evenings for hours. In fact, she saw me walking up the footpath before I rang the bell. She can see far into the street. In the seven years I have known her, I have witnessed the outside of her home slowly turn from a welcoming space where popping by seemed possible into a fortress. She is suspicious of strangers, and her suspicion has led her to stay home more, watching the video monitors. She is more isolated. She has experienced not only the trauma of her son, my client, being sentenced to death but also of losing another son to murder. And while she often talks about these losses, the pervasive fear she expresses about the world is general and ever-present and disconnected from any particular experience.

I wonder how much of her fear is manufactured by the screens she watches all day. As a person who has lived nearly a century, she exists at a time when crime rates are historically low.[1] She fears people from Mexico, though American citizens, not immigrants, commit most crimes.[2] She is preoccupied by the existence of transgender people. Neither immigrants nor transgender people are the cause of suffering in America or of her own personal hardships, but her focus on them fuels her separation from others in her community. There is an "us" and there is a "them," and in this calculus the "them" is to blame. In response to the information she receives throughout the day, she wants harsher penalties for the strangers vilified on the news. At the same time, she wants her son to be released from death row.

My client's mother, like most people I connect with, describes continual anxiety and the exhaustion it causes. She experiences a very real physical and psychological response to sustained stress. I am tired too, and in that moment despondent, watching television reports detailing the cruelty of politicians who are in the process of dismantling already insufficient but essential safety nets. My despair sits heavy like a rock in my chest; I know these actions will be the catalyst to more death, more ruin. And I know that when the murder rate rises, the same people who stole the safety of our communities will lay the blame squarely on those who committed these irreversible acts, directing all of us to look away from our role in this sequence of events. A modern-day gaslighting so well designed. I see it extending far out into the American horizon. I am full of dread.

The screens can blot out all sense of history and context, two things mitigation works to reincorporate into any narrative. Working as a mitigation specialist has taught me that the past is always walking with us in the present, whether or not we choose to acknowledge it. Each individual life is a product of experiences and decisions made by previous generations, invisible hands that shift both the individual and collective trajectory. The journalist Isabel Wilkerson likens living in America to the experience of residing in an old house:

> Wind, flood, drought, and human upheavals batter a structure that is already fighting whatever flaws were left unattended in the original foundation. When you live in an old house, you

may not want to go into the basement after a storm to see what the rains have wrought. Choose not to look, however, at your own peril. The owner of an old house knows that whatever you are ignoring will never go away. Whatever is lurking will fester whether you choose to look or not. Ignorance is no protection from the consequences of inaction. Whatever you are wishing away will gnaw at you until you gather the courage to face what you would rather not see.

Enslavement, torture, degradation, and theft. This is our inheritance. As Wilkerson rightly concludes, "Our immediate ancestors may have had nothing to do with it, but here we are, the current occupants of a property with stress cracks and bowed walls and fissures built into the foundation. We are the heirs to whatever is right or wrong with it. We did not erect the uneven pillars or joists, but they are ours to deal with now. And any further deterioration is, in fact, on our hands."

American history, including the rules of its criminal legal system, starts with the theft of land, the genocide of Native people, and the capture, kidnapping, and enslavement of people. This is not hyperbole; it is fact. Think about what it means to steal land, to kill its rightful inhabitants, enslave others, separate parent from child, view another human as property. How must the displaced, captive, or separated have been viewed? Only as something less than fully human. Ours was never going to be a system of equal access, human rights, or universal dignity. It was designed as a system with two tiers: for those who deserve opportunities and for those who do not. The deserving and the undeserving.

We are making the decisions about where to invest resources that create the situations described in this book—and countless others that do not appear in these pages. The agonizing decisions that a parent like Maria makes: to stop working and providing or to leave her son chained to a bed. The walk from the vestibule of the public housing towers to the elevator and eventually, hopefully, to the fifteenth floor, where some form of safety might live for George and his family. The family members who have lost their loved ones to execution or to prison, like the families of Ledell Lee and Wes Purkey, who mourn the men the world has condemned and forgotten. These are not merely difficult situations; they are impossible.

American democracy has been built to exclude and severely limit access to resources, and therefore to justice, for those the powerful deem undeserving. A two-party political system cannot capture coalitions, which would allow for a wider range of engagement and potential for legislative progress rather than gridlock. Likewise, other structures—such as the electoral college, lifetime appointments of politicized justices, and the election of prosecutors—all give the appearance of access but enforce exclusion. Improvements are possible. A report by the Brennan Center for Justice suggests that Supreme Court justices be limited to staggered eighteen-year terms, which would allow a vacancy on the court every two years, ensuring that a sitting president would get to pick two, and only two, justices each term.[3] This would address court-packing, the ability of one of the two parties to dramatically change the ideological position of the court. It would enhance judicial independence and better protect and reflect the collective values of a majority of citizens. This is but one suggestion, but others exist that can enhance broader access to justice, if we truly want that.[4]

The legal system is but one type of social structure that operates within a broader system that includes education, housing, health care, employment, immigration, transportation, and on and on. To silo the criminal legal system as particularly in need of reform is to fail to understand the true causes of crime. For there to be real sustained change, we must take stock of the values that undergird our institutions. Do we truly want everyone in America to have the opportunity to live a safe, healthy, and flourishing life? If the answer is yes, there is great work ahead. If the answer is no, we can continue to march down the current path of retribution, devastation, and ruin, knowing that it will not get better or right itself—that avoidable death and unfathomable grief will come.

IN 2020, WHILE the world suffered the traumas wrought by the pandemic, Attorney General William Barr and President Donald Trump carried out thirteen federal executions. Five executions were carried out between November, after he lost the election to incoming president Joe Biden, and January, five days before the inauguration. In the history of America, no lame-duck president has spent his final weeks ensuring as many American citizens were killed as President Trump. Four of the dead were men of color and one was Lisa Montgomery, a survivor of brutal sex-trafficking who had been terribly represented by Frederick Duchardt, the same attorney who represented Wes at his capital trial. Lisa was the only woman on federal death row and the first woman to be executed by the U.S. government in seventy years.[5]

The continuation of this cruelty and focus on retribution started on day one of the second Trump administration with the signing of executive order 14164, "Restoring the Death Penalty and Protecting Public Safety."[6] It includes the following language:

> These efforts to subvert and undermine capital punishment defy the laws of our nation, make a mockery of justice, and insult the victims of these horrible crimes. The Government's most solemn responsibility is to protect its citizens from abhorrent acts, and my Administration will not tolerate efforts to stymie and eviscerate

the laws that authorize capital punishment against those who commit horrible acts of violence against American citizens.

Euphemisms allow atrocities to continue, so I will speak clearly: the executive order is full of lies. I use that word specifically, because to call the description inaccurate or false is to signal a belief that its author could have made a simple mistake. There was no mistake here. The order is referring to, among other lawful decisions, that of outgoing president Biden to grant commutation to thirty-seven of the forty people remaining on federal death row. Those thirty-seven are now serving sentences of life without the possibility of parole. The president has the power to grant commutations and pardons—as President Trump also did on his first day in office at the start of his second term. President Biden had been presented with clemency applications: details of the lives of the men he pardoned, information that he weighed in the balance of harm and justice. Yes, some of the victims of those who were commuted were angry with the decision and felt victimized again by a system that did not and cannot dispense justice. Other victims of the same offender were relieved.[7] No victim received what they deserved. That is the point: the criminal legal system cannot deliver an end to suffering. But we could have built a society that prevented it in the first place.

There is a long history in our nation of debating the legality of capital punishment, with vastly different opinions existing on the issue. The decision in 1972 to suspend the death penalty in *Furman v. Georgia* illustrated an array of views about the death penalty held among the Supreme Court justices. Every justice penned his own opinion, totaling more than two hundred pages of thought and analysis on the topic. It is a lie to state that those who do not view the law—a living and breathing structure—through a retributive lens have nefarious intentions and seek to "make a mockery of justice and insult victims." Rather, a return to more "tough on crime" policies and efforts to roll back reforms that could *truly* protect American citizens from abhorrent acts represents a choice to control people, to punish, to harm, rather than seek to respond to the experiences that cause the behavior in the first place.

Some politicians are emboldened by the call to seek the death and ruin of others espoused in these orders. The governor of Louisiana Jeff Landry has carried out the first execution in Louisiana by suffocation: gassing using nitrogen hypoxia, evoking the way the Nazis carried out murders in their state-sanctioned death chambers.[8] It is worth noting that this form of killing is not even permitted for veterinarians who put down animals.[9] Louisiana is following the protocol of Alabama, which has carried out four nitrogen hypoxia executions since 2024.[10] South Carolina pursued another return to savagery: the killing by firing squad of sixty-seven-year-old Brad Sigmon on March 7, 2025.[11]

New laws are also demonstrating how scores of politicians are leaning into retribution to the detriment of their constituents, including children, who will be made far less safe by the passing of these laws. Florida and Tennessee have passed laws authorizing death sentences for people convicted of rape or sodomy of a child under twelve or thirteen, respectively. Arizona, Arkansas, and Idaho have passed similar legislation. A person who has experienced abuse is often less likely to report the abuse or more likely to minimize it, especially since the person who caused harm is often a family member or family friend.[12] Simply, fear of negative consequences for the person who caused the harm helps drive underreporting of child sexual abuse. Consider someone like Connor and how his fear animated reporting. If a child understood that by reporting abuse a family member could be killed, that would just become another barrier to the disclosure.

These laws are also unambiguously unconstitutional: the U.S. Supreme Court in *Kennedy v. Louisiana* (2008) ruled that rape does not make one eligible for the death penalty. Prosecutions that go forward under these laws will therefore waste limited resources that could be directed toward other areas, like solving open crimes. Even though these laws actually go beyond that wastefulness and make victims less safe, some politicians lie about the justification. Here is Florida governor Ron DeSantis's statement about passing a law that is illegal:

> In Florida we stand for the protection of children. And unfortunately in our society you have very heinous sex crimes that are committed against children under the age of twelve years old.... We think that in the worst of the worst cases, the only appropriate punishment is the ultimate punishment. And so this bill sets up a procedure to be able to challenge that precedent and to be able to say that in Florida we believe that the worst of the worst crimes deserve the worst of the worst punishment.[13]

Euphemisms allow harm to continue. Governor DeSantis is saying that he knows this law is illegal but nonetheless will put victims through the adjudicative process in the hopes that eventually a case will go to the U.S. Supreme Court, which has been packed with conservatives who will undo almost twenty years of legal precedent. It is a callous experiment that only extends suffering.

In public statement after public statement from the president down to local legislators, words that signal more safety and security are being used to justify unnecessary harm, when in fact, it is the passage of these policies that is the catalyst for the pain people will feel. Some know they lie, and others are ignorant. Both roads lead to the same place.

I can imagine the moments in the lives of my clients and their families when things could have been different. If Edward, whose mother left him chained to a bed as an infant for as many as fifteen hours a day, had had a safe, affordable place, his life would have been different. And George and William, who were left to live in the killing fields of public housing or youth facilities, if they had known safety, known what it was like to run free and joyful without the thought of dropping to the ground or having to carry knives to school for protection, would have been free to contemplate a future and a path to get there. They could have been good neighbors, loving friends, and supportive partners. Connor's life would have been entirely different if the counselor he was sent to had tried to understand his behavior rather than slap a diagnostic label on him, marking him as the problem and setting him on a path of torture through the Straight program. If the Straight program had focused on true trauma healing rather than profits, Connor and thousands of other children whose families were desperate for help might actually have seen their children change in healthy ways. Connor could have been a great father, a present brother, and a supportive son. If Tony had been taken out of that trailer and raised in a safe home, he would have graduated from high school, gone to college, and contributed to his community through writing or other creative endeavors. The same would have been true for Wes, who was so bright and had a deep capacity for love and care. And Ledell, who would have reveled in becoming a grandfather and taking care of his parents by washing their cars, cooking family meals, and helping them navigate the final stages of life.

These could have been the stories of the men I have known. And for each one of these alternate outcomes, the stories of the victims who were harmed—those whose lives my clients took, but also the lives of the many who were forever changed because of murder—would have been different too. Everyone deserved a chance at those outcomes, at those lives.

Mitigation evidence—the fact that it exists as a way to infuse humanity into the criminal justice process—is paradoxical. Its existence is proof of the problem and also the solution. Each human being I have had the honor of connecting with through my work, in nearly every state in this nation, wants the same thing: to be loved, safe, and valued. If that were the goal for our society—making sure that every single person has access to the resources that can help them flourish—such a goal, taken seriously, would radically transform the criminal legal system. Further, it would radically transform the quality of and access to education, medical and mental health services, employment opportunities, safe and affordable housing, and all the other components of our society, because each of these is its own form of a justice system.

True criminal justice reform requires structuring our society to have as its end the ability of every single person to reach their potential. This is not a piecemeal solution but a long-term project that places human dignity and generational safety at the center of decision-making. It is the opposite of what is currently taking place.

Criminal justice policy in the United States has always been highly vulnerable to the public—through the federalist system, through the election of prosecutors and judges, and through malleable views about the trustworthiness of elected officials. This is why solutions cannot be entirely policy-driven. A progressive prosecutor will not make a permanent difference; nor will changes in the law that provide for bail reform, discretionary sentencing, or other immediate ways to limit interaction with the criminal legal system. All of those can, have been, and will be undone as the pendulum swings.

For things to change, *we* must change. We must change how we see people from the moment they are born—their unique and unmatched potential—and we must invest in creating a community that facilitates growth regardless of income, origin, race, religion, or any other aspect of a person that we have designed to facilitate difference.[14] We have to cultivate the capacity to understand that when crime happens, the act signifies more than the crime itself; it gives us information about what that person needed to develop in order to live their fullest life, and where that connection failed. The choice we have is how to take those tragedies and create the kind of society each human life deserves.

As a starting point for this kind of lasting and sustained change within our culture, we must place a new question at the center of our policies and laws. What resources or supports are necessary for any person in this community to thrive? When we think specifically about crime and punishment, we must move beyond retribution, which has provided no meaningful safety for communities and has stolen vast amounts of human potential from all of us.

We must align resource investment with the spaces we believe are crucial to the success of our society. In the criminal legal system this would mean equitable funding and resourcing for agencies that prosecute and those that defend individuals accused of crimes. Currently prosecutorial agencies have vastly more financial and human resource support than public defenders. Equal funding, pay, staffing, caseloads, and other resources are essential to ensure that outcomes are reliable and fair.[15]

We must dispense with the death penalty. It is a failed public policy that does not promote public safety and strips communities of needed resources. Likewise, sentences of natural life should no longer be used. Every human deserves an opportunity for release. When the time comes for assessing whether a person is ready for release, that person should be judged by a board of pardons and parole that includes formerly incarcerated members who can be a part of the process and add perspective on readiness for release and suitability of reentry plans. Should someone be denied, there ought to be an opportunity for the incarcerated person to work with someone within the system (a social worker, for example) who can better ready them for release by providing the support to grow in the areas needed for a successful return to the wider community.

The maximum sentence for the most severe crimes (murders, attempted murders, rape, for example) should be no more than twenty years before there is an opportunity for release.[16] This would be the floor and not a guarantee of release, but a guarantee of consideration. And because indefinite sentencing can be used to keep a person incarcerated for their natural life, the ceiling or maximum before automatic release should be no more than forty years of incarceration. Setting the maximum punishment at a specific number of years would incentivize our communities to provide the type of programming aimed at growth and change, rather than the bare minimum to survive incarceration. In other words, if we knew that someone who had committed murder was going to be released in twenty, thirty, or forty years, what would we do to make sure they could return to our communities and contribute? We wouldn't leave humans to languish in closets with no human contact for decades; we know the damage that causes.

We must change how we treat the confined. The punishment bestowed on an incarcerated person should be the loss of freedom that comes with incarceration, not more than that. Our carceral facilities are nearly all unfit for human habitation, and these conditions lead to devastating results, including the deaths of other incarcerated persons and staff members. These facilities should be invested in returning incarcerated individuals to the community. Their primary aim should be providing support to ensure the success of that return: free dignified housing upon release, healthy meals, exercise, education, assistance with job acquisition, and trauma treatment. Trauma treatment should address preexisting issues and more recent experiences from incarceration.

Some may suggest that providing these opportunities could encourage people to break the law in order to go to prison or jail. The concern reveals the problem. If obtaining this baseline quality of life in the richest nation in the world is out of reach for many within free society, that is a problem and means the options for living in free society must improve.

We cannot allow the use of solitary confinement as a regular method of incarceration.[17] Over sixty thousand people, like Edward, are living in long-term solitary confinement, shuttered inside cells with no human contact beyond the occasional touch of a correctional officer hooking belly chains and shackles on their bodies. Due to the fact that many of those currently on death row or serving life without the possibility of parole sentences have serious mental health issues in addition to complex traumatic experiences that have never been adequately addressed, the use of solitary confinement is objectively psychically damaging. The combination of illness, trauma, and solitude is soul-crushing and mind-altering. It is simply a form of torture, one that exemplifies the dehumanization and brutality of our carceral institutions. It has no place in a civilized society.

With the gutting of mental health facilities and the criminalization of illness, too many people with treatable conditions are shunted into prisons. Once there, these individuals, who need adequate treatment, often violate rules and receive additional punishments. Our priorities are reflected in the financial investment we make; we have invested in prisons at the expense of other systems. An adequate and accessible mental health system must be provided so those who can benefit from such support are not left to the legal system.

The lack of connection between the incarcerated and the free breeds misconception and fear. We must create opportunities for incarcerated citizens and those who are free to connect. This can be through work programs, educational opportunities, religious or spiritual programming, dog programs, yoga and mindfulness work, arts and theater, and culinary classes. By creating connections and shaping incarceration to better reflect the experiences of the wider community, we are preparing people for a smoother transition and building a support system. We are also building empathy, which is essential to prevent a return to the dehumanizing practices that created the environment for treating each other so poorly in the first place.

The values of mitigation extend to everyone, including victims. Victims need to be treated with dignity, not used as a means to an end, as is often the case in our current system. We should consider what victims need in the aftermath of a harm, from their viewpoint, recognizing that punishment via a penal system is just one potential avenue. There are other paths possible: the opportunity to ask the offender questions; to partner with an offender in programming and activities that could prevent them from engaging in similar actions in the future; to have a say in how descriptions of the harm are presented in the media, if at all; and to have access to trauma support for a substantial period of time in the aftermath of harm. Victims should also have meaningful independent support through the litigation of a case, including someone who can fairly explain the process and ensure notification of court hearings or outcomes before they become public knowledge.

Mitigation is concerned first and foremost with the inherent dignity of a person and with creating space where that dignity is honored and shared. Reshaping our society to encompass these values would provide the type of life and opportunity everyone deserves. It is something we can do, starting now by choosing compassion, care, and investment.

ONE MORNING, UNCEREMONIOUSLY, a court order vacated Edward's death sentence; based on evidence provided by his defense team, the court deemed him to be a person living with intellectual disability. At the time of his conviction and sentence, the law allowed the execution of those living with intellectual disability. That changed in 2002. Just like that, he was no longer under the threat of death.

"I am waiting for the other shoe to drop," Edward says to me on the phone.

"It won't. This is done. No one can take this from you. The court order takes away your death sentence. It is over. You are automatically serving life."

Edward says he's been bringing the order with him wherever he goes inside the prison—a bit of proof of his new life. Still in prison, but a life.

I am going to visit Edward in a new facility. It has been over twenty years of drives to prisons to visit clients. This time is different. I haven't seen Edward since he took it as a matter of course that he would be left in a cell for days without a shower, that he would be left in a closet to defecate, that he would have to go without the touch of his loved ones. I haven't seen him in his new life. How strange that after so many years, so much work, the change came in an instant.

I have a roll of quarters. I am excited to see my friend and looking forward to witnessing the person he can become. At least he has the chance now to try. I hope we'll be able to shake hands.

Acknowledgments

I have been lucky in life, and the fact that this book lives in the world is further evidence of my good fortune.

I met Matthew Hefti, who wrote a wonderful book and was kind enough to introduce me to his literary agent, Kate Johnson. Kate generously read the beginning of this work, which I penned as the pandemic wore on and my concerns for the future grew. That she saw something in those pages still feels amazing to me. Her gentle guidance through the process of refining my thinking about the book allowed me to develop the threads pulled together here.

I was lucky to work with two incredible editors at Bloomsbury. Ben Hyman, who advocated for this project, was my book doula, giving me the encouragement and support I needed to get the ideas out of my mind and into a form that could build connection between the reader and my clients. I wanted people to feel the cascade of emotions that I do as I carry out my work, and Ben saw it so clearly. He gave me confidence that I could succeed in doing justice to these stories and that the stories could make lasting change. Callie Garnett provided masterful edits of the manuscript. As a poet, she showed me how to make movement with my words.

Erin Fiaschetti, my original editor and support, who read every word of every draft, spent her weekends and evenings pushing me to think about how to do more and do better. There is nothing that I do without the counsel of Erin as my copartner at Advancing Real Change, and the same has held true here.

The J.M. Kaplan Fund and board member Quina Fonseca provided financial support without which I would not have been able to develop the book proposal. As in most things the J.M. Kaplan Fund has provided me, it is not just the financial support but also the psychological support of knowing that people believe in my vision for how to make society more just. I am grateful beyond words to Justin Goldbach for encouraging me to share the idea with the Fund and for his unwavering support and friendship.

Jill Patterson and Maurice Chammah, two writers who I trust dearly and admire enormously, reviewed the manuscript and provided thoughtful feedback. I thank Ethan Corey, who provided fact-checking and took great care to ensure the privacy of those in this book and the accuracy of the facts contained within.

My husband, Jonny Kerr, who shouldered the load at home with our two beautiful and energetic children, also carved out time to review the work. He is the most sensible and clear-minded person I know. I am a better person and this is a better book because of him.

To my clients, their loved ones, and my named and unnamed colleagues. Hope is what I carry. Thank you for adding to this mosaic.

And to my mother, father, and brother. For all the experiences that shaped me. This book would not exist without you.

Notes

FOREWORD

1. C. D. Wright, "Stripe for Stripe," preface to *One Big Self: An Investigation* (Copper Canyon Press, 2007).
2. Incarceration Transparency, https://www.incarcerationtransparency.org /louisiana/.
3. Deborah Luster, "The Reappearance of Those Who Have Gone," introduction to *One Big Self: Prisoners of Louisiana* (Twin Palms, 2003).
4. The photograph first appeared in Luster and Wright's collaboration *One Big Self*.
5. Elizabeth Bruenig, "Witness," *Atlantic*, July 2025.
6. Bruenig, "Witness."

INTRODUCTION

1. For the rise and easing of capital punishment in Texas, see Maurice Chammah, *Let the Lord Sort Them: The Rise and Fall of the Death Penalty* (Crown, 2021).
2. For a graphic of death sentences imposed throughout the country, with the peak being in the 1990s, see "History of the Death Penalty," Death Penalty Information Center, accessed June 12, 2025, https://deathpenaltyinfo.org/ facts-and-research/history-of-the-death-penalty. For specific information related to Texas, see statistics from the Texas Department of Criminal Justice: "Total Number of Inmates Sentenced to Death from Each County,"

Texas Department of Criminal Justice, updated May 7, 2024, https://www
.tdcj.texas.gov/death_row/dr_number_sentenced_death_county.html;
and "County of Conviction for Executed Inmates," Texas Department of
Criminal Justice, updated May 28, 2025, https://www.tdcj.texas.gov/death
_row/dr_county_conviction_executed.html. One Texas county (Harris)
has accounted for 298 death sentences and 135 executions since 1976. Texas
has executed the most people in the United States since 1976.

3. Juan A. Lozano, "US Carries Out 25 Executions This Year as Death Penalty
Trends in Nation Held Steady," Associated Press, December 19, 2024,
https://apnews.com/article/death-penalty-annual-report-historic-lows
-1bfe20e3c69da803f01ff63029028e64.

4. Russell Stetler, "*Lockett v. Ohio* and the Rise of Mitigation Specialists,"
ConLawNOW 10, no. 1 (2018): 51–63, https://ideaexchange.uakron
.edu/conlawnow/vol10/iss1/4/; and Russell Stetler, "The Past, Present,
and Future of the Mitigation Profession: Fulfilling the Constitutional
Requirement of Individualized Sentencing in Capital Cases," *Hofstra Law
Review* 46, no. 4 (2017): 1161–256, https://scholarlycommons.law.hofstra
.edu/hlr/vol46/iss4/5.

5. Mitigation specialists are now employed in many public defender offices
to assist in nonhomicide cases. Elizabeth S. Vartkessian et al., "When
Justice Depends on It: The Need for Professional Standards for Mitigation
Development in All Criminal Cases," *University of Baltimore Law Review*
52, no. 3 (2022): 449–88, https://scholarworks.law.ubalt.edu/ublr/vol52/
iss3/4.

6. Mikko Kautto and Kati Kuitto, "The Nordic Countries," in *The Oxford Handbook of the Welfare State*, ed. Daniel Béland et al., 2nd ed. (Oxford Handbooks,
2021), 803–25, https://doi.org/10.1093/oxfordhb/9780198828389.013.46.

7. "Estimates of Rates of Homicides per 100,000 Population," World
Health Organization Global Health Observatory, accessed June 12, 2025,
https://www.who.int/data/gho/data/indicators/indicator-details/GHO
/estimates-of-rates-of-homicides-per-100-000-population.

8. American Bar Association, "Guidelines for the Appointment and
Performance of Defense Counsel in Death Penalty Cases, Revised Edition,
February 2003," *Hofstra Law Review* 31, no. 4 (2003): 1022, https://scholarly

commons.law.hofstra.edu/hlr/vol31/iss4/2/. It is quoted in and references *Brown v. State*, 526 So. 2d 903, 908 (Fla. 1988), citing *Hitchcock v. Dugger*, 481 U.S. 393, 394 (1987). See also *Eddings v. Oklahoma*, 455 U.S. 104, 113–15 (1982), and *Lockett v. Ohio*, 438 U.S. 586, 604 (1978).

9. American Bar Association, "Guidelines for the Appointment and Performance of Defense Counsel in Death Penalty Cases," 1989, https:// www.americanbar.org/groups/committees/death_penalty_representation /resources/aba_guidelines/1989-guidelines/.

10. Stetler notes that the first official mention was the 1985 National Legal Aid & Defender Association Standards for the Appointment of Defense Counsel in Death Penalty Cases; these guidelines, in turn, formed the basis for the 1989 ABA guidelines, which applied nearly identical language to describe mitigation specialists. Stetler, "*Lockett v. Ohio.*"

11. American Bar Association, "Guidelines, February 2003."

12. It took another five years for standards specific to the expectations of the mitigation function to be published. "Supplementary Guidelines for the Mitigation Function of Defense Teams in Death Penalty Cases," *Hofstra Law Review* 36, no. 3 (2008): 677–92, https://scholarlycommons.law.hofstra .edu/hlr/vol36/iss3/.

13. American Bar Association, "Guidelines, February 2003," 959.

14. Todd C. Peppers and Margaret A. Anderson, *A Courageous Fool: Marie Deans and Her Struggle Against the Death Penalty* (Vanderbilt University Press, 2017).

15. David Von Drehle, *Amongst the Lowest of the Dead* (University of Michigan Press, 2006).

16. Maurice Chammah, "We Saw Monsters. She Saw Humans," Marshall Project, July 13, 2017, https://www.themarshallproject.org/2017/07/13 /we-saw-monsters-she-saw-humans.

17. As of 2024. Becky Feldman, "The Second Look Movement: A Review of the Nation's Sentence Review Laws," The Sentencing Project, March 24, 2025, https://www.sentencingproject.org/reports/the-second-look-movement -a-review-of-the-nations-sentence-review-laws/.

18. Mitigation is directly called for in federal cases after the decisions in *United States v. Booker*, 543 U.S. 220 (2005); all federal sentencing, which was

highly prescribed by formula, is now discretionary. See Amy Baron-Evans, "Sentencing by the Statute," Defender Services Office Training Division, April 27, 2009, revised December 21, 2010, https://www.fd.org/sites/default /files/criminal_defense_topics/essential_topics/sentencing_resources/ sentencing-by-the-statute.pdf. For calls to make mitigation a part of non-capital sentencing more broadly, see Miriam Gohara, "Grace Notes: A Case for Making Mitigation the Heart of Noncapital Sentencing," *American Journal of Criminal Law* 41 (2013), http://hdl.handle.net/20.500.13051/4732. Gohara argues for the expanded use of mitigation in criminal sentencing to encourage individualized punishment and for sentencing evidence to explore social factors that contribute to crime.

19. Reginald Dwayne Betts is the founder of Freedom Reads, a nonprofit that builds libraries inside prisons. To learn more about the work of the organization, visit https://freedomreads.org/.

CHAPTER ONE: THE LONG WAY AROUND

1. Houston was a particular hot spot for the use of wet, or fry, as it was commonly known. Edward was raised on the north side of the city, which corresponded to a concentrated-use area: "Dealers obtain embalming fluid from distributors on Houston's Near North Side, a working-class neighborhood populated mostly with African American and Hispanics." William N. Elwood, *"Fry": A Study of Adolescents' Use of Embalming Fluid with Marijuana and Tobacco* (Texas Commission on Alcohol and Drug Abuse, 1998), https://erowid.org/chemicals/pcp/pcp_info3.pdf.

2. Texas Penal Code Sec. 7.01, https://statutes.capitol.texas.gov/Docs/PE/htm /PE.7.htm.

3. Edward's trial attorney represented more than a dozen people who were sentenced to death. Michael Graczyk, "Houston Lawyer Labeled 'Worst Lawyer in the United States,'" *Houston Chronicle*, August 13, 2016, https:// www.chron.com/news/article/Texas-lawyer-who-lost-all-death-penalty -cases-9140712.php.

4. "Epigenetics and Child Development: How Children's Experiences Affect Their Genes," Harvard University Center on the Developing Child,

February 19, 2019, https://developingchild.harvard.edu/resources/what
-is-epigenetics-and-how-does-it-relate-to-child-development/.

5. "The Link Between Cortisol and PTSD (and How to Balance It)," PTSD
UK, accessed June 12, 2025, https://www.ptsduk.org/the-link-between
-cortisol-and-ptsd/.

6. Rachel Condry, *Families Shamed: The Consequences of Crime for Relatives
of Serious Offenders* (Willan, 2007).

7. Phenomenon noted in Bruce D. Perry and Maia Szalavitz, "Tina's World,"
chapter 1 in *The Boy Who Was Raised as a Dog: And Other Stories from a
Child Psychiatrist's Notebook—What Traumatized Children Can Teach Us
About Loss, Love, and Healing* (Basic Books, 2007), 7–30.

8. Barbara Maranzani, "Ernest Hemingway: How Mental Illness Plagued the
Writer and His Family," Biography.com, April 1, 2021, https://www.biogra-
phy.com/authors-writers/ernest-hemingway-mental-illness-family.

9. "Immigration Reform and Control Act (IRCA) (1986)," Immigration
History, accessed June 11, 2025, https://immigrationhistory.org/item
/1986-immigration-reform-and-control-act/.

10. At the time, Texas was a leader in providing victim services relative to
much of the country. See Alyssa Linares and Taylor D. Robinson, "The
History of Victim Rights and Services," Crime Victims' Institute Newsletter,
April 2024, https://dev.cjcenter.org/_files/cvi/The%20History%20of%20
Victim%20Rights%20and%20Services.pdf_1712759747.pdf. Even in
Texas, however, victim services programs were underfunded and only
supported a small fraction of crime victims. This remains true today.
The vast majority of crime victims do not receive services for which
they're eligible, which was even more common in the late 1980s, when
such support was in a relatively embryonic form. Ralph Chapoco, "Many
Crime Victims Unaware of Financial Assistance Available to Them,"
Alabama Reflector, June 10, 2025, https://alabamareflector.com/2025
/06/10/most-crime-victims-unaware-of-financial-assistance-available-to-
them/.

11. Research has shown that sexual assault cases involving victims of color are
often taken less seriously by law enforcement and the legal system. Cassia
Spohn and Jeffrey Spears, "The Effect of Offender and Victim Characteristics

on Sexual Assault Case Processing Decisions," *Justice Quarterly* 13, no. 4 (1996): 649–79, https://doi.org/10.1080/07418829600093141.

12. Traumatic brain injuries are common among domestic violence victims. Glynnis Zieman et al., "Traumatic Brain Injury in Domestic Violence Victims: A Retrospective Study at the Barrow Neurological Institute," *Journal of Neurotrauma* 34, no. 4 (2017), https://doi.org/10.1089/neu.2016.4579.

13. Emma Platoff, "Years After a Judge Ordered Fixes, Texas' Child Welfare System Continues to Expose Children to Harm, Federal Monitors Say," *Texas Tribune*, June 16, 2020, https://www.texastribune.org/2020/06/16 /texas-child-welfare-harm-federal-monitors/. I am reminded of the Netflix docuseries on Gabriel Fernandez. See Mahita Gajanan, "The Heartbreaking Story Behind Netflix's Documentary Series *The Trials of Gabriel Fernandez*," *Time*, February 26, 2020, https://time.com/5790549/ gabriel-fernandez-netflix-documentary/. If Fernandez had lived, he would have been at serious risk of being directly involved in the criminal legal system.

14. Dale L. Johnson and James N. Breckenridge, "The Houston Parent-Child Development Center and the Primary Prevention of Behavior Problems in Young Children," *American Journal of Community Psychology* 10, no. 3 (1982), https://www.uh.edu/~psycp2/PC_Behavior_Problems_82.htm. The main predecessor to Head Start was the Social Services Amendments Act of 1974, which provided matching funds for states that provided child care services. Social Services Amendments Act of 1974, Pub. L. No. 93-647, https://www.congress.gov/bill/93rd-congress/house-bill/17045 /text. Even today, federally funded childcare programs serve far fewer children than are eligible: Antoinette J. Waller et al., "Lack of Access to Child Care Subsidies Is a Barrier to Student-Parent Completion & Success," EdTrust, December 19, 2022, https://edtrust.org/blog/lack-of-access-to-child -care-subsidies-is-a-barrier-to-student-parent-completion-success/.

15. Texas was the first state to pass a so-called Baby Moses law, but that didn't happen until 1999, after Edward was an adult and already incarcerated. Even then, the law only applied to infants less than sixty days old. Otherwise, child abandonment is a state jail felony (and it was a third-degree felony at

the relevant period of Edward's life). Jaden Edison, "Texas Has a Law That Allows Parents to Give Up Newborns at Fire Stations or Hospitals. Hardly Anyone Uses It," *Texas Tribune*, June 26, 2022, https://www.texastribune .org/2022/06/26/texas-safe-haven-law/.

16. Joan A. Reid et al., "Contemporary Review of Empirical and Clinical Studies of Trauma Bonding in Violent or Exploitative Relationships," *International Journal of Psychology Research* 8, no. 1 (2013): 37–73, https:// digitalcommons.usf.edu/fac_publications/325/.

17. H. Stefan Bracha, "Freeze, Flight, Fight, Fright, Faint: Adaptationist Perspectives on the Acute Stress Response Spectrum," *CNS Spectrums* 9, no. 9 (2004): 679–85, https://doi.org/10.1017/s1092852900001954.

18. "The fact that decades of increased investments in criminal justice have been justified in service of protecting victims of crime, when most crime victims haven't seen the justice system offer any real protection or help, is perhaps the most sinister aspect and irony of mass incarceration." Lenore Anderson, *In Their Names: The Untold Story of Victims' Rights, Mass Incarceration, and the Future of Public Safety* (New Press, 2022).

CHAPTER TWO: CONDUCT

1. Leah Roemer, " 'I Just Wanted . . . to Stay Alive': Who Was William Henry Furman, the Prisoner at the Center of a Historic Legal Decision?" Death Penalty Information Center, May 15, 2024, https://deathpenaltyinfo.org/i -just-wanted-to-stay-alive-who-was-william-henry-furman-the-prisoner -at-the-center-of-a-historic-legal-decision.

2. Elmer H. Johnson, "Selective Factors in Capital Punishment," *Social Forces* 36, no. 2 (1957): 165–69, https://doi.org/10.2307/2573854.

3. *Woodson v. North Carolina*, 428 U.S. 303–5 (1976), https://supreme.justia .com/cases/federal/us/428/280/#303.

4. *Lockett v. Ohio*, 438 U.S. 586 (1978), https://supreme.justia.com/cases /federal/us/438/586/.

5. *Eddings v. Oklahoma*, 455 U.S. 104 (1982), https://supreme.justia.com/cases /federal/us/455/104/; *Skipper v. South Carolina*, 476 U.S. 1 (1986), https://

supreme.justia.com/cases/federal/us/476/1/; *Penry v. Lynaugh*, 492 U.S. 302 (1989), https://supreme.justia.com/cases/federal/us/492/302/.

6. *Barefoot v. Estelle*, 463 U.S. 880 (1983), https://supreme.justia.com/cases /federal/us/463/880/; *Payne v. Tennessee*, 501 U.S. 808 (1991), https:// supreme.justia.com/cases/federal/us/501/808/.

7. Linda Greenhouse, "Death Penalty Is Renounced by Blackmun," *New York Times*, February 23, 1994, https://www.nytimes.com/1994/02/23/us/death -penalty-is-renounced-by-blackmun.html.

8. There is no right to counsel for postconviction proceedings. "Law Regarding Capital Representation," Death Penalty Information Center, accessed June 12, 2025, https://deathpenaltyinfo.org/policy-issues/policy /death-penalty-representation/law-regarding-capital-representation.

9. Most cases are filed in state courts, eleven to thirteen million each year, compared with fewer than one hundred thousand federal criminal prosecutions. The system is overwhelmed. "Data for Court Professionals," National Center for State Courts, accessed June 12, 2025, https://www.ncsc.org/resources- courts/data; "Federal Judicial Caseload Statistics 2024," U.S. Courts, accessed June 12, 2025, https://www.uscourts.gov/data-news/reports/statistical-reports /federal-judicial-caseload-statistics/federal-judicial-caseload-statistics-2024.

10. Mark D. Cunningham and Mark P. Vigen, "Death Row Inmate Characteristics, Adjustment, and Confinement: A Critical Review of the Literature," *Behavioral Sciences & the Law* 20, nos. 1–2 (2002): 191–210.

11. Elliot C. Nelson et al., "Association Between Self-Reported Childhood Sexual Abuse and Adverse Psychosocial Outcomes: Results from a Twin Study," *JAMA Psychiatry* 59, no. 2 (2002), https://doi.org/10.1001/archpsyc .59.2.139. Childhood sexual abuse is associated with increased risk for many adverse life outcomes.

12. Massachusetts Legislative Task Force on Child Sexual Abuse Prevention, *Guidelines and Tools for the Development of Child Sexual Abuse Prevention and Intervention Plans by Youth-Serving Organizations in Massachusetts* (Massachusetts State Legislature and the Children's Trust, 2017, updated 2020), https://safekidsthrive.org/the-report/introduction/; and Ateret Gewirtz-Meydan and David Finkelhor, "Sexual Abuse and Assault in a

Large National Sample of Children and Adolescents," *Child Maltreatment* 25, no. 2 (2019): 203–14, https://www.unh.edu/ccrc/sites/default/files /media/2022-03/sexual-abuse-and-assault-in-a-large-national-sample-of -children-and-adolescents.pdf. Police reports corroborated the abuse of 19.1 percent of interviewed children.

13. This is the definition given by the American Psychiatric Association in the *Diagnostic and Statistical Manual* (*DSM-5-TR*).

14. "Just Say No," History, updated May 28, 2025, https://www.history.com /articles/just-say-no.

15. Straight was renamed Drug Free America and continues to operate in the United States. A massive collection of stories from the children who survived the experience can be found on various websites, in media sources, and in published books. Surviving Straight Inc., accessed June 12, 2025, https://survivingstraightinc.com/.

16. Alfred S. Friedman et al., "Outcome of a Unique Youth Drug Abuse Program: A Follow-up Study of Clients of Straight, Inc.," *Journal of Substance Abuse Treatment* 6, no. 4 (1989): 259–68, https://www.jsatjournal. com/article/0740-5472(89)90051-2/pdf.

17. "Veterans' Diseases Associated with Agent Orange," U.S. Department of Veterans' Affairs, accessed June 12, 2025, https://www.publichealth.va.gov /exposures/agentorange/conditions/.

18. Matt Shea, "Teens Are Being Trapped in Abusive 'Drug Rehab Centers,'" *Vice*, May 22, 2013, https://www.vice.com/en/article/thousands-of-american -teens-are-trapped-in-abusive-cult-like-treatment-centres/; and Nora Ashleigh Barrie, "Closure: Outback Therapeutic Expeditions," Surviving the Troubled Teen Industry, May 4, 2023, https://thetroubledteenindustry .com/investigation-program-closures-outback-therapeutic-expeditions.

19. Maia Szalavitz, *Help at Any Cost: How the Troubled-Teen Industry Cons Parents and Hurts Kids* (Riverhead Books, 2006).

20. *The Last Stop*, written and directed by Todd Nilssen (2017), https://www .imdb.com/title/tt6508926/.

21. "The Troubled Teen Industry," Unsilenced Project, accessed July 28, 2025, https://www.unsilenced.org/the-industry/.

CHAPTER THREE: HIGH-RISE

1. This was essentially the same legal error in Connor's case. Both courts found each of the men's trial attorneys to have provided ineffective assistance of counsel during the punishment phase of the trial.

2. Teenage incontinence is a red flag of trauma. Naomi Warne et al., "Mental Health Problems, Stressful Life Events and New-Onset Urinary Incontinence in Primary School-Age Children: A Prospective Cohort Study," *European Child and Adolescent Psychiatry* 33, no. 3 (2024): 871–9, https://doi.org/10.1007/s00787-023-02211-x.

3. The building of expressways after World War II was both an act of "development" and often intentionally cut through Black neighborhoods as a means of busting up slums rather than addressing the conditions that made the areas hard to inhabit. "One of the most influential post-World War II urban planners," writes Farrell Evans, "was New York City's 'construction coordinator' Robert Moses, who oversaw all public works projects in the nation's largest metropolis, including an astonishing array of its roadways, bridges, tunnels, housing projects and parks. Not only was Moses arguably the most powerful unelected official in the state's history, but his influence on federal highway policy extended well beyond New York. He was a leading proponent of the idea that the best way to eradicate the supposed slums where Black people lived was to build highways through them." Evans, "How Interstate Highways Gutted Communities—and Reinforced Segregation," History, October 20, 2021, https://www.history.com/news/interstate-highway-system-infrastructure-construction-segregation.

4. Sebastian Haumann, "Crosstown Expressway," Encyclopedia of Greater Pennsylvania, 2015, https://philadelphiaencyclopedia.org/essays/crosstown-expressway/; "Crosstown Expressway (Unbuilt)," Philly Roads, accessed June 12, 2025, http://www.phillyroads.com/roads/crosstown/.

5. Jane Stevens, "The Adverse Childhood Experiences Study—the Largest, Most Important Public Health Study You Never Heard of—Began in an Obesity Clinic," ACEs Too High, October 3, 2012, https://acestoohigh.com/2012/10/03/the-adverse-childhood-experiences-study-the-largest-most-important-public-health-study-you-never-heard-of-began-in-an-obesity-clinic/.

6. Stevens, "Adverse Childhood Experiences."

7. V. J. Felitti et al., "Relationship of Childhood Abuse and Household Dysfunction to Many of the Leading Causes of Death in Adults: The Adverse Childhood Experiences (ACE) Study," *American Journal of Preventive Medicine* 14, no. 4 (1998): 245–58, https://doi.org/10.1016/s0749-3797(98)00017-8.

8. "About the CDC-Kaiser ACE Study," CDC, accessed June 12, 2025, https://www.cdc.gov/violenceprevention/aces/about.html.

9. Nadine Burke Harris, *The Deepest Well: Healing the Long-Term Effects of Childhood Adversity* (Houghton Mifflin, 2018).

10. Charles L. Whitfield et al., "Adverse Childhood Experiences and Hallucinations," *Child Abuse & Neglect* 29, no. 7 (2005): 797–810, https://doi.org/10.1016/j.chiabu.2005.01.004.

11. David Lisak and Sara Beszterczey, "The Cycle of Violence: The Life Histories of 43 Death Row Inmates," *Psychology of Men & Masculinity* 8, no. 2 (2007): 118–28, https://doi.org/10.1037/1524-9220.8.2.118. The findings of self-reports included all participants reporting being neglected as children, 95 percent being physically abused, 59 percent being sexually abused, and 84 percent having witnessed violence.

12. "Martin Luther King Plaza Hope VI," MDesigns, accessed June 12, 2025, https://mdesigns.consulting/portfolio_project/martin-luther-king-plaza-hopevi/.

13. Angela Taurino, "Little Park, Long View," Hidden City, February 1, 2012, https://hiddencityphila.org/2012/02/little-park-long-view/.

14. A high concentration of poverty exacerbated by the physical and social isolation of the plaza from the rest of the neighborhood led to it becoming, in the 1980s and 1990s, one of Philadelphia's most crime-ridden areas. Elijah Anderson, *Code of the Street: Decency, Violence, and the Moral Life of the Inner City* (Norton, 1999).

15. *The Final Report of the National Commission on Severely Distressed Public Housing* (National Commission on Severely Distressed Public Housing, 1992), https://www.huduser.gov/portal//portal/sites/default/files/pdf/The-Final-Report-of-the-National-Commission-on-Severely-Distressed-Public-Housing-.pdf.

16. Philadelphia Home Owners' Loan Corporation, "Area Description," February 3, 1937, https://upload.wikimedia.org/wikipedia/commons/d /d4/Philadelphia_HOLC_Redlining_Zone_Descriptions%2C_1937.pdf. The tract is D-18. "Philadelphia, Area D-18," Mapping Inequality, accessed June 12, 2025, https://dsl.richmond.edu/panorama/redlining/map/PA /Philadelphia/area_descriptions/D18#loc=15/39.938/-75.1851&adview=full.

17. Taurino, "Little Park, Long View."

18. This is the number reported by the FBI, which relies on self-reports from local law enforcement agencies. In 2023, about 94 percent of agencies throughout the United States submitted data, so this is likely lower than the actual number. Likewise, the quoted number includes murders and nonnegligent homicides, many of which would not necessarily qualify for a capital prosecution, slightly overrepresenting the potential number of homicides that would allow for a capital prosecution. "FBI Releases 2023 Crime in the Nation Statistics," Federal Bureau of Investigation, September 23, 2024, https://www.fbi.gov/news/press -releases/fbi-releases-2023-crime-in-the-nation-statistics.

19. *The Death Penalty in 2023: Year End Report* (Death Penalty Information Center, 2023), https://deathpenaltyinfo.org/research/analysis/reports/year -end-reports/the-death-penalty-in-2023-year-end-report.

20. *Death Penalty in 2023*.

21. Keri Blakinger and Maurice Chammah, "They Went to Prison as Kids. Now They're on Death Row," Marshall Project, February 1, 2022, https:// www.themarshallproject.org/2022/02/01/they-went-to-prison-as-kids -now-they-re-on-death-row; and Alex Hannaford, "Letters from Death Row: The Biology of Trauma," *Texas Observer*, June 22, 2015, https://www .texasobserver.org/letters-from-death-row-childhood-trauma/.

22. Andrew Kenney, "The Three Men Polis Spared from Death," March 23, 2020, Colorado Public Radio, https://www.cpr.org/2020/03/23/the -three-men-polis-spared-from-death/.

23. Tracy L. Snell, *Capital Punishment, 2012—Statistical Tables* (Bureau of Justice Statistics, 2014), https://bjs.ojp.gov/content/pub/pdf/cp12st.pdf.

24. "In the community of Holocaust concentration camp survivors in Antwerp Belgium where I grew up, there were two groups: those who didn't die,

and those who came back to life. And those who didn't die were people who lived tethered to the ground, afraid, untrusting. The world was dangerous, and pleasure was not an option. You cannot play, take risks, or be creative when you don't have a minimum of safety, because you need a level of unself-consciousness to be able to experience excitement and pleasure." Esther Perel, "Esther Perel on Mating in Captivity," interview by Lori Schwanbeck, Psychotherapy.net, 2012, https://www.psychotherapy.net /interview/couples/esther-perel-mating-captivity.

25. Layla A. Jones, "Homicides Dropped After Philly Gangs Signed a 1974 Peace Pact. What Can We Learn from the Org That Brokered the Truce?" *Philadelphia Tribune*, December 14, 2020, https://www.phillytrib.com /homicides-dropped-after-philly-gangs-signed-a-1974-peace-pact-what -can-we-learn-from/article_fbd72433-4b7a-569a-847e-ba9276cecfc5.html.

26. "Anosognosia," Cleveland Clinic, accessed June 12, 2025, https://my .clevelandclinic.org/health/diseases/22832-anosognosia.

27. Stephanie V. Phan, "Medication Adherence in Patients with Schizophrenia," *International Journal of Psychiatry Medicine* 51, no. 2 (2016): 211–19, https:// doi.org/10.1177/0091217416636601.

28. "From Restrictive Covenants to Racial Steering: A Special Exhibit on the Fight for Fair Housing in Washington, D.C.," Mapping Segregation in Washington D.C., accessed June 12, 2025, https://mappingsegregationdc.org/.

29. David Alpert, "Where DC Used to Bar Black People from Living," Greater Greater Washington, May 5, 2016, https://ggwash.org/view/41615 /where-dc-used-to-bar-black-people-from-living; and Sarah Shoenfeld, "The History and Evolution of Anacostia's Barry Farm," D.C. Policy Center, July 9, 2019, https://www.dcpolicycenter.org/publications/barry -farm-anacostia-history/.

30. Humanities Council of Washington, *Kenilworth: A DC Neighborhood by the Anacostia River* (Humanities Council of Washington, D.C., 2006), 21–22, https://planning.dc.gov/sites/default/files/dc/sites/op/publication /attachments/Kenilworth_Brochure.pdf.

31. Environmental Protection Agency, *Burn, Bury or What? Filmscripts on Solid Waste Management* (Environmental Protection Agency, 1972), 1, https://nepis.epa.gov/Exe/ZyPURL.cgi?Dockey=910210VL.TXT.

32. Humanities Council of Washington, *Kenilworth*, 21–22.
33. Justin Lini, "The Feds Made Kenilworth Park a Toxic Waste Site. Muriel Bowser Wants to Clean It Up," Greater Greater Washington, April 12, 2017, https://ggwash.org/view/63046/the-feds-made-kenilworth-park-a-toxic -waste-site-muriel-bowser-wants-to-clean-.
34. Paul Duggan, "After 35 Years, a Lawsuit over 'Inhumane' Juvenile Detention in D.C. Has Led to Major Reforms," *Washington Post*, February 17, 2020, https://www.washingtonpost.com/local/public-safety/after-35-years-a -lawsuit-over-inhumane-juvenile-detention-in-dc-has-led-to-major -reforms/2020/02/17/1eea122c-4d89-11ea-bf44-f5043eb3918a_story.html.
35. Greg Allen, "Florida's Dozier School for Boys: A True Horror Story," NPR, October 15, 2012, https://www.npr.org/2012/10/15/162941770/floridas -dozier-school-for-boys-a-true-horror-story.
36. News Service of Florida, "Florida Inmate Cites Dozier Abuse as He Argues to Vacate His Death Sentence," *Tampa Bay Tribune*, August 7, 2024, https://www.tampabay.com/news/crime/2024/08/07/florida-inmate-cites -dozier-abuse-he-argues-vacate-his-death-sentence/. There are 270 people on Florida's death row: "Death Row Roster," Florida Department of Corrections, accessed June 12, 2024, https://pubapps.fdc.myflorida.com /OffenderSearch/deathrowroster.aspx.
37. Ashley Nellis and Celeste Barry, "A Matter of Life: The Scope and Impact of Life and Long Term Imprisonment in the United States," Sentencing Project, January 8, 2025, https://www.sentencingproject.org /reports/a-matter-of-life-the-scope-and-impact-of-life-and-long-term -imprisonment-in-the-united-states/.
38. Marc Mauer, "Long-Term Sentences: Time to Reconsider the Scale of Punishment," *UMKC Law Review* 87, no. 1 (2022): 113–31, https://www .sentencingproject.org/app/uploads/2022/08/UMKC-Law-Review-Scale -of-Punishment.pdf.
39. Shawn D. Bushway, "Incapacitation," *Reforming Criminal Justice* 4, ed. Erik Luna (Academy for Justice, 2017), https://law.asu.edu/sites/default /files/pdf/academy_for_justice/3_Criminal_Justice_Reform_Vol_4 _Incapacitation.pdf.

40. Dana Goldstein, "Too Old to Commit Crime?" Marshall Project, March 20, 2015, https://www.themarshallproject.org/2015/03/20/too-old-to-commit-crime.

41. Laura Bennett, "Deterrence and Incapacitation: A Quick Review of the Research," Center for Just Journalism, accessed June 12, 2025, https://justjournalism.org/page/deterrence-and-incapacitation-a-quick-review-of-the-research.

CHAPTER FOUR: DEATH QUALIFICATION

1. "Lua," by Bright Eyes, track 4 on *I'm Wide Awake, It's Morning*, Saddle Creek Records, released January 25, 2005, https://www.youtube.com/watch?v=TSBs-hiapo4.

2. "About Us," Treatment Advocacy Center, accessed June 12, 2025, https://www.tac.org/about-tac/.

3. "Serious Mental Illness Prevalence in Jails and Prisons," Treatment Advocacy Center, September 2016, https://www.tac.org/reports_publications/serious-mental-illness-prevalence-in-jails-and-prisons/.

4. Jennifer Bronson and Marcus Berzofsky, *Indicators of Mental Health Problems Reported by Prisoners and Jail Inmates, 2011–12* (Bureau of Justice Statistics, 2017), https://bjs.ojp.gov/content/pub/pdf/imhprpji1112.pdf.

5. "Studies: 21st-Century Executions Disproportionately Involve Defendants with Mental Illness," Death Penalty Information Center, April 3, 2017, updated March 14, 2025, https://deathpenaltyinfo.org/studies-21st-century-executions-disproportionately-involve-defendants-with-mental-illness. The studies included a small sample size (which reflects the relatively small number of people sentenced to death), though some found rates as high as 88 percent for PTSD. Mark D. Cunningham, "Death Row Inmate Characteristics, Adjustment, and Confinement: A Critical Review of the Literature," *Behavioral Sciences & the Law* 20, nos. 1–2 (2002): 191–210, https://doi.org/10.1002/bsl.473.

6. Charlotte Humphrey et al., "Childhood Interpersonal Trauma and Paranoia in Psychosis: The Role of Disorganised Attachment and Negative Schema," *Schizophrenia Research* 241 (2022): 142–8, https://doi.org/10.1016/j.schres.2022.01.043.

7. Scharlette Holdman, who was largely credited with starting mitigation, died at the age of seventy. David von Drehle, "Remembering America's 'Angel of Death Row,' " *Time*, July 14, 2017, https://time.com/4858368/death-row -angel-scharlette-holdman/. Life expectancy for women was eighty-one years in 2017 when she died. Elizabeth Arias and Jiaquan Xu, *United States Life Tables, 2017* (Centers for Disease Control, 2017), https://stacks.cdc.gov /view/cdc/79487.

8. Janet Foster, "The Emotional Impact of Homicide Investigation," in *The Routledge International Handbook of Homicide Investigation*, ed. Cheryl Allsop and Sophie Pike (Routledge, 2023), https://doi .org/10.4324/9781003195283-30.

9. Charles M. Balch et al., "Stress and Burnout Among Surgeons: Understanding and Managing the Syndrome and Avoiding the Adverse Consequences," *JAMA Surgery* 144, no. 4 (2009): 371–76, https://doi.org/10.1001/archsurg.2008.575.

10. Joe Sexton, "The Hardest Case for Mercy," Marshall Project, September 17, 2024, https://www.themarshallproject.org/2024/09/17/school-shooting -death-penalty-parkland-nikolas-cruz; Susannah Sheffer, *Fighting for Their Lives: Inside the Experience of Capital Defense Attorneys* (Vanderbilt University Press, 2013); and David R. Lynch, "The Nature of Occupational Stress Among Public Defenders," *Justice System Journal* 19, no. 1 (2014): 17–35, https://doi.org/10.1080/23277556.1997.10871248.

11. Franklin E. Zimring et al., *Punishment and Democracy: Three Strikes and You're Out in California* (Oxford Academic, 2003). The original three-strikes law in California mandated twenty-five-to-life sentences, and laws in other states prescribed a variety of punishments (and also differed in terms of which offenses counted as "strikes"): John Clark et al., " 'Three Strikes and You're Out': A Review of State Legislation," *National Institute of Justice Research in Brief*, September 1997, https://www.ojp.gov/pdffiles/165369.pdf.

12. William J. Bowers and Wanda D. Foglia, "Still Singularly Agonizing: Law's Failure to Purge Arbitrariness from Capital Sentencing," *Criminal Law Bulletin* 39, no. 1 (2003): 51–86.

13. Wanda D. Foglia, "They Know Not What They Do: Unguided and Misguided Discretion in Pennsylvania Capital Cases," *Justice Quarterly* 20, no. 1 (2003): 187–211, https://doi.org/10.1080/07418820300095501.

14. 1 Texas Code of Criminal Procedure Article 37.07, Section 3(a)(1), https://statutes.capitol.texas.gov/docs/CR/htm/CR.37.htm.

15. Ronald C. Dillehay and Marla R. Sandys, "Life Under *Wainwright v. Witt*: Juror Dispositions and Death Qualification," *Law and Human Behavior* 20, no. 2 (1996): 147–65, http://links.jstor.org/sici?sici=0147-7307%28199604%2920%3A2%3C147%3ALUWVWJ%3E2.0.CO%3B2-V.

16. Claudia L. Cowan et al., "The Effects of Death Qualification on Jurors' Predisposition to Convict and on the Quality of Deliberation," *Law and Human Behavior* 8, nos. 1–2 (1984): 53–79, https://doi.org/10.1007/BF01044351.

17. Robert Fitzgerald and Phoebe C. Ellsworth, "Due Process vs. Crime Control: Death Qualification and Jury Attitudes," *Law and Human Behavior* 8, nos. 1–2 (1984): 31–51, https://doi.org/10.1007/BF01044350.

18. Phoebe C. Ellsworth et al., "The Death-Qualified Jury and the Defense of Insanity," *Law and Human Behavior* 8, nos. 1–2 (1984): 81–93, https://doi.org/10.1007/BF01044352.

19. Logan A. Yelderman et al., "Capital-izing Jurors: How Death Qualification Relates to Jury Composition, Jurors' Perceptions, and Trial Outcomes," in *Advances in Psychology and Law*, vol. 2, ed. Brian H. Bornstein and Monica K. Miller (Springer, 2016), https://doi.org/10.1007/978-3-319-43083-6_2.

20. William J. Bowers, "The Capital Jury: Is It Tilted Toward Death?" *Judicature* 79, no. 5 (1995): 220–24, https://heinonline.org/HOL/LandingPage?handle=hein.journals/judica79&div=63.

21. William J. Bowers, "The Capital Jury Project: Rationale, Design, and Preview of Early Findings," *Indiana Law Journal* 70, no. 4 (1994): 1043–1102, https://ilj.law.indiana.edu/articles/70/70_4_Bowers.pdf.

22. Elizabeth Vartkessian, "Fatal Distraction: Does the Texas Capital Sentencing Statute Discourage the Consideration of Mitigating Evidence?" (PhD diss., University of Oxford, 2011).

23. Amir A. Gilmore and Pamela J. Bettis, "Antiblackness and the Adultification of Black Children in a US Prison Nation," in *Oxford Research Encyclopedia of Education*, March 25, 2021, https://doi.org/10.1093/acrefore/9780190264093.013.1293.

CHAPTER FIVE: CRUELTY

1. "The 'Arkansas Eight' Update: Three Stays Remain in Place, One Granted Clemency," American Bar Association, December 1, 2017, https://www.americanbar.org/groups/committees/death_penalty_representation/project_press/2017/year-end/the-arkansas-eight-update-three-stays-remain-in-place/.

2. Lee Kovarsky, "The American Execution Queue," *Stanford Law Review* 71 (2019): 1163–1228, https://review.law.stanford.edu/wp-content/uploads/sites/3/2019/05/Kovarsky-71-Stan.-L.-Rev.-1163-2019.pdf.

3. Describing the three executions, which took place in rapid succession, Associated Press, "Arkansas Executes 3 Killers in 1 Night," *Deseret News*, January 9, 1997, https://www.deseret.com/1997/1/9/19288390/arkansas-executes-3-killers-in-1-night/.

4. Justin McCarthy, "New Low of 49% in U.S. Say Death Penalty Applied Fairly," Gallup, October 22, 2018, https://news.gallup.com/poll/243794/new-low-say-death-penalty-applied-fairly.aspx.

5. Ed Pilkington, "Europe Moves to Block Trade in Medical Drugs Used in US Executions," *Guardian*, December 20, 2011, https://www.theguardian.com/world/2011/dec/20/death-penalty-drugs-european-commission; and Manny Fernandez, "Executions Stall as States Seek Different Drugs," *New York Times*, November 8, 2013, https://www.nytimes.com/2013/11/09/us/executions-stall-as-states-seek-different-drugs.html.

6. Lincoln Caplan, "The End of the Open Market for Lethal-Injection Drugs," *New Yorker*, May 21, 2016, https://www.newyorker.com/news/news-desk/the-end-of-the-open-market-for-lethal-injection-drugs.

7. Oklahoma was the first state to adopt lethal injection as a method of execution in 1977, but Texas was the first state to carry it out, in 1982, with the execution of Charles Brooks. "Execution Method Descriptions," Death Penalty Information Center, accessed June 12, 2025, https://deathpenaltyinfo.org/executions/methods-of-execution/description-of-each-method.

8. This includes U.S.-based companies like Pfizer, which banned the use of its drugs in execution in 2016. Erik Eckholm, "Pfizer Blocks the Use of Its Drugs in Executions," *New York Times*, May 14, 2016, https://www.nytimes.com/2016/05/14/us/pfizer-execution-drugs-lethal-injection.html.

9. "Compounding and the FDA: Questions and Answers," Food and Drug Administration, accessed June 12, 2025, https://www.fda.gov/drugs/human -drug-compounding/compounding-and-fda-questions-and-answers.

10. The protocols could have changed to use other drugs, or lawmakers could have sought other methods, like firing squad or gas, as other states have recently. These state actors simply did not want to wait and get it done in more lawful or safe ways. *Hearings on H. 658—A Bill Exempting from Disclosure Information Relating to Executions*, 66th Idaho Legislature (2022) (testimony of Robert B. Dunham, executive director of the Death Penalty Information Center), https://legislature.idaho.gov/wp-content/uploads /sessioninfo/2022/standingcommittees/220309_sj&r_0130PM-Minutes _Attachment_1.pdf.

11. Andrew Hosken, "Lethal Injection Drug Sold from UK Driving School," BBC News, January 6, 2011, http://news.bbc.co.uk/today/hi/today/newsid _9342000/9342976.stm. According to the Death Penalty Information Center, Arizona used the drugs to kill Jeffrey Landrigan and Eric King. Arizona planned to use them for the execution of Donald Beaty as well but swapped it out at the last moment after the U.S. Department of Justice complained that the state had illegally obtained the drugs. "Lethal Injection: Justice Dept. Orders Arizona Not to Use Imported Drug, Staying Execution," Death Penalty Information Center, May 25, 2011, https://deathpenaltyinfo.org /lethal-injection-justice-dept-orders-arizona-not-to-use-imported-drug -staying-execution. See also "DOJ Tells Arizona It Illegally Obtained Death Penalty Drug," ABC News, May 24, 2011, https://abcnews.go.com/Politics /doj-tells-arizona-illegally-obtained-death-penalty-drug/story?id=13679827.

12. Kevin Fixler, "Cash Buys, Private Flights, Changing Rules: How Idaho Hides from Execution Oversight," *Idaho Statesman*, January 19, 2022, https:// www.idahostatesman.com/news/local/crime/article257310422.html.

13. Gregg Zoroya, "Death Penalty Spurs Wild West Scramble for Drugs," *USA Today*, March 9, 2014, https://www.usatoday.com/story/news/nation/2014 /03/09/executions-lethal-injection-drugs-prisons-death-penalty/5866947/.

14. Anna Meisel and Melanie Stewart-Smith, "Death Row: The Secret Hunt for Lethal Drugs Used in US Executions," BBC News, October 21, 2023, https:// www.bbc.com/news/world-us-canada-67150566.

15. Matthew C. Bergs, "Execution by . . . Heroin?: Why States Should Challenge the FDA's Ban on the Importation of Sodium Thiopental," *Iowa Law Review* 102, no. 2 (2017): 761–91, https://ilr.law.uiowa.edu/sites/ilr.law.uiowa.edu /files/2023-02/ILR-102-2-Bergs-updated.pdf.

16. Jeffrey E. Stern, "The Cruel and Unusual Execution of Clayton Lockett," *Atlantic*, June 2015, https://www.theatlantic.com/magazine/archive /2015/06/execution-clayton-lockett/392069/.

17. "Procedures for the Execution of Offenders Sentenced to Death," Oklahoma Department of Corrections, effective April 14, 2014, https://graphics8 .nytimes.com/packages/pdf/20140421_OK_protocol-4-14-14.pdf.

18. Katie Fretland, "Oklahoma plans to use untested three-drug combination in two executions," *Guardian*, April 1, 2014, https://www.theguardian.com /world/2014/apr/01/oklahoma-execution-untested-drug-combination- death-row; and Stern, "The Cruel and Unusual Execution of Clayton Lockett."

19. Corinna Barrett Lain, *Secrets of the Killing State: The Untold Story of Lethal Injection* (New York University Press, 2025), 11–2.

20. Lain, *Secrets of the Killing State*, 24.

21. Dakin Andone, "Arkansas Plans to Execute 8 Men over 11 Days," CNN, March 3, 2017, https://edition.cnn.com/2017/03/02/health/arkansas-eight -executions/; and " 'Arkansas Eight' Update," American Bar Association.

22. More than a dozen states require "ordinary" or "respectable" citizen witnesses. And Arkansas requires six. Candace Rondeaux, "Witnessing Execution a Matter of Duty, Choice," NBC News, December 10, 2006, https:// www.nbcnews.com/id/wbna16131655; and Patrik Jonsson, "Witnesses to Execution Test a 'Somber' Civic Duty," *Christian Science Monitor*, April 24, 2017, https://www.csmonitor.com/USA/Justice/2017/0424 /Witnesses-to-execution-test-a-somber-civic-duty.

23. For instance, North Carolina's execution protocol emphasizes the importance of rehearsals: "The purpose of each rehearsal is to ensure that each Execution Team Member is proficient in carrying out the role to which they have been assigned, in understanding the roles of each other Execution Team Member, and in describing the interaction between the role to which they have been assigned and the roles of each

other Execution Team Member." See "Execution Procedure Manual for Single Drug Protocol (Pentobarbital)," North Carolina Department of Public Safety, October 24, 2013, https://www.dac.nc.gov/documents/files /execution-procedure-manual-single-drug-protocol-pentobarbital.

24. Rebecca Boone, "Idaho Halts Execution by Lethal Injection After 8 Failed Attempts to Insert IV Line," Associated Press, February 28, 2024, https:// apnews.com/article/idaho-execution-creech-murders-serial-killer-91a12d 78e9301adde77e6076dbd01dbb.

25. Alexander H. Updegrove and Michael S. Vaughn, "Evaluating Competency for Execution After *Madison v. Alabama*," *Journal of the American Academy of Psychiatry and the Law* 53, no. 2 (2025), https://doi.org/10.29158 /JAAPL.200003-20; *Ford v. Wainwright*, 477 U.S. 399 (1986), https://supreme .justia.com/cases/federal/us/477/399/.

26. Author's analysis of data from "Death Penalty Census," Death Penalty Information Center, accessed June 12, 2025, https://deathpenaltyinfo.org /facts-and-research/data/death-penalty-census.

27. Author's analysis of data from "Death Penalty Census," Death Penalty Information Center.

28. Author's analysis of "Death Penalty Census," Death Penalty Information Center; see also James S. Liebman et al., *A Broken System: Error Rates in Capital Cases, 1973–1995*, Columbia Law School, Public Law Research Paper no. 15 (2000), https://www.columbia.edu/cu/pr/00/06/lawStudy.html.

29. "O'Connor Questions Death Penalty," CBS News, July 3, 2001, https://www .cbsnews.com/news/oconnor-questions-death-penalty/.

30. "Justice Backs Death Penalty Freeze," CBS News, April 10, 2001, https:// www.cbsnews.com/news/justice-backs-death-penalty-freeze/.

31. *Lee v. State*, CR99-1116, February 22, 2001, https://case-law.vlex.com/vid /lee-v-state-99-887277668.

32. Bernadette Rabuy and Daniel Kopf, "Prisons of Poverty: Uncovering the Pre-Incarceration Incomes of the Imprisoned," Prison Policy Initiative, July 9, 2015, https://www.prisonpolicy.org/reports/income.html; "Not only are the median incomes of incarcerated people prior to incarceration lower than non-incarcerated people, but incarcerated people are dramatically concentrated at the lowest ends of the national income distribution";

most people charged with a crime are likely to be represented by public defenders, Caroline Wolf Harlow, *Defense Counsel in Criminal Cases* (Bureau of Justice Statistics, 2000), https://bjs.ojp.gov/content/pub/pdf /dccc.pdf.

33. "ACLU Praises Supreme Court Refusal of 'Sleeping Lawyer' Case as 'Acknowledgment and Reminder' of Death Penalty Problems," American Civil Liberties Union, June 3, 2002, https://www.aclu.org/press-releases/aclu -praises-supreme-court-refusal-sleeping-lawyer-case-acknowledgment-and -reminder.

34. "Ledell Lee: What You Should Know About His Case and Execution," Innocence Project, January 23, 2020, https://innocenceproject.org/news /ledell-lee-what-you-should-know-about-his-case-and-execution/.

35. "Executive Clemency," Arkansas Department of Corrections, accessed June 12, 2025, https://doc.arkansas.gov/post-prison-transfer-board /executive-clemency/.

36. Leona D. Jochnowitz and Tonya Kendall, "Analyzing Wrongful Convictions Beyond the Traditional Canonical List of Errors, for Enduring Structural and Sociological Attributes (Juveniles, Racism, Adversary System, Policing Policies)," *Touro Law Review* 37, no. 2 (2021): 579–663, https://digitalcommons.tourolaw.edu/cgi/viewcontent.cgi?params=/ context/lawreview/article/3313/&path_info=Jochnowitz_Kendall__ FORMATTED.pdf.

37. "You'll never hear another sound like a mother wailing whenever she is watching her son be executed. There's no other sound like it. It is just this horrendous wail. You can't get away from it. That wail surrounds the room. It's definitely something you won't ever forget." Stacy Abramson and David Isay, "Inside the Death Chamber," *In These Times*, April 16, 2007, https:// inthesetimes.com/article/inside-the-death-chamber.

38. Robert Perkinson, *Texas Tough: The Rise of America's Prison Empire* (Metropolitan Books, 2010), 40.

39. Heather Murphy, "4 Years After an Execution, a Different Man's DNA Is Found on the Murder Weapon," *New York Times*, May 7, 2021, https://www .nytimes.com/2021/05/07/us/ledell-lee-dna-testing-arkansas.html.

CHAPTER SIX: PUBLIC SAFETY

1. Newspaper article about the incident: Linda Loyd and Thomas J. Gibbons Jr., "Suspect Is Taken into Custody, Emerges from Police Van Paralyzed," *Philadelphia Inquirer*, April 17, 1997, https://www.newspapers.com/image/178298595/. Lawsuit filed against the officers and city: *Saunders v. City of Philadelphia*, 97–3251, United States District Court for the Eastern District of Pennsylvania, https://web.archive.org/web/20201023181933/http://www.paed.uscourts.gov/documents/opinions/97D0825P.pdf.

2. Justine Barron, "Freddie Gray, Five Years Later," The Appeal, April 23, 2020, https://theappeal.org/freddie-gray-five-years-later/.

3. I have left the last names off the list for privacy.

4. Gracie Martinez and Jeffrey S. Passel, "Facts About the U.S. Black Population," Pew Research Center, January 23, 2025, https://www.pewresearch.org/social-trends/fact-sheet/facts-about-the-us-black-population/.

5. Heather Warnken and Janet L. Lauritsen, *Who Experiences Violent Victimization and Who Accesses Services? Findings from the National Crime Victimization Survey for Expanding Our Reach* (Center for Victim Research, 2019), https://navaa.org/wp-content/uploads/2021/02/CVR-Article_Who-Experiences-Violent-Victimization-and-Who-Accesses-Services-1.pdf.

6. *Crime Survivors Speak: National Survey of Victims' Views on Safety and Justice* (Alliance for Safety and Justice, 2022), https://allianceforsafetyandjustice.org/wp-content/uploads/2022/09/Alliance-for-Safety-and-Justice-Crime-Survivors-Speak-September-2022.pdf.

7. Brian A. Reaves, *Felony Defendants in Large Urban Counties, 2009—Statistical Tables* (Bureau of Justice Statistics, 2013), https://bjs.ojp.gov/content/pub/pdf/fdluc09.pdf.

8. John Gramlich, "Only 2% of Federal Criminal Defendants Went to Trial in 2018, and Most Who Did Were Found Guilty," Pew Research Center, June 11, 2019, https://www.pewresearch.org/short-reads/2019/06/11/only-2-of-federal-criminal-defendants-go-to-trial-and-most-who-do-are-found-guilty/.

9. "FBI Releases 2023 Crime in the Nation Statistics," https://www.fbi.gov/news/press-releases/fbi-releases-2023-crime-in-the-nation-statistics.

CHAPTER SEVEN: SPIRIT

1. Laurence Steinberg, "Cognitive and Affective Development in Adolescence," *Trends in Cognitive Sciences* 9, no. 2 (2005): 69–74, https://doi.org/10.1016/j.tics.2004.12.005.

2. Bessel A. Van der Kolk, *Psychological Trauma* (American Psychiatric Publications, 2003); Bessel A. Van der Kolk, *The Body Keeps the Score: Brain, Mind, and Body in the Healing of Trauma* (Penguin, 2014).

3. *Juvenile Life Without Parole Project: Using International Law and Advocacy to Give Children a Second Chance* (American Civil Liberties Union of Michigan, 2007), https://www.aclumich.org/sites/default/files/pdfs/JWLOPpacket.pdf.

4. Maladaptive responses such as emotional disorders, self-mutilation, suicide attempts, and prison misbehavior are most common during the early phases of incarceration. Kenneth Adams, "Adjusting to Prison Life," *Crime and Justice* 16 (1992): 275–359, https://doi.org/10.1086/449208.

5. Andrew Coyle, "Replacing the Death Penalty: The Vexed Issue of Alternative Sanctions," in *Capital Punishment: Strategies for Abolition*, ed. Peter Hodgkinson and William A. Schabas (Cambridge University Press, 2004).

6. *Bureau of Prisons: Growing Inmate Crowding Negatively Affects Inmates, Staff, and Infrastructure* (Government Accountability Office, 2012), https://www.gao.gov/assets/650/648123.pdf.

7. *Juvenile Life Without Parole Project.*

8. Kate Wells, "Settlement Reached for Michigan's Juvenile Lifers, Schedules 'Prompt' Resentencings," Michigan Public Radio, September 30, 2020, https://www.michiganpublic.org/news/2020-09-30/settlement-reached-for-michigans-juvenile-lifers-schedules-prompt-resentencings.

9. *Miller v. Alabama*, 567 U.S. 460 (2012), https://supreme.justia.com/cases/federal/us/567/460/. In 2016, *Miller* was made retrospective , which meant that people like Tony, who were already sentenced to LWOP and under the age of eighteen at the time of the crime, could have the chance for mitigation to be considered. *Montgomery v. Louisiana*, 577 U.S. 190 (2016, https://supreme.justia.com/cases/federal/us/577/190/.

10. "Michigan Juvenile Life Without Parole: Laws and Updates," LegalClarity Michigan, January 16, 2025, https://legalclarity.org/michigan-juvenile-life -without-parole-laws-and-updates/.

11. Leslie Kellam, *Targeted Programs: Preliminary Analysis of the Impact of Prison Program Participation on Community Success* (New York Department of Correctional Services, 2005), https://books.google.com /about/Targeted_Programs.html. Participating in prison programming increased reentry success (i.e., not returning to prison).

12. "What happens inside jails and prisons does not stay inside jails and prisons. Formerly incarcerated people and corrections officers carry the effects of violence home to their families and communities. Reducing violence and improving safety and health behind bars is thus essential for the prosperity of all communities": *Confronting Confinement: A Report of the Commission on Safety and Abuse in America's Prisons* (Vera Institute of Justice, 2006), https://www.vera.org/publications /confronting-confinement/.

13. Brandi Grissom, "Inmates Complain of Sweltering Prison Conditions," *Texas Tribune*, August 9, 2011, https://www.texastribune.org/2011/08/09 /lawsuit-could-cool-sweltering-prisons/. In 2023, two thirds of inmates still lacked air-conditioning. Jolie McCullough, "Inmates Are Dying in Stifling Texas prisons, but the State Seldom Acknowledges Heat as a Cause of Death," *Texas Tribune*, June 28, 2023, https://www.texastribune .org/2023/06/28/texas-prisons-heat-deaths/.

14. McCullough, "Inmates Are Dying in Stifling Texas Prisons."

15. Since 2023, there's been some limited investment in expanding air-conditioning in Texas prisons, and a judge recently ruled that keeping Texas prisoners in units without air-conditioning was unconstitutional. Pooja Salhotra, "Federal Judge Rules Prison Heat Conditions Are Unconstitutional, but Doesn't Require Air Conditioning," *Texas Tribune*, March 27, 2025, https:// www.texastribune.org/2025/03/26/texas-prison-air-conditioning-lawsuit/.

16. Lester Krames and Gordon L. Flett, *Jail/Holding Cell Design: Proposals for Modification and Design Changes to Jail/Holding Cells Psychological Impact on Aggressive and Self Destructive Behaviour* (Canadian Police Research

Centre, 2005), https://www.publicsafety.gc.ca/lbrr/archives/cnmcs-plcng /cn27084-eng.pdf.

17. Andreea Matei, *Solitary Confinement in US Prisons* (Urban Institute Justice Policy Center, 2022), https://www.urban.org/sites/default/files/2022-08 /Solitary%20Confinement%20in%20the%20US.pdf; and "Settlement Reached to End Permanent Solitary Confinement for People Sentenced to Death in Pennsylvania," American Civil Liberties Union of Pennsylvania, November 18, 2019, https://www.aclupa.org/en/press-releases/settlement -reached-end-permanent-solitary-confinement-people-sentenced-death. Pennsylvania death row inmates sued over their prison conditions and won in 2018. Those conditions, which were not as restrictive as those applied in Texas, were found by the courts in Pennsylvania to be akin to torture and not necessary for the safety of the inmates or officers.

18. Laura Rice, "This Company Recorded Thousands of Prisoners' Phone Calls to Their Attorneys," *Texas Standard*, November 12, 2015, https:// www.texasstandard.org/stories/prisoners-leaked-phone-records-breach -attorney-client-privilege/; and Tonya Riley, "A Private Prison Company Gave 1,300 Recordings of Confidential Inmate Phone Calls to Prosecutors," *Mother Jones*, June 8, 2018, https://www.motherjones.com/criminal-justice /2018/06/securus-corecivic-kansas-prison-phone-calls/.

19. Germany: Maurice Chammah, "German Prisons Are Kinder, Gentler, and Safer Than the Ones in America," Vice News, July 9, 2015, https://www .vice.com/en/article/german-prisons-are-kinder-gentler-and-safer-than -the-ones-in-america-617/. Denmark, Norway, and Sweden: Peter Scharff Smith and Thomas Ugelvik, "Punishment and Welfare in Scandinavia," in *Scandinavian Penal History, Culture and Prison Practice*, ed. Peter Scharff Smith and Thomas Ugelvik (Palgrave, 2017), https://doi.org/10.1057/978 -1-137-58529-5_21. There appears to be a connection between a stronger community-oriented social policy state (versus the American model of individualism) and rehabilitative models of punishment.

20. "Empowering Change: Transforming an American Prison Unit with Scandinavian-Inspired Policies," Scandinavian Prison Project, accessed June 12, 2025, https://www.scandinavianprisonproject.com/.

21. Albert Bandura, *Moral Disengagement: How People Do Harm and Live with Themselves* (Worth, 2015).

CHAPTER EIGHT: THE TORRENT

1. *Compassion*, accessed June 12, 2025, https://www.compassionondeathrow .org/. An inmate-published newsletter aimed to develop healing communication between offenders sentenced to death and murder victims' families. The founders of the newsletter also established a college scholarship fund for family members of murdered victims. "In no way are the scholarships to the immediate family members of murdered victims meant to atone for the loss they have experienced," Hasan wrote in his first editorial. "Scholarships are . . . a compassionate gesture to those who have had a significant and unfortunate tragedy befall them." Quoted in "About Us," *Compassion* newsletter, accessed June 12, 2025, https://www.compassionondeathrow.org/about-us/.

2. Errors contained within the original correspondence have been corrected.

3. A fourth man, Lezmond Mitchell, also received a stay of execution over allegations of racial bias by the jury that convicted him. "Execution of Navajo Man Placed on Hold," *Arizona Daily Star*, October 9, 2019, https://www.news-papers.com/article/arizona-daily-star-execution-of-navajo-m/111561472/.

4. Derrick Bryson Taylor, "A Timeline of the Coronavirus Pandemic," *New York Times*, March 17, 2021, https://www.nytimes.com/article/coronavirus -timeline.html.

5. Carrie Johnson, "Lawsuit Seeks Delay in Pending Federal Execution, Citing COVID-19 Infection Risks," NPR, July 2, 2020, https://www.npr.org /2020/07/02/886403059/lawsuit-seeks-delay-in-pending-federal-execution -citing-covid-infection-risks.

6. Austin Sarat, "William Barr Uses Victims and Their Families to Prop Up America's Failing Death Penalty System," Verdict, September 14, 2020, https://verdict.justia.com/2020/09/14/william-barr-uses-victims-and -their-families-to-prop-up-americas-failing-death-penalty-system.

7. "Records Disclose Taxpayers Picked Up a Nearly Million Dollar Price Tag for Each Federal Execution," Death Penalty Information Center, February

3, 2021, https://deathpenaltyinfo.org/records-disclose-taxpayers-picked -up-a-nearly-million-dollar-price-tag-for-each-federal-execution/.

8. Daniel LaChance, "Last Words, Last Meals, and Last Stands: Agency and Individuality in the Modern Execution Process," *Law & Social Inquiry* 32, no. 3 (2007): 701–24, https://www.jstor.org/stable/20108722.

EPILOGUE: CHOICES

1. John Gramlich, "What the Data Says About Crime in the U.S.," Pew Research Center, April 24, 2024, https://www.pewresearch.org/short-reads /2024/04/24/what-the-data-says-about-crime-in-the-us/.

2. Jasmine Garsd, "Immigrants Are Less Likely to Commit Crimes Than U.S.-Born Americans, Studies Find," NPR, March 8, 2024, https://www.npr .org/2024/03/08/1237103158/immigrants-are-less-likely-to-commit-crimes -than-us-born-americans-studies-find.

3. Alicia Bannon and Michael Milov-Cordoba, "Supreme Court Term Limits," Brennan Center for Justice, June 20, 2023, https://www.brennancenter.org /our-work/policy-solutions/supreme-court-term-limits.

4. Jamal Greene, *How Rights Went Wrong: Why Our Obsession with Rights Is Tearing America Apart* (Houghton Mifflin, 2021), https://scholarship.law .columbia.edu/books/302/.

5. Erik Ortiz, "Spree of Federal Executions During Trump's Lame-Duck Period and Pandemic Is Unprecedented," NBC News, December 9, 2020, https://www.nbcnews.com/news/us-news/spree-federal-executions -during-trump-s-lame-duck-period-pandemic-n1250565.

6. "Restoring the Death Penalty and Protecting Public Safety," *Federal Register* 90, no. 20 (January 30, 2025): 8463–65, https://www.govinfo.gov/app /details/FR-2025-01-30/2025-02012.

7. Bailey Gallion, "Family, Police React to Biden Commuting Death Sentence for Ohio Cop Killer," *Columbus Dispatch*, December 23, 2024, https://www .dispatch.com/story/news/local/2024/12/23/biden-commutes-37-death -sentence-daryl-lawrence-bryan-hurst-columbus-cop-killer/77168818007/.

8. Jeff Brumley, "Louisiana Jews Form Alliance to Oppose Gassing as Means of Execution," Baptist News Global, May 13, 2024, https://baptistnews.com

/article/louisiana-jews-form-alliance-to-oppose-gassing-as-means-of
-execution/.

9. Marlo Lacen, "Nitrogen Hypoxia Discontinued in Euthanizing Animals,
Why Is It Ok for Humans?" WJTV 12 News, February 25, 2025, https://
www.wjtv.com/news/regional-news/nitrogen-hypoxia-discontinued-in
-euthanizing-animals-why-is-it-ok-for-humans/.

10. Sarah Clifton, "Alabama Executes Demetrius Frazier by Nitrogen Gas
for 1991 Murder," *Montgomery Advertiser*, February 6, 2025, https://www
.montgomeryadvertiser.com/story/news/local/alabama/2025/02/06
/alabama-executes-demetrius-frazier-by-nitrogen-gas-for-1991-murder
/78282236007/.

11. Erik Ortiz, "South Carolina Prepares for First Firing Squad Execution,
Ushering Return of Rare Method," NBC News, March 2, 2025, https://
www.nbcnews.com/news/us-news/south-carolina-prepares-firing-squad
-execution-brad-sigmon-rcna193920.

12. Rosaleen McElvaney et al., "To Tell or Not to Tell? Factors Influencing
Young People's Informal Disclosures of Child Sexual Abuse," *Journal of
Interpersonal Violence* 29, no. 5 (2014): 928–47, https://doi.org/10.1177
/0886260513506281.

13. "Florida Gov. Ron DeSantis Pushes Law to Give Death Penalty to Child
Rapists," Forbes Breaking News, May 2, 2023, https://www.youtube.com
/watch?v=5QSUYExqXl4.

14. This is taken from philosopher John Rawls and his influential theory of how
to make society just by applying a "veil of ignorance." John Rawls, *A Theory
of Justice* (Harvard University Press, 1971).

15. "Editorial: An Indefensible Lapse of Justice," *Anchorage Daily News*,
February 4, 2023, https://www.adn.com/opinions/editorials/2023/02/04
/editorial-an-indefensible-lapse-of-justice/.

16. Liz Komar et al., "Counting Down: Paths to a 20-Year Maximum
Prison Sentence," Sentencing Project, February 15, 2023, https://www
.sentencingproject.org/reports/counting-down-paths-to-a-20-year
-maximum-prison-sentence/.

17. Stephanie Wykstra, "The Case Against Solitary Confinement," Vox,
April 17, 2019, https://www.vox.com/future-perfect/2019/4/17/18305109

/solitary-confinement-prison-criminal-justice-reform; and Ram Subramanian, "How Some European Prisons Are Based on Dignity Instead of Dehumanization," Brennan Center for Justice, November 29, 2021, https://www.brennancenter.org/our-work/analysis-opinion/how-some -european-prisons-are-based-dignity-instead-dehumanization.

Index

A Note on the Author

Mitigation specialist **Elizabeth Vartkessian** has been investigating the life histories of those facing the most severe penalties possible in the United States since 2004. She holds a PhD in law from the University of Oxford, an MS in comparative social policy from Oxford, and BAs in philosophy and political science from the George Washington University, where she was a Presidential Scholar. In 2015 she was awarded the J.M.K. Innovation Prize for her efforts to bring mitigation to all areas of the criminal justice process. In 2018 the Baltimore City Council passed a resolution praising her efforts to bring human dignity into the justice system. After launching a successful private practice, Vartkessian and several colleagues created Advancing Real Change, Inc., a national nonprofit dedicated to conducting life history investigations in criminal cases. She has spoken widely on the criminal legal system and written about it in the *Baltimore Sun* and numerous peer-reviewed publications and law reviews. She lives in Baltimore.